CAMBRI...

CA...

CHINUA ACHEBE

This book provides a detailed and up-to-date examination of the writings of Chinua Achebe, Africa's best-known and most widely read author. Dr Innes studies his writings, lectures and activities chronologically, in the context of Nigerian cultures and politics and their interaction with western cultures and powers. Her analysis goes beyond that of previously published studies, to examine Achebe's short stories, essays and poetry, and his most recent publications *Anthills of the Savannah* (1987) and *Hopes and Impediments* (1988). Particular emphasis is placed upon Achebe's departure from European literary models in order to create a new kind of fiction which seeks to challenge the preconceptions of African and western audiences alike, and which is of considerable literary and political significance.

CAMBRIDGE STUDIES IN AFRICAN AND CARIBBEAN LITERATURE

Series Editor: Professor Abiola Irele, Ohio State University

Each volume in this unique new series of critical studies will offer a comprehensive and in-depth account of the whole *oeuvre* of one individual writer from Africa or the Caribbean, in such a way that the book may be considered a complete coverage of the writer's expression up to the time the study is undertaken. Attention will be devoted primarily to the works themselves – their significant themes, governing ideas and formal procedures; biographical and other background information will thus be employed secondarily, to illuminate these aspects of the writer's work where necessary.

The emergence in the twentieth century of black literature in the United States, the Caribbean and Africa as a distinct corpus of imaginative work represents one of the most notable developments in world literature in modern times. This series has been established to meet the needs of this growing area of study. It is hoped that it will not only contribute to a wider understanding of the humanistic significance of modern literature from Africa and the Caribbean through the scholarly presentation of the work of major writers, but also offer a wider framework for the ongoing debates about the problems of interpretation within the disciplines concerned.

First title in the series
Chinua Achebe, by C. L. Innes, University of Kent at Canterbury

Other titles in preparation
Mongo Beti, by Richard Bjornson, Ohio State University
Aimé Césaire, by Gregson Davis, Stanford University
Rene Depestre, by Joan Dayan, City University of New York
Edouard Glissant, by Michael Dash, University of the West Indies
Nicolás Guillén, by Josaphat Kubayanda, Ohio State University
George Lamming, by Rhonda Cobham, Amherst College
V. S. Naipaul, by Fawzia Mustafa, Fordham University
Léopold Sédar Senghor, by Abiola Irele, Ohio State University
Wole Soyinka, by Biodun Jeyifo, Cornell University

Chinua Achebe

CHINUA ACHEBE

C. L. INNES

*Senior Lecturer in English, African and
Caribbean Literature, University of Kent
at Canterbury*

Published by the Press Syndicate of the University of Cambridge
The Pitt Building, Trumpington Street, Cambridge CB2 1RP
40 West 20th Street, New York, NY 10011–4211, USA
10 Stamford Road, Oakleigh, Victoria 3166, Australia

First published 1990
First paperback edition 1992

British Library cataloguing in publication data

Innes, C. L.
Chinua Achebe – (Cambridge studies
in African and Caribbean literature:1)
1. Fiction in English. Nigerian writers. Achebe, Chinua – Critical studies
I. Title
823

Library of Congress cataloguing in publication data

Innes, Catherine Lynnette.
p.   cm. – (Cambridge studies in African and Caribbean literature: 1)
Bibliography.
Includes index.
ISBN 0 521 35623 7
1. Achebe, Chinua – Criticism and interpretation.   I. Title.   II. Series.
PR9387.9.A3Z7   1990
823 – dc 19   89–31432 CIP

ISBN 0 521 35623 7 hardback
ISBN 0 521 42897 1 paperback

Transferred to digital printing 1999

GG

For Martin, Robin and Rachel
and for Chinelo and Ik

Language, for the individual consciousness, lies on the borderline between oneself and the other. The word in language is half someone else's. It becomes 'one's own' only when the speaker populates it with his own intention, his own accent, when he appropriates the word, adapting it to his own semantic and expressive intention. Prior to this moment of appropriation, the word does not exist in a neutral and impersonal language (it is not, after all, out of a dictionary that the speaker gets his words!), but rather it exists in other people's mouths, in other people's contexts, serving other people's intentions: it is from there that one must take the word, and make it one's own.

Mikhail Bakhtin, 'Discourse in the Novel'

Contents

Acknowledgements   *page* xiii
List of abbreviations   xiv
Chronology   xv

Introduction   1
1 Origins   4
2 'A less superficial picture': *Things Fall Apart*   21
3 'The best lack all conviction': *No Longer at Ease*   42
4 Religion and power in Africa: *Arrow of God*   64
5 Courting the voters: *A Man of the People*   83
6 The novelist as critic: politics and criticism,
     1960–1988   102
7 Marginal lives: *Girls at War and Other Stories*   121
8 Poetry and war: *Beware Soul Brother and Other*
     Poems   134
9 The critic as novelist: *Anthills of the Savannah*   150
Conclusion   165

Notes   174
Bibliography   186
Index   197

Acknowledgements

I would like to thank Abiola Irele and a number of other people who have read this manuscript at various stages and whose comments and suggestions have helped me fashion the final draft. They include Michael Black, Ernest Emenyonu and Abdul JanMohamed. Some of the ideas were developed and then modified in lively discussion with students and colleagues at the University of Kent, and also with faculty and postgraduate students at a seminar at the University of Nigeria in Nsukka, which I visited on a trip sponsored by that university and the British Council. My work has been assisted by Professor Molly Mahood who gave me useful notes and information on Joyce Cary and Bernth Lindfors who has generously sent me much of the bibliographical information I needed. In particular, I am deeply grateful to Chinua Achebe, not only for providing the subject for the study itself, but also for checking and correcting the biographical and bibliographical sections of this book.

Permission to quote from Chinua Achebe's works has kindly been given by William Heinemann Ltd and Heinemann Educational Books Ltd.

Abbreviations

Abbreviated references in the text and notes are to the following editions of Achebe's works. Initials are followed by a page number.

AG	*Arrow of God*, revised ed., London: Heinemann, 1974
AS	*Anthills of the Savannah*, London: Heinemann, 1987
BSB	*Beware Soul Brother*, London: Heinemann, 1972
GW	*Girls at War and Other Stories*, London: Heinemann, 1972
HI	*Hopes and Impediments: Selected Essays 1965–87*, London: Heinemann, 1988
MOP	*A Man of the People*, London: Heinemann, 1966
MYCD	*Morning Yet on Creation Day*, London: Heinemann, 1975
NLAE	*No Longer at Ease*, London: Heinemann, 1975
TFA	*Things Fall Apart*, London: Heinemann, 1976
TWN	*The Trouble with Nigeria*, Enugu: Fourth Dimension, 1983

Chronology

1930   Achebe born 16 November in Eastern Nigeria.

1944–8   Attended Government College, Umuahia.

1948–53 Student at University College, Ibadan.

1954   Appointed Talks Producer with the Nigerian Broadcasting Corporation.

1956   Studied with the BBC in London.

1958   Publication of *Things Fall Apart*.

1959   Awarded the Margaret Wrong Memorial Prize for his contribution to African literature.

1960   Nigerian independence.
Publication of *No Longer at Ease*. Awarded Nigerian National Trophy for Literature.

1960–1 Visited East Africa on a Rockefeller Fellowship.

1961   Married Christie Chinwe Okoli. Appointed Director of External Broadcasting for the Nigerian Broadcasting Corporation.

1962   Achebe becomes founding editor of African Writers Series for Heinemann Educational Books.
Birth of daughter, Chinelo.

1963   Travelled in the United States, Brazil and Britain on a UNESCO fellowship.

1964   Publication of *Arrow of God*. Received Jock Campbell *New Statesman* Award for this novel.
Birth of son, Ikechukwu.

1966   Publication of *A Man of the People*.
Military coup in January installing General Ironsi as Head of State. Second coup in July led by General Gowon. Achebe's cousin is one of the military officers assassinated. Massacre of Igbos in North. Achebe leaves Lagos and returns to Eastern Nigeria.

1967   Biafra declares secession from federation of
        Nigeria. Achebe visits a number of African
        states, Europe and North America as spokesman
        for Biafra.
        Birth of son, Chidi.
        Senior Research Fellow at the University of
        Nigeria, Nsukka.
        Death of Christopher Okigbo fighting with
        Biafran army.

1970   Biafra surrenders.
        Birth of daughter, Nwando.

1971   First issue of *Okike: An African Journal of New
        Writing*.
        Publication of *Beware Soul Brother* in Nigeria.

1972   Awarded Commonwealth Poetry Prize for *Beware
        Soul Brother*. Publication of *Girls at War and Other
        Stories*.

1972–5 Visiting Professor of Literature, University of
        Massachusetts, Amherst, USA.

1975   Coup by Murtala Muhammed replaces General
        Gowon's government.
        Publication of *Morning Yet on Creation Day*.

1975–6 Visiting Professor of Literature, University of
        Connecticut, Storrs, USA.

1976   Assassination of Murtala Muhammed. Obansan-
        jo regime begins.
        Achebe returns to Nigeria. Professor of
        Literature at University of Nigeria, Nsukka.

1979   Elections in Nigeria. Inauguration of Second
        Republic with Shehu Shagari as President.
        Achebe receives the Nigerian National Merit
        Award (NNMA) and the Order of the Federal
        Republic (OFR). Elected Chairman of the
        Association of Nigerian Authors.

1982   Publication of *Aka Weta*, edited with Obiora
        Udechukwu, an anthology of 'egwu' verse.

1983   Death of Mallam Aminu Kano, Leader of the
        People's Redemption Party. Achebe elected
        Deputy National President of the People's
        Redemption Party.

Publication of *The Trouble with Nigeria*.
Military coup, 31 December. General Buhari becomes Head of State.

1984   First issue of *Uwa ndi Igbo: a Journal of Igbo Life and Culture* published by Achebe.

1985   Military coup. Major General Babangida's regime begins.

1986   Appointed Pro-Vice-Chancellor, State University of Anambra, Enugu.

1987   Publication of *Anthills of the Savannah*.

1987–8   Visiting Fellow at the University of Massachusetts, Amherst, USA.

1988   Publication of *Hopes and Impediments: Selected Essays 1965–87*.

1989   Distinguished visiting Professor of Literature, City College of New York. Nominated for President, PEN International.

1990   Visiting Professor of Literature, Bard College, Annandale-on-Hudson, New York.

Introduction

CHINUA ACHEBE is Africa's most widely read novelist and the first to be taken seriously by both African and European readers. His novels and critical pronouncements have profoundly influenced his readers' understanding of Africans and their lives and have formed the basis for many a discussion of 'the African novel'. They have also provided a model for succeeding African novelists to follow and contend with. Yet, although Achebe's first and most influential novel, *Things Fall Apart*, was published thirty years ago, critical discussion of his work as a whole has rarely moved beyond books designed as introductions. Three of those books were first written more than fifteen years ago – although they have been revised since to take into account Achebe's short fiction and poetry – and they are concerned chiefly with describing the novels in terms of their central themes, conflicts and characters.[1] The fourth book, Robert M. Wren's *Achebe's World*, was published in 1980 and provides important historical and anthropological background and annotation for the novels.[2] These four critical works have served and continue to serve a useful purpose for new students of Achebe's writing. The present study seeks to build upon the foundation they have constructed.

That foundation contains some now solidly entrenched concepts and assumptions about the nature of Achebe's achievement, a foundation to which Chinua Achebe's own essays and lectures – notably 'The Role of the Writer in a New Nation' and 'The African Writer and the English Language' – have contributed much of the framework. For, *as* a writer, says Achebe, his 'fundamental theme' must be 'that African peoples did not hear of culture for the

1

first time from Europeans'.[3] And so many critics have
revealed Achebe's fundamental theme in *Things Fall Apart*
and *Arrow of God* to be the demonstration of the dignity and
validity of Igbo culture. 'With great skill Achebe in his
novels of traditional life combines the role of novelist and
anthropologist, synthesising them in a new kind of fiction.
This is where his essential genius lies', affirms David
Carroll,[4] and many other critics of the individual novels
agree with this conclusion and approach.[5]

'I feel that the English language will be able to carry the
weight of my African experience. But it will have to be a
new English, still in full communion with its ancestral
home but altered to suit its new African surroundings',
Achebe declared.[6] Critics such as Bernth Lindfors, Gareth
Griffiths and Felicity Riddy have analysed and
demonstrated Achebe's skill in fashioning 'a new English',
while his use of Igbo proverbs and pidgin English has constantly delighted or dismayed reviewers.[7]

What has received less attention is Achebe's creation of
a new English *literature*, his use of the novel form and the
alterations he has made to it 'to suit its new African surroundings'. In this study, therefore, while giving due
attention to the concerns with language and historical
change which are central to Achebe's works, I shall also
place particular emphasis on Achebe's Africanization of
the novel, trying to discern what elements he has used and
what innovations he has made in his development as a
novelist. And I shall use as my point of departure the
African novels of Joyce Cary, particularly his much ac-
claimed *Mister Johnson*, which provoked Achebe into
becoming a writer so that he could tell the story of Nigeria
'from the inside'.[8]

Between 1955 and 1965, Achebe wrote four novels which
many have seen as a kind of tetralogy covering the history
of Nigeria from colonization until the first military coup. It
was to be another twenty years before Achebe completed a
fifth novel, *Anthills of the Savannah*, published in 1987.
Nevertheless, the intervening years were very full ones.
Achebe has described the Nigerian Civil War (1967–70) as
a watershed for him, as for many Nigerians, which led

to radical rethinking about Nigeria's past and future.[9] In the latter part of this study, I will seek to show how the fruits of that rethinking can be seen not only in the short stories collected in *Girls at War and Other Stories* (1972) and the poems published in *Beware Soul Brother* (1971) and *Okike* magazine, but also in the numerous lectures and essays which Achebe wrote in those years. For Achebe, new thoughts and new insights are to be discovered in new forms of language and discourse. The varied forms and modes with which he has experimented – literary and political, analytical and rhetorical, poetry and prose – come together in his long-awaited fifth novel.

1

Origins

ACHEBE WAS BORN IN Eastern Nigeria on 16
November 1930. He was christened Albert
Chinualumogu. His father, Isaiah Okafor Achebe, a
catechist for the Church Missionary Society, had as a
young man been converted to Christianity and had been an
evangelist and church teacher in other parts of Eastern
Nigeria before returning to settle in his ancestral village,
Ogidi, five years after the birth of his fifth child. His
mother, Janet, had also been a convert to Christianity.
When Isaiah and Janet Achebe were married in 1909, the
service was conducted by Isaiah Achebe's teacher, super-
visor and friend, the eminent missionary and amateur anthropologist, G. T. Basden, who was to be the model for
Mr. Brown, the more tolerant and tolerable missionary in
Things Fall Apart.

Achebe describes growing up in Ogidi in the thirties as
living 'at the crossroads of cultures':[1]

On one arm of the cross we sang hymns and read the bible night
and day. On the other my father's brother and his family, blind-
ed by heathenism, offered food to idols. That was how it was supposed to be anyhow.[2]

But the 'supposed' parting of the ways between heathen
and Christian was not absolute. As a small child, Achebe
moved between both sides of his family, finding himself intrigued by the differing rituals and tempted by the
'heathen' food. Dismissing the popular notion of the
modern African as 'a soul torn between cultures', Achebe
affirms the benefit of his dual experience, giving him a
slight distance from each culture:

The distance becomes not a separation but a bringing together

4

like the necessary backward step which a judicious viewer might take in order to see a canvas steadily and fully.[3]

It was by that time some eighty years since the coming of the first missionaries to Eastern Nigeria. They had been given hospitality in Ogidi by Achebe's great-uncle, who allowed them to stay in his compound until their mournful hymns caused him to ask them to leave – lest his neighbours think the hymns were dirges for his funeral. This same great-uncle raised Achebe's father, whose parents had died when he was a child. He did not make 'any serious objections' when his nephew joined the Christians and although he firmly resisted conversion, the uncle, so Achebe tells us, remained very close to his nephew.[4]

Situated just a few miles from the market town of Onitsha on the River Niger, Ogidi was not untypical of Igbo villages at that time. Traditional titles and forms of authority existed side by side with those conferred or imposed by the church and the British colonial administration. Unlike other groups in Nigeria, such as the Hausa and the Yoruba, the Igbos had no centralized institutions or figureheads in the form of chiefs or kings. Each village, consisting of a small cluster of hamlets, was autonomous. Legal judgements and decisions which concerned the village as a whole were made by the village elders – titled men who gained their status through their rectitude, their material success and other achievements. Other decisions were made by age groups and women's groups as appropriate. Village meetings were held in the market place, and here all could participate in the debate and express their approval or disapproval of the points made.

The Igbo people share a common language (although there are differences of dialect in various regions) and common religious beliefs and practices. A number of anthropologists and commentators have asserted that they also worship a supreme deity, Chukwu, the Creator, but in recent years this assertion has been challenged by Donatus Nwoga.[5] One of the most important of a number of deities is Ala, also called Ani, the goddess of the earth and arbiter of morality. Ala also controls the coming and going of the ancestors who look after the spiritual and material welfare of their descendants and are in turn sustained by them.

A significant aspect of Igbo theology is the belief that at birth, each person acquires a *chi* or spiritual double. Achebe has described the concept thus:

Every person has an individual *chi* who created him, its natural home is somewhere in the region of the sun but it may be induced to visit an earthly shrine; a person's fortunes in life are controlled more or less completely by his *chi*.[6]

It is this cosmology which, in Achebe's view, provides the source not only for the Igbo's individualism and independence but also for his tolerance and egalitarianism, and at one time encouraged a society which held a fine balance between the material and the spiritual:

And finally, at the root of it all lies that very belief we have already seen: a belief in the fundamental worth and independence of every man and of his right to speak on matters of concern to him and, flowing from it, a rejection of any form of absolutism which might endanger those values. It is not surprising that the Igbo held discussion and consensus as the highest ideals of the political process. This made them argumentative and difficult to rule. But how could they suspend for the convenience of a ruler limitations which they impose even on their gods?[7]

When the British took control of Nigeria in the late nineteenth century, they assumed that together with trade in palm oil they brought enlightenment and progress to a people they deemed to have no valid social, religious or political institutions, and no history of their own. The beliefs and shrines of the Igbos, like those of other peoples in Africa, were dismissed as mere superstitions and 'fetishes'; and the British failed to acknowledge any system of government which did not fit their preconceived notions about chiefs and emirs. In 1900, the British imposed their administration upon the Igbos by dividing South-eastern Nigeria into areas ruled by District Commissioners and appointed selected Igbos to act as warrant chiefs, clerks and messengers to assist them, a system resented by the Igbos not only because it was an alien imposition violating their own more democratic structures, but also because those who accepted the appointments were men without status conferred by the villagers and without allegiance to their own communities. They were often regarded as contemptible collaborators. While the decentralization of Igbo society contributed to some of its more admirable qualities and sustained the independence of small communities, it also made organized group resistance to the imposition of British rule more difficult. But nor could there be any surrender on the part of Igbos as a group, and the British were 'embroiled in endless village-to-village skirmishes in Igboland'.[8] Villages which did resist were sometimes 'pacified', either by the razing of the village and the shooting or arrest of those villagers who had not fled beforehand, or by the arrest and imprisonment, sometimes execution, of the village elders.[9] In 1918, Lord Lugard introduced 'indirect rule' as a policy for the whole of Nigeria, ignoring the differences between the political structures of Hausa, Yoruba, Igbo and other peoples. The District Commissioners were removed and the warrant chiefs given greater power, often leading to greater abuse of that power. These abuses resulted in a number of protests, and in 1930 further reorganization took place in Eastern Nigeria to comply more closely with traditional Igbo groupings and institutions. This system survived until Independence in 1960.

As a child in Ogidi, and later at Owerri, Achebe attended church schools. His first lessons were in Igbo, and like Oduche in *Arrow of God*, he studied *Azu Ndu* ('Fresh Fish' or 'Green Back', according to the accent on *Azu*), the Church Missionary Society text for beginners. At about eight, he began to learn English; after the two years of Infants' schooling, all instruction was in English. There were a few books in his father's house, and Achebe read all of them – including an Igbo adaptation of *Pilgrim's Progress*, stories of missionaries in Africa and ecclesiastical exhortations in *The West African Churchman's Pamphlet*, a simplified version of *A Midsummer Night's Dream*, as well as the discarded primers and readers of his older brothers and sister. He also listened to stories in Igbo told by the old men in his village, his mother and his elder sister. Achebe writes that he had 'always been fond of stories and intrigued by language'.[10]

From the church school, Achebe was selected in 1944 to attend the prestigious secondary school, Government College in Umuahia. Fellow students included Christopher Okigbo and Vincent Chukwuemeka Ike; Gabriel Okara, Elechi Amadi and I. N. C. Aniebo are also well-known African writers who were alumni of the college. Here Achebe studied for the Cambridge School Certificate, following a course of studies almost identical to that of secondary school pupils in England at that time. He matriculated in 1948 with a scholarship to study medicine at University College, Ibadan, at that time affiliated to the University of London. After one year, Achebe decided to switch from Medicine to a course in English Literature, Religious Studies and History. The decision cost him his scholarship, but his older brother John generously supported him and Achebe was able to pursue his chosen course.

As an Arts student, Achebe encountered a syllabus similar to that taught in British universities, but with some additions. He read Shakespeare, Milton, and Wordsworth, but he also read writers considered 'relevant' to Nigerian students: Conrad, Joyce Cary and Graham Greene. The history classes he attended were taught from a British point of view, but they, together with the course taught by Dr J. Parrinder, a pioneer in the study of West African religions, stirred him to investigate further the history and theology of his own people, mainly through oral accounts but also through written records of missionaries, administrators and anthropologists. The post-war period was a time of political and intellectual ferment in Nigeria, and this first group of students at Ibadan were part of that ferment. Not that British rule had gone unquestioned previously: as a schoolboy during World War II, Achebe shared the view held by many of his peers that if Hitler was an enemy of the British, he deserved support. The recruiting of large numbers of Nigerians and other Africans to fight with the

British armed forces against dictatorship and racism not surprisingly led Nigerians to think that dictatorship and racism should also be eliminated in their own country. In 1944, the Igbo leader Dr Nnamdi Azikiwe became General Secretary of the National Council of Nigeria and the Cameroons (NCNC), a confederation of trade unions, ethnic groups, smaller parties and literary groups whose aim was 'to achieve internal self-government for Nigeria'.[11]

In 1951–2, Nigeria's first general election was held to choose representatives for a Legislature with limited powers and Azikiwe's NCNC won the east with a large majority. The limited constitution was severely criticized, and between 1952 and 1954, when new elections under a new constitution were held, the energetic debate about the future of Nigeria and the questions of ethnic and regional representation continued.

The ferment was also a cultural one. Dr Azikiwe had included poetry in his daily newspaper, *The West African Pilot* (founded in 1937), and other papers and magazines followed suit. In 1950, Nigeria held its first Arts Festival, including drama and literary contributions.[12] At University College, Ibadan, the student magazines began to reflect an increasing interest in Nigerian culture. The *University Herald*, an occasional Student Union paper called *The Bug*, and *Eagle*, a cyclostyled sheet, saw the earliest publications of Chinua Achebe and Wole Soyinka, both of whom were students at Ibadan between 1949 and 1954. Achebe in his third year became editor of Ibadan's *University Herald*.[13]

One of Achebe's earliest contributions to the *University Herald*, 'Polar Undergraduate', is reprinted in *Girls At War and Other Stories*. First published in 1950, it is a witty and urbane piece on the sleeping (or non-sleeping) habits of his fellow students. With hindsight one can glimpse some of the traits which would distinguish the later novelist – a coolly amused (sometimes masquerading as bemused) view of the future educated elite of his country, a propensity for contrast worked into a carefully balanced structure, and a pleasure in parodying and satirizing various modes of discourse, in this case the would-be scientific. Absurd play with the language of science is carried to even greater lengths in another piece published in the *University Herald* in 1951, 'An Argument Against the Existence of Faculties', in which the crowning absurdity in an argument for allowing students to take a mixture of scientific and arts courses is the demonstration that a botanical diagram for fruit and the family tree of the Dukes of Lorraine are identical in all important aspects.[14] But the humour and parody are also directed against compartmentalization of the *intellectual* faculties, foreshadowing Achebe's insistent critique in later years of those who are unable to see or tolerate the dualities in their societies and in themselves.

In 1951 the *University Herald* also published 'In a Village Church'. This too is a coolly detached and amused piece in which the writer establishes his distance from the village 'characters' – not only by his ironic stance but also through the language which displays his literary education and contrasts the semi-literate fumblings of the elderly bible reader with his own easy acquaintance with Wordsworth. Nevertheless, this piece marks a shift from the earlier preoccupation with his fellow students at Ibadan to an interest in rural Nigeria and the uneasy coming together of two cultures. The narrative voice is implicated in that uneasiness, shifting from a 'we' at the beginning – which involves him with the villagers – to the detached 'I' of later paragraphs in the sketch. Here, too, the developing writer is learning to let incidents and scenes work on the reader's imagination without anxious instruction from the author. Such an incident occurs at the end of the first paragraph:

An old woman suddenly cried out and we stopped at the door to look back at her. 'I forgot to wear my shoes,' she explained piteously. (*GW*, p. 74)

In addition to essays, sketches, editorials, and letters, Achebe published two short stories while still an undergraduate, both reprinted in *Girls at War and Other Stories*. These stories, 'Marriage Is a Private Affair' (first published in 1952) and 'Dead Man's Path' (first published without any title in 1953), foreshadow later works and preoccupations. Like *No Longer at Ease*, 'Marriage Is a

10

Private Affair' takes as its theme the conflict between traditional Igbo and European concepts of marriage, the one
demanding obedience to family and community concerns,
the other assuming the right to individual choice and marriage for love. Unlike the later novel, however, this story
ends optimistically, with the implication that the father's
stubborn resistance and hardness of heart will be overcome
by the persistence and unremitting goodness of the son and
daughter-in-law and especially by the presence of grand-
children. 'Dead Man's Path', a story about a young school
teacher determined to replace 'old-fashioned ways' with
'modern methods', gives rather more force and substance
to the traditional Igbo world. Achebe endows the priest of
Ani with dignity and authenticity of speech. (We find here
the first appearance of a proverb which will recur in variant
forms in later works: 'Let the hawk perch and let the eagle
perch.') Moreover, the priest's admonition is given weight
by the subsequent death of a baby and the anger of the
villagers. Also typical of the later fiction is the swift and
ironic ending, for here the white inspector joins with the
'primitive' villagers to rebuke the 'progressive' young head
teacher. And this story reveals a sharper ear for differing
speech forms – some, like the priest's, given the flavour
of Igbo idiom; others, like Nancy's imitation of women's
magazines, lightly satirized. Achebe's use in this story of
the indirect third-person narrative is flexible and
accomplished, suggesting the language and cultural experiences which have formed the consciousness of the
characters described, while retaining the slight detachment
which encourages the reader not to take that consciousness
for granted. So he describes Michael Obi in the opening
paragraph:

He had many wonderful ideas and this was an opportunity to put
them into practice. He had had sound secondary school education which designated him a 'pivotal teacher' in the official
records and set him apart from the other headmasters in the mission field. He was outspoken in his condemnation of the narrow
views of these older and often less-educated ones.   (*GW*, p. 78)

On the next page, he will describe Nancy's thoughts
in a language and style drawn from schooling and

literature which seeks to cultivate 'proper feminine behaviour':

> Nancy was downcast. For a few minutes she became skeptical about the new school; but it was only for a few minutes. Her little personal misfortune could not blind her to her husband's happy prospects. (*GW*, p. 79)

It is a technique which Achebe will use with particular skill in his first three novels and a number of the later stories.

By this time, Achebe had not only decided to become a writer, but had also found the subject and the story that would preoccupy him. As part of his studies at Ibadan he read 'some appalling novels about Africa' and decided that 'the story we had to tell could not be told for us by anyone else, no matter how gifted and well-intentioned'.[15] One of those novels was Conrad's *Heart of Darkness* which Achebe dissected and accused of racism at its own heart in a lecture delivered at the University of Massachusetts in 1974.[16] But it was Cary's *Mister Johnson* which provided the chief starting point for his first novels:

> I know around '51, '52, I was quite certain that I was going to try my hand at writing, and one of the things that set me thinking was Joyce Cary's novel, set in Nigeria, *Mister Johnson*, which was praised so much, and it was clear to me that it was a most superficial picture of – not only of the country – but even of the Nigerian character, and so I thought if this was famous, then perhaps someone ought to try and look at this from the inside.[17]

The relationship between Cary's *Mister Johnson* and Achebe's first two novels, originally planned as one, has received surprisingly little critical attention. Yet as one can see from Achebe's later comments on the role of the African writer and his aims as a cultural nationalist, he was aware that the decision to retell Joyce Cary's story had implications only partially suggested by the contrast between 'a most superficial picture' and a look 'from the inside'. For Cary was not merely an 'outsider' observing Nigeria in a disinterested manner; his view was scarcely an objective one. He came to Nigeria as a colonial administrator and his depiction of Nigeria and Nigerians can be understood most fully in the light of the often inconsistent policies and attitudes of the British government and of colonial officials caught between those policies and the day-to-day realities of their work in Africa.[18] The stories Cary tells – the linear narratives – and the pictures he paints of an unchanging and static Africa develop from his own particular vision as an English official of Irish birth, writing within the traditions of a culture and a political system which sought to justify colonialism either as it was or as reformers thought it should be. The title of Achebe's first novel, *Things Fall Apart*, with its reference to Yeats' concept of vast historical cycles, implies that in challenging Cary's story he knew that he was also challenging a whole vision of history, a set of values and a particular ordering of society and literature.

Within the context of colonial structures and the literature which emanated from them, Frantz Fanon's analysis of the psychology of colonialism provides a particularly useful framework for understanding the literary representations of 'natives' and colonizers.[19] Fanon argues that it is race rather than class that matters in a colonial situation:

In the colonies the economic substructure is also a superstructure. The cause is the consequence; you are rich because you are white, you are white because you are rich. This is why Marxist analysis should always be slightly stretched every time we have to do with the colonial problem . . . It is neither the act of owning factories, nor estates, nor a bank balance which distinguishes the governing classes. The governing race is first and foremost those who come from elsewhere, those who are unlike the original inhabitants, 'the others'.[20]

That 'otherness' is maintained mentally and physically by an insistence on cultural and intellectual superiority on the one hand and by segregation on the other. And the physical separation is in turn maintained by enforceable law, bringing threats of violence on both sides. The insistence on racial otherness, together with the economic demand for the black man's *manual* labour, leads to an emphasis on the body: 'In the web of race prejudice, the Negro symbolizes the biological danger, the Jew, the

13

intellectual danger.'[21] Fanon follows Freud in assuming that civilization demands sublimation, and so sees racism as in part a projection of the European's repressed desires on to the Negro, who becomes allegorized as the id in subjection to the European superego. Renate Zahar gives such racial psychology a particular emphasis in a colonial situation:

The historico-economic process of colonization which racism helps to rationalize demands of the ruling group that they renounce any display of spontaneity. Society imposes on its members a repressive regimentation of their instinctual economy.[22]

Most of the aspects of colonial psychology described by Fanon and Zahar can be found in Cary's four novels set in Africa.[23] Each of them includes at least one Englishman or woman who seeks to fulfil the civilizing mission and/or encourage prosperity and trade. It is a mission wholeheartedly embraced by the most sympathetically portrayed African characters – Aissa in *Aissa Saved*, Louis Aladai in *The African Witch* and Mister Johnson in the novel named after him. But the consequences of this embrace are in each case disastrous, with the consequent implication that the colonial task must be a long and arduous one. The main reason for these disastrous consequences is the inevitable reabsorption of these African protagonists into their racially defined role. The critic A. R. JanMohamed has demonstrated that Cary's African characters can best be understood in terms of 'racial romance', using the term 'romance' as Northrop Frye does in *The Anatomy of Criticism* to describe a literature emanating from a static feudal society (like that established by the colonial hierarchy) in which characters function as archetypal or allegorical figures with fixed qualities, rather than as 'realistic' characters.[24] Cary's European characters belong to history; their psychology is understood in terms of cause and effect, and they learn and change within specific social and historical situations. In contrast, his African characters like Aissa and Mister Johnson do not learn; they behave in certain ways because they are what they are, and ultimately they remain true to their assigned racial characteristics. Louis Adalai, at first sight the most 'civilized' of them with his Oxford education, proves the most awful example of all when at the end of *The African Witch* he responds to the call of his 'blood instinct' and reverts to crocodile worship and human sacrifice. In the end, he is shot by the British soldiers in what is portrayed as a foolhardy and foolish nationalist gesture towards the liberation of his country (Rimi).

Violent physical or psychological obliteration is the usual fate of those in Cary's novels who aspire to be like the British, whether as Christians or as part of an educated elite – the deaths of Aissa and Mister Johnson, the psychological disintegration of Akande Tom in *The African Witch* and of Ulu in *The American Visitor* are other examples of this. As JanMohamed argues, this treatment of those who seek to 'ape' Europeans betrays the degree to which Cary's novels are caught up in the contradictions of a colonial policy which on the one hand claimed to educate the natives, bringing the 'benefits' of British religion, education and 'democratic' institutions, and on the other sought to maintain and justify the autocratic and non-egalitarian rule of those who represented the colonial power, and to preserve the economic privileges and psychological superiority which accrued from being a colonist. Thus, in *The African Witch* and *Mister Johnson*, the perception by the native protagonists that British rule and education are desirable is endorsed by the *narrator*, who comments on and commends the opportunity given to the natives to step from a world which he asserts to be hemmed in by superstition and fear, governed by the likes of Elizabeth (the African witch of the title), into an adult world, offering widening horizons and the riches of civilization. Yet the actual *story* brings upon those who seek to embrace such opportunities ridicule or destruction or, more usually, both. In all cases, acculturation is shown to be superficial – most dramatically in the case of Louis Aladai, with his almost-completed Oxford degree and the continued guidance in Africa of his Oxford tutor. This superficiality is symbolized by the shedding of western clothes. Just as Mister Johnson gives away his suit, umbrella and shoes, so Louis gradually changes from suit or blazer to native dress, while Akande Tom is bereft of his newly acquired suit and reduced to naked subjugation by Elizabeth.

Cary maintained that his characters were 'real people in a real world or they [were] nothing'.[25] His assertion is valid only with regard to his European characters. His characterization of Africa and Africans can be seen in the context of colonial interests and a whole tradition of colonial writing which contributed to the justification of the colonial presence in Africa. That tradition has been explored in detail by a number of scholars, most notably Dorothy Hammond and Alta Jablow in *The Africa That Never Was: Four Centuries of British Writing About Africa*.[26] One might ask why Achebe 'picked on' Cary rather than any number of other colonialist writers. Why not rewrite Conrad, for example? One reason may be that Conrad's *Heart of Darkness* is in part an allegorical and symbolic novel, while Cary is *primarily* concerned with historical and social rather than psychological and metaphysical questions, despite his ambivalence about the role of Africans in the movement of history.[27] A corollary of that concern is the situation of his novels in specific localities; these are all Nigerian and the reader is expected to believe in their reality. Cary writes as a man who 'knows' his Africa; Conrad's narrator is allowed to express some doubts as to the extent of his knowledge. We are never allowed to learn what 'unspeakable rites' Kurtz became a part of in Conrad's tale; Cary is explicit about the rites Louis participates in when he journeys up the river Rimi. Achebe shares with Cary an interest in specific moments of historical and cultural change and the ways in which specific characters may be caught up in such change. And so he also writes about particular Nigerian localities, challenging as he does so, Cary's 'knowledge' of Nigeria and Nigerians.

Moreover, Cary takes up questions about the relationship between individuals and history, the interaction between personal and political motives – questions which also arouse Achebe's deepest interest. Both novelists explore the problem of personal responsibility in a world in which individual power must be limited by forces outside one's control and knowledge. Those questions of power, responsibility and knowledge are in turn related to the problem of self-knowledge, the conflict between intellect and feeling, the difficulties of understanding and perceiving one's own motives, and the ways in which knowledge of others may be obscured by self-interest. And both novelists believe that artists and politicians share a common responsibility to their society – though it is precisely about these matters that Cary and Achebe differ. What *are* the implications of the artist's responsibility and – a closely connected issue – what weight should be given to individual fulfilment? Whereas Cary's overriding interest is in the freedom of the individual and his need to overcome the barriers to self-fulfilment and self-expression, Achebe's central concern is with the continuity and survival of a decent community threatened by self-interested individuals.

Cary's stories and characters and the form and technique of his novels can be seen as a product not merely of his colonial experience but also of the European literary tradition; specifically a novelistic tradition fashioned both by romanticism – with its emphasis on individual experience and sensibility – and by realism – which has tended to encourage individualism within a specific social framework while discouraging the active participation of the reader in either constructing or questioning the characters and the choice he or she makes. The readers of Cary's novels must suspend judgement and disbelief and remain unquestioning participants in a self-contained fictional world. In his preface to the Carfax edition of *Mister Johnson*, Cary distinguishes thus between the roles of reader and critic:

For a reader (who may have as much critical acumen as you please, but is not reading in order to criticize), the whole work is a single continuous experience. He does not distinguish style from action and character . . .

With a story in the present tense, when he too is in the present, [the reader] is carried unreflecting on the stream of events; his mood is not contemplative but agitated . . . But as Johnson does not judge, so I did not want the reader to judge. And as Johnson swims gaily on the surface of life, so I wanted the reader to swim, as all of us swim, with more or less courage and skill, for our lives. [28]

In challenging Cary's 'superficial picture', a representation to be observed on the surface without critical intervention, Achebe challenged not only the vision depicted but also the manner of the depiction, not only the story but the mode of storytelling, and the consequent relationship between reader and writer. Achebe's concern with community, together with his experience of a culture whose storytelling traditions are oral and communal, led him to radically re-form the novel in such a way that the reader is provoked into thoughtful awareness of the problems his characters face and evaluation of the responses made to those problems. His approach to the form and function of the novel is comparable to Brecht's approach to epic theatre, which itself was influenced by folk and oral forms and conventions. To put it another way, using the terms employed by the Russian critic Mikhail Bakhtin, Achebe rejects the 'monologic' form of Cary's novels to create his own kind of 'dialogic' novel. [29]

In 1971 the English novelist and critic David Caute lamented the division between politically committed novelists who cling to realism and the illusion of a self-contained fictional world, and modernist novelists who use the techniques of alienation only to endorse sensibilities contemptuous of all political and social involvement:

By and large the radical, committed impulse among novelists remains stubbornly harnessed to the realist, illusionist impulse. And whereas in the theatre many of the writers and artists whose work is of genuine *aesthetic* importance are men and women with an obvious *political* orientation to the Left, the most interesting or influential contemporary novelists are almost without exception writing about 'private' lives. Today's young radical student finds voices speaking to him and for him in the theatre; but if he has a passion for novels he must either accept kitchen-sink naturalism (or worn-out socialist realism) or else stare into space. Clearly that space ought to be, must be, filled. [Caute's italics] [30]

Had David Caute's student been staring in the direction of the African continent, he might have noticed that the space

18

was already being filled – by novelists such as Chinua Achebe and the writers who were to follow him.

With some justice Achebe may be deemed the 'father of the African novel in English'. His influence both as a creative writer and a critic has been considerable, not only on his fellow Nigerian authors but also on East African novelists such as Ngugi wa Thiong'o and Nuruddin Farah. His influence is most obviously apparent in the work of younger Igbo novelists such as Nkem Nwankwo, John Munonye, Chukwuemeka Ike, and Flora Nwapa, who follow Achebe in choosing for their settings traditional or changing rural communities, exploring the theme of the conflict between old and new values. In particular, Achebe's use of 'African English', drawing on the proverbs, tales and idiom of a traditional Igbo culture, becomes the norm. As Bernth Lindfors has noted, even older novelists such as Onuora Nzekwu 'whose first two novels had been written in a stiff, formal prose occasionally spiced with quotations from Sir Walter Scott, Robert Southey and Shakespeare, suddenly discovered how to write in an African vernacular style in his third novel, *Highlife for Lizards* (1965)'.[31] The Yoruba novelist, T. M. Aluko, also changed to an African English style after encountering Achebe's work, and Chukwuemeka Ike told Lindfors of the importance of Achebe's first two novels as models for the themes and techniques in his own work. Elechi Amadi is another Nigerian novelist whose early novels suggest Achebe's influence.

Although there are greater and more obvious differences between Achebe and the two most prominent contemporary East African novelists, they too acknowledge his importance. *Things Fall Apart* is mentioned as a key work for particular characters in their novels (for Munira in Ngugi's *Petals of Blood* and for Medina in Farah's *Sardines*). Neither of these novelists uses language in quite the same way as Achebe and the Nigerians who followed him, but for both the colonial encounter, the tension between African and western cultures and values, and the emphasis on the novel as a means of political understanding and change are central. And after their earliest fiction, both move closer and closer to novelistic forms which by no means mimic Achebe's, but which arguably are suggested by his in their multiplicity of voices and perspectives, in their frequent echoing of oral narrative forms, in their interweaving of past and present, and in their call upon the reader's intellectual participation and judgement as well as his or her concern.

2

'A less superficial picture':
Things Fall Apart

JOYCE CARY'S *Mister Johnson* tells the story of a young
Nigerian clerk who takes a bribe, loses his job, regains it,
helps and encourages the young British colonial officer
Rudbeck build a road, embezzles taxes to do so, murders
a white storekeeper, and is subsequently tried and executed
by Rudbeck. The novel seeks above all to celebrate the
character of Johnson, who is portrayed as a Dionysian
character, bursting with emotion, song, dance and spontaneity, and enamoured of European civilization. He is
contrasted both with the self-interested and unimaginative
pagan and Muslim Africans and with the British colonial
officers, who are characteristically tight-lipped, constrained
by reason and the letter of the law. Johnson provides
Rudbeck with the inspiration and energy as well as the
labour force and the money to build a road through his
district. Cary's implication is that Johnson's qualities must
be linked to and put to the service of Rudbeck's vision and
technological knowledge, and that Rudbeck can become
more humane and more creative by learning from
Johnson, although Johnson's anarchic and destructive
tendencies must be suppressed. At the end of the novel,
Rudbeck follows the letter of the law in trying and condemning Johnson, but bends the law by agreeing to personally
execute Johnson, who pleads with him to do so, reminding
Rudbeck that he (Johnson) has always regarded him as 'his
father and mother'.

Achebe originally planned his first novel as another version of *Mister Johnson*. However, the rewriting turned into
two novels, *Things Fall Apart* and *No Longer at Ease*, and it

is the second which seems at first glance to carry the burden of responding to Cary's story of a clerk who takes bribes while working for the British administration and is disgraced. But while the plots of *Mister Johnson* and *No Longer At Ease* are similar, thematically *Things Fall Apart* takes up the issues raised by Cary's novel. It is an attempt to give a less 'superficial' picture 'not only of the country – but even of the Nigerian character';[1] it also dramatizes the conflict between intuitive feeling and rigid social codes, between liberalism and conservatism, and between creativity and sterility. As Cary's novel opposes the spontaneous African man of feeling inspired by the romance of European civilization to the iron rule of native conservatism or of European law, so *Things Fall Apart* contrasts Okonkwo's rigidity and refusal to acknowledge feeling (a trait shared by the District Commissioner) with the intuitive knowledge and imaginative sympathy felt by Unoka and Nwoye, which the latter imagines to be a property of the western missionaries. Whereas in Cary's novel these opposing tendencies cluster around European and African respectively, in *Things Fall Apart* they become associated in Okonkwo's mind – and also in the reader's – with masculine and feminine principles.

The fact that the conflicts are located *in* the African community and then shadowed by the British characters makes an important difference, for at once the Africans become something more than symbols of qualities which, however important, are nevertheless subordinate elements in the total complex of the European psyche. Achebe's characters are complex individuals, types rather than archetypes, the resolution of whose conflicts is central to the plot. Okonkwo's role is not to save the British administrator and it is clear that Achebe's Europeans, even the more liberal ones like Mr. Brown, will never dream that they have anything to learn from Africans – who may be studied but never imitated. That is part of the tragedy for the Africans, who find it almost impossible to comprehend the depth and consequences of the white man's arrogance.

Part 1 of *Things Fall Apart* focuses on two things: the portrayal of Okonkwo and his psychology, and the portrayal

of the social, political and religious life of Umuofia, the
Igbo village to which Okonkwo belongs. On reading *Things
Fall Apart* after *Mister Johnson* one becomes aware of a
number of specific ways in which Achebe's version of
African society contrasts with Cary's. One of the earliest
scenes in *Mister Johnson* involves the bartering of Bamu, the
young woman Johnson seeks to marry, by her 'pagan'
family who equate her with a choice piece of horseflesh.
Her family is motivated by sheer greed, and family loyalty
is seen chiefly as the exercise of property rights. Bamu
herself has no feeling other than contempt for Johnson, and
stoically accepts her fate as a counter in the bargaining.
She will stay with him only as long as the terms of the
bargain are kept. One may contrast Achebe's depiction of
the agreement and discussion over the marriage contract
for Obierika's daughter, Akueke. First there is a long
period of drinking and chatting before the business of sett-
ling the bridal dowry is brought up. As if to make the contrast quite explicit, one of the men compares their traditional method of using a bundle of sticks to settle the dowry
with the customs of other clans such as Abame and Aninta:
'All their customs are upside down. They do not decide
bride price as we do, with sticks. They haggle and bargain
as if they were buying a goat or a cow in the market.'[2]
Achebe does not let the point rest, for we are shown yet
another part of a marriage ceremony in part 2, the con-
summation of the marriage of Uchendu's youngest son
(pp. 92–3); in part 3 the question of the marriage of
Okonkwo's daughters is discussed, and we learn of their
willing agreement to await their return to Umuofia. We are
also reminded several times of the special relationship between Okonkwo and Ekwefi.

Bamu regards her marriage to Mister Johnson as no
more than a business proposition; she will cook and breed
for him only as long as he can provide for her, and she
prepares to leave him as soon as he is in trouble. There is
never any question that Okonkwo's wives would desert
him – especially when he is in trouble – despite his hasty
and sometimes cruel treatment of them. Relationships between Igbo husbands and wives in *Things Fall Apart* are as

complex and varied as the relationship between Rudbeck and his wife, Celia, in *Mister Johnson*. In the same chapter telling of Akueke's betrothal, there is the story of Ndulue, whose wife Ozoemena died immediately after she learned of his death. ' "It was always said that Ndulue and Ozoemena had one mind." said Obierika. "I remember when I was a young boy there was a song about them. He could not do anything without telling her" ' (pp. 47–8). Then there is the relationship between Ekwefi and Okonkwo, his gruff affection for her and his concern when she follows Chielo and her daughter, and the story of her coming to him when he had been too poor to marry her earlier. We are shown also the settlement by the elders of a marriage dispute – an attempt to bring about reconciliation in the best interests of the couple and the community – very different from the self-interested commands of Bamu's brother, Aliu, or of the Waziri who supposedly governs Fada, where Cary's novel is set.

The scene showing the deliberation and judgement of the elders, along with other such scenes in the novel, also contrasts Achebe's version of African government with Cary's. Whereas *Mister Johnson* shows only despotic and greedy native rulers with little concern for the welfare of the people they govern, *Things Fall Apart* portrays a group of elders who share decision making, who are trusted by the people, and whose primary concern is the maintenance of a peaceful, prosperous and respected community for all. Moreover, their decisions are neither arbitrary nor individualistic, as Cary's novel asserts, but grow out of a long tradition and a finely interwoven set of beliefs – religious, social and political.

Perhaps one of the most significant things about *Things Fall Apart* is the way in which it demonstrates the intricate relationship between a man's individual psychology and the social context in which he has grown up. And that is where the novel makes its firmest response to Cary. Mister Johnson is representative of the free and unfettered spirit; he is an earlier version of Gulley Jimson, the carefree artist in Cary's later and more successful novel, *The Horse's Mouth*. So in terms of the theme of the novel it is appropriate that he have no family, no background, no social context other than the vague suggestion of a mission education. He is a man without roots, belonging to romance rather than to historical narrative. The European reader, long accustomed to such figures in literature if not in life – wandering poets, Synge's tramps and playboys, bohemian artists – does not readily question Mister Johnson's rootlessness. But Mister Johnson is essentially a European creation. To the Nigerian reader, according to Achebe, such a figure is hard to imagine; no Southern Nigerian (as Johnson is supposed to be) in the early part of the twentieth century could be without a family or relatives to care for him and come to his assistance when he is in trouble.[3]

However, after encountering Chinua Achebe's novels even the European reader may be struck by the discontinuity between Mister Johnson's character and his origins. Cary's novel rests on an opposition between the archetypal force Johnson suggests – id, or feeling and instinct – and the Europeans – who are associated with superego, or moral and intellectual qualities – so matching closely the kind of colonialist psychology and projection described by Fanon and Zahar and referred to in the previous chapter. Nowhere in *Mister Johnson* does Cary suggest that the African might have his own system of values, intelligently conceived and based on a long and evolving tradition, comprehending concern for others and the welfare of the community as a whole. The theme and project of *Mister Johnson* demand that the African possess not even a 'primitive' set of beliefs, for any action in terms of mind rather than feeling or sensual gratification would spoil the series of contrasts. It might also question the assumptions upon which colonial rule is based.

The Igbo community presented to us in *Things Fall Apart* is one which has established a balance, though sometimes an uneasy one, between the values clustered around individual achievement and those associated with community, or between materialism and spirituality. Those groups of values tend to be identified as masculine and feminine respectively and are epitomized in the two proverbs, 'Yam is King', and 'Mother is supreme', which dominate the first and second parts of the novel. Okonkwo prizes 'manliness' above all, and judges action and talk by that criterion, classifying everything he admires as 'manly' and everything he despises as 'womanly'. Fear of being called, like his father, an *agbala*, meaning both a man without a title and an old woman, is shown to be the motivating force in his life. He continually regrets that Ezinma, his favourite daughter, is a girl, laments that Nwoye 'has too much of his mother in him'; and it is fear of being thought effeminate that drives him to participate in the killing of Ikemefuna. In the use of these opposing categories of male and female, Okonkwo shares the thinking of his people, although he is less respectful than they are to the values embodied by the Earth Goddess, Ani, the priestess Chielo, and the sympathy, comfort and solace offered by his motherland. But the reader never doubts that he is the product of his society's system, and from the very beginning we are told that he is one of the great men of the village. The texture of his mind is made up of the proverbs, the sayings, the imagery, the rituals, the language which embody that system. He is, as A. R. JanMohomed argues, a *type* of his society, and Achebe is careful to show us how he has come into being through a combination of social moulding and family circumstance.[4] In this abstract sense he is much closer to Cary's Rudbeck and Bulteel and Rackham than he is to Mister Johnson whose most consistent trait is his lack of any social or psychological roots.

There is in *Things Fall Apart* one character who bears some resemblance to Mister Johnson, and that is Unoka, Okonkwo's father. Like Johnson, he is a man who refuses to accept responsibility for his debts, who is childlike and charming and exasperating. Like Johnson he is essentially an artist:

Unoka, for that was his father's name, had died ten years ago. In his day he was lazy and improvident and was quite incapable of thinking about tomorrow. If any money came his way, and it seldom did, he immediately bought gourds of palmwine, called round his neighbours and made merry. He always said that whenever he saw a dead man's mouth he saw the folly of not eating what one had in one's own lifetime. Unoka was, of course,

a debtor, and he owed every neighbour some money, from a few
cowries to quite substantial amounts.   (p. 8)

Unlike Mister Johnson, Unoka *does* have a family which
is obliged, though shamefacedly, to take care of him. And
one of the themes in the novel deals with the importance
of kin to the Igbo. Unoka is taken care of by his son and
the community does not let him starve. In his trouble
Okonkwo is sustained materially and psychologically by his
mother's relatives, and one of the bitterest things for
Okonkwo to envision is the breaking up of clan and the
family system through the influence of missionaries like Mr
Kiaga who praise Nwoye for leaving his family: 'Blessed is
he who leaves his father and his mother in my name', he
quotes from the New Testament – a declaration which, we
are told, 'Nwoye did not understand fully' (p. 142).

Unoka is also unlike Mister Johnson in that he is a conscious rather than an unconscious artist. His music does
not just well instinctively from some primitive source, nor
is Unoka unaware of the effect he is creating and the
techniques which he is using. Whereas Mister Johnson is
presented as a youth who creates in a kind of trance, whose
consciousness is submerged in a Dionysian state of oneness
with his audience, nature and the work of creation, Unoka
is both creator and critic, he is a craftsman and teacher as
well as a man of feeling. Although Unoka is a minor
character, sketched in briefly in the passage above, he is
given a context: a social and natural environment,
memories of childhood, of past festivals and seasons, images of bright skies, hovering kites, snatches of folk tale,
anecdote and everyday conversation about the weather and
village affairs. And so Unoka emerges not as an archetypal
character, but as a realistic one, not a rootless free spirit,
but a believable human being, differing in degree rather
than essence from the norms of his own and other
communities.

But *Things Fall Apart* does continue Cary's identification
of intuitive knowledge and feeling with music and poetry.
As Mister Johnson in some sense embodies the feeling and
imagination that Rudbeck often tries to suppress, so
Unoka is identified with the tenderness and humanity with

27

which the inarticulate Okonkwo wrestles. We are told that Okonkwo's whole life is dominated by the fear of being thought effeminate like his father, that he discourages his son from listening to 'womanly' folk tales and songs, and that the unspoken fear that Nwoye will turn out like Unoka haunts him. Both Okonkwo and Rudbeck are commanded to execute the boys who call them father, and both determine to participate in that execution in ways unacceptable to the elders in their communities. In both novels, this incident takes a crucial place and significance: in *Mister Johnson* it is the final act, approved wholeheartedly by Johnson and apparently intended to suggest new hope for Rudbeck who has allowed Johnson's 'inspiration' to supersede the exact letter of the law.

Johnson, seeing his gloom and depression, exerts himself. 'Don' you mind, sah, about dis hanging. I don't care for it one lil bit. Why' – he laughs with an air of surprise and discovery – 'I know fit nutting about it – he too quick. Ony I like you do him youself, sah. If you no fit to shoot me. I don' 'gree for dem sergeant do it, too much. He no my frien'. But you my frien'. You my father and my mother. I tink you hang me youself' . . .

Johnson knows then that he won't have to get up again from his knees. He feels the relief like a reprieve, unexpected, and he thanks Rudbeck for it. He triumphs in the greatness, the goodness, and the daring inventiveness of Rudbeck. All the force of his spirit is concentrated in gratitude and triumphant devotion; he is calling at the world to admit that there is no god like his god. He burst out aloud 'Oh Lawd, I tank you for my frien' Miser Rudbeck – de bigges' heart in de worl'.'

Rudbeck leans through the door, aims the carbine at the back of the boy's head, and blows his brains out. Then he turns and hands it back to the sentry. 'Don't forget to pull it through.'

He is surprised at himself, but he doesn't feel any violent reaction. He is not overwhelmed with horror. On the contrary, he feels a peculiar relief and escape, like a man who, after a severe bilious attack, has just been sick.[5]

As a number of critics have argued, Cary wishes to indicate that Rudbeck, in the narrator's words at the end of the novel 'growing ever more free in the inspiration which seems already his own idea', has moved away from mechanical rationalism, signified by the weighing of Johnson and establishing of his equivalent in bags of money and goods, to acknowledging Johnson's humanity and Rudbeck's own sense of responsibility to the boy who calls him his 'father and mother'.

The boy who is executed in *Things Fall Apart* is Ikemefuna, to whose significance readers are alerted in the very first chapter of *Things Fall Apart* when we are told in the final sentence of that chapter that Okonkwo was asked to 'Look after the doomed lad who was sacrificed to the village of Umuofia by their neighbours to avoid war and bloodshed. The ill-fated lad was called Ikemefuna' (p. 6). We are reminded again in chapter 2 that Ikemefuna's story is a sad one, 'still told in Umuofia unto this day' (p. 9). Hence the reader watches Ikemefuna's appearance and developing relationship with Nwoye and Okonkwo with apprehension and alert attention. It becomes apparent that Ikemefuna, although an outsider, is the ideal type of the clan. As a skilful hunter *and* musician, sympathetic to the troubles of his adopted sister when she carelessly breaks her water pot, encouraging Nwoye to develop the 'manly' virtues that please Okonkwo, he succeeds in balancing masculine and feminine attributes. Hence the killing of Ikemefuna is not only a tragic destruction of a promising and guiltless individual, it connotes the murder of the clan's potential; Ikemefuna's sacrifice is both a symbol of what the clan lacks and a realistic dramatisation of the clan's inability to maintain a harmonious balance between male and female principles, rather than an uneasy dialectic without synthesis. The image of tension between opposites, of a taut balance destroyed, is taken up and emphasized when we are told of Nwoye's reaction to the killing: 'Something seemed to give way inside him, like the snapping of a tightened bow' (p. 43). The sacrifice of Ikemefuna and his father's participation in it is the focal act which finally alienates Nwoye from the clan and Okonkwo and leads him to seek a more humane community among the Christians.[6]

Whereas Mister Johnson accepts his fate without question and is full of gratitude to Rudbeck for taking the execution into his own hands, an act which for Rudbeck is a courageous one, Ikemefuna instinctively turns to Okonkwo for salvation, and Okonkwo's intervention is portrayed as an act of cowardice: 'Dazed with fear, Okonkwo drew his matchet and cut him down. He was afraid of being thought weak' (p. 43). For Rudbeck, the shooting is cathartic: 'he feels a peculiar relief and escape, like a man who, after a severe bilious attack, has just been sick' (p. 249), and he returns to his house feeling hungry and ready for breakfast. The final lines of the novel indicate that he feels (and that the reader should approve) a certain pride in his action: 'But Rudbeck, growing ever more free in the inspiration which seems already his own idea, answers obstinately, "I couldn't let anyone else do it, could I?" ' Okonkwo, on the other hand, is unable to eat for three days, drinks heavily to avoid self-condemnation, and the reader endorses Obierika's disapproval (p. 46). The contrasts between the two scenes subtly undermine stock European assumptions about the relative humanity of Africans and Europeans. (Cary's *Aissa Saved* and *The African Witch* dwell repeatedly on callous murders and tortures, including Aissa's death as she is eaten alive by ants.) Moreover, these contrasts subvert the closing scenes of *Mister Johnson*, which now seem overwritten, quite unconvincing in the portrayal of a young man's response to death and his executioner, and callous in their turning of the loss of one human life so quickly to another man's profit. This final point is also underlined in the ending of *Things Fall Apart* when the District Commissioner turns from the body of Okonkwo to meditate upon the usefulness of this death for his planned book for the edification of Europeans.

The novelist and his reader

Although Cary's reader is to be 'carried unreflecting on the stream of events' and to refrain from judging Johnson or from 'distinguishing style from action or character', he is not expected to *identify with* Johnson. The narrative tone is generally one of slightly amused, sometimes bemused detachment, and the reader is rarely allowed to view the characters or the action from any other perspective. Indeed, the vision of Africa presented by Cary in his novels is not unlike the view Cary ascribes to Celia, Rudbeck's wife, in *Mister Johnson*:

But to Celia Africa is simply a number of disconnected events which have no meaning for her at all. She gazes at the pot-maker without seeing that she has one leg shorter than the other, that she is in the first stages of leprosy, that her pot is bulging on one side. She doesn't really see either woman or pot, but only a scene in Africa. Even Mr. Wog [Mister Johnson] is to her a scene in Africa.[7]

For Johnson, on the other hand, 'Africa is simply perpetual experience, exciting, amusing, alarming or delightful, which he soaks into himself through all his five senses at once, and produces again in the form of reflections, comments, songs and jokes'.

The reader is placed somewhere between the position of Celia for whom 'Africa is simply a number of disconnected events', and Mister Johnson for whom 'Africa is simply perpetual experience . . . soaked in through the senses'; 'simply' so in both cases. The reader is given no space or provision for reflection, criticism or judgement. The pace of the narrative is breathless. Only at the end of the novel is there time to stop and ask about meaning, significance, connection, morality, with the result that the reader is left to ponder the significance of Rudbeck's action and encounter with Johnson, not the significance and morality of Johnson's actions.

For Achebe, the relationship between reader and subject, and hence the relationship between narrative voice and subject, as well as the pace of the story, must be very different. His narrative persona is characterized from the opening paragraphs of the novel:

Okonkwo was well known throughout the nine villages and even beyond. His fame rested on solid personal achievements. As a young man of eighteen he had brought honour to his village by throwing Amalinze the Cat. Amalinze was the great wrestler who for seven years was unbeaten, from Umuofia to Mbaino. He was called the Cat because his back would never touch the earth. It was this man that Okonkwo threw in a fight which the old men agreed was one of the fiercest since the founder of their town engaged a spirit of the wild for seven days and seven nights.

The drums beat and the flutes sang and the spectators held their breath. Amalinze was a wily craftsman, but Okonkwo was as slippery as a fish in water. Every nerve and every muscle stood out on their arms, on their backs and their thighs, and one almost heard them stretching to breaking point. In the end Okonkwo threw the Cat.

Not only does this passage introduce Okonkwo as a heroic figure and wrestler (who will be seen to wrestle with others, with his *chi*, his father's heritage, his own character, and with the white man), but it also reveals the primary characteristics of the narrative voice. His world is that of the nine villages, from Umuofia to Mbaino; areas outside of these boundaries have little significance as yet, belonging simply to that vague realm 'beyond'. His values are those of his society, recognizing 'solid personal achievements' and approving those who thus bring honour to their village, values which in turn emphasize the close tie between individual success and the welfare of the community. And he is the recorder of a legend which will link up with the legends (of other great heroes and wrestlers) remembered by the old men. As in other tales developed from oral sources, such as *The Iliad* or *Beowulf*, history, myth and legend are closely connected; poetry and history are intertwined. The narrative voice is primarily a recreation of the persona heard in tales, history, proverbs and poetry belonging to an oral tradition; it represents a collective voice through which the artist speaks *for* his society, not as an individual apart from it – he is the chorus rather than the hero. As such he embodies not only the values and assumptions of his community, but also its traditions, its history, its past; and the present must be seen as growing out of that past, a product of it, as Okonkwo is seen as a product of his community and its structures.

The opening paragraph also suggests a kinship between the speaker and his implicit audience, for instance in the assumption that values are shared in regard to what constitutes worthwhile achievements. A sharp awareness of the needs of the audience, its call upon the speaker, is implied in the very qualities which make both the opening paragraph and the work as a whole, with its numerous digressions and episodic structure, reminiscent of oral composition. Explanations like that concerning the identity of Amalinze and the source of his nickname are inserted as the speaker feels his fictive audience's need for them, not with regard to a preconceived structure and sense of proportion typical of the written work planned by the District Commissioner at the end of the novel.

The language used by the narrator is also closely related to the speech of the Igbo characters who are at the centre of the novel. Expressions and proverbs used by Okonkwo, Obierika and others are repeated or echoed by the narrator, and thus the identity of the narrator as spokesman for the Igbo community is emphasized. At the same time, the dialogue is seasoned with proverbs which give the conversation flavour (for 'proverbs are the palm-oil with which words are eaten') and at the same time characterize the speaker, his mood, and the values of the society he represents.

Cary's narrative voice is quite distinct from the voices of any of his characters. It is furthest in tone and style from Johnson's childlike babble; nowhere does it approximate his idiom or his accent. Likewise it avoids the sentiment and romanticism of Johnson's songs. In tone and idiom it is closer to the language of the British administrators, but it is also much more flexible, concrete and precise than the threadbare clichés Rudbeck, Bulteel and Celia use as conversational counters and as substitutes for thinking and seeing. But Cary's breathless pace almost allows him to obscure the question of language: How and in what languages do the characters in *Mister Johnson* communicate? Pagans such as Bamu and her family utter animal-like screeches and grunts; their speech, like their comprehension, is represented as extremely simple and limited. It is emphasized again and again that Johnson is an outsider from the south, yet he has no *linguistic* difficulty in communicating with the natives of Fada and the interior, whether Muslim or pagan. Most of his conversation is characterized by a dialect somewhere between southern Afro-American speech and West African pidgin, but it becomes clear that Bamu does not understand any form of English when Johnson introduces her to Celia, and all remarks have to be translated. Such explicit references to the fact that the people of Fada speak a different language are rare, however.

In contrast, Achebe rarely lets his reader forget the otherness of Igbo culture and the language which embodies it. His use of Igbo words is one means of insisting on this otherness, of bringing the reader up against the barriers of non-English sounds and concepts. In general, the Igbo words such as *ilo, obi, jigida, agbala* and *ndichie* are immediately translated or explained in the text itself. Their function is not to mystify the reader but to remind him that the Igbo possess a language of their own, and that their culture, ranging from everyday surroundings and artefacts (*obi, jigida*) to complex religious and philosophical concepts (*ndichie, agbala*) is expressed through it. Many critics have analysed one of the most striking aspects of *Things Fall Apart*: the use of idioms, imagery and proverbs which suggest a non-English and specifically Eastern Nigerian culture, and there is no need to go over such ground again.[8] What may be emphasized for the purposes of this discussion is Achebe's repeated reminder of the linguistic barriers to communication and understanding, in contrast with Cary's implication that the barriers are ones of civilization and intelligence rather than language. In *Things Fall Apart* almost every encounter with the white man or his emissaries involves some reference to the alien language or dialect: there is the white man who repeats something incomprehensible at Abame; the ludicrous confusion of 'himself' and 'his buttocks' by the missionary; Obierika's bitter reply to Okonkwo's question, 'Does the white man understand our custom about land?' – 'How can he when he does not even understand our tongue?'; the difference in syntax and idiom between the speech of the District Commissioner and that of the Igbo. Like Obi, who felt it necessary to remind Londoners that Africans have languages of their own, Achebe reminds his readers that Igbo is the language of his community.[9]

Paradoxically, Achebe uses the written word brought by the colonizers in order to record and recreate the oral world obliterated or denied by them. This paradox is related to the irony that although Achebe shows the failure of language to enlarge understanding, to become a means of communication, and to break out of a self-enclosed system, nevertheless the novel itself *is* an attempt to reach, through self-conscious use of the language of one culture, the culture of another. The paradox is highlighted by direct reference to the western literary tradition which now belongs also to the author: the title, *Things Fall Apart*, from Yeats' 'The Second Coming', is not only a reminder of that tradition but is also appropriate to the novel's record of the destruction of a civilization; at the same time, one recalls that Yeats' theory of the cycles of history ignores African history, as does European thought generally. A further irony of course is that Yeats' poem foresees the end of the Christian era, while Achebe's novel records the end of the non-Christian era in Eastern Nigeria. Yet that non-Christian tradition, its religion and culture, is in part validated for the western or westernized reader by indirect parallels with biblical tales; for instance, the parallel between Okonkwo's sacrifice of Ikemefuna and the story of Abraham and Isaac is brought to the surface when Nwoye takes Isaac as his Christian name. Within the text itself, the occasional inclusion of phrases such as 'nature . . . red in tooth and claw' from Tennyson's *In Memoriam*, or of literary words such as 'valediction' in the otherwise non-British and non-literary idiom, serve to remind the reader of the contrasting worlds that have finally come together in the authorial consciousness. That consciousness is to be distinguished from the epic voice discussed earlier, and it is closer to the questioning and alienated vision of Nwoye than the unquestioning and integrated culture which Okonkwo fights desperately to preserve. (The Hungarian critic Georg Lukács maintains in his *Theory of the Novel* that such a conflict between the nostalgia for epic totality and the consciousness alienated from its society is the core of the novel form.)

The reference to the poetry of the British and Christian cultural tradition and Achebe's use of the novel form also suggest the importance of the poetic as a means of bridging the gap between languages, of going beyond the Logos – the authoritative, self-enclosed and self-validating discourse – of each culture.[10] *Things Fall Apart* is a commentary on the ways in which language can become rigid and incapable of communication, but at the same time demonstrates the creative possibilities of language. The very proverbs and phrases which have become clichés for their Igbo speakers, which no longer have a living relation to the things signified, are yet for the western reader creative of a world in which the tension between word and referent, the awareness of metaphor as such, is alive and vibrant. When Okonkwo says, 'Let the kite and the eagle perch together', we are made aware of the ritualistic nature of those words for him; but this same sentence helps to create a world and its value system for us, and gains significance as the novel proceeds.

For Cary the barriers to understanding between Africans and Europeans arise mainly in the gap between what he sees as a static, undeveloped group, and an advanced, civilized and changing society. His natives have neither a past nor a future; they live from moment to moment. Therefore, cause and effect, development and change, and concepts of time are alien to them. Cary's African characters exist only in the present tense, from one isolated event to the next. They react – passively, indifferently, or with excitement – to events and people, but they never learn from them. And like Mister Johnson, Cary's narrative charges headlong from episode to episode, with exuberance but without dignity, until it comes to a shocking halt. Here again, Achebe's opposing vision leads him to adopt an entirely different narrative style and technique. The qualities exhibited in the opening passages of *Things Fall Apart* serve as a model for the structure of the novel as a whole as it moves backward and forward in time. Okonkwo is introduced at the height of his fame, although the story is set in the past, and is in turn related to a more

36

distant historical and mythical past. His fame as the story begins, when he was about forty, rests on his achievements, including the memorable wrestling match when he was eighteen. The third paragraph returns to the forty-year-old Okonkwo of the beginning of the story, the fourth moves back again to the death of his father ten years previously, the fifth to Unoka's childhood, the sixth to his irresponsible adulthood at a time parallel to Okonkwo's present, and the final paragraph of the chapter returns to Unoka's death, to Okonkwo's achievement, and looks forward to the fate of Ikemefuna. Chapter 2 takes up the story of Okonkwo in his prime when he is responsible for Ikemefuna, but chapter 3 moves back again in time to Okonkwo's boyhood and difficult struggle as a young man. Such narrative movement is characteristic of Achebe's novels. All five begin at one moment in time and then move further back before moving forward, frequently returning to more or less distant pasts as the story proceeds. There is an irony in this, since most of his protagonists seek to break free of their pasts and create themselves anew. (In *Arrow of God*, however, Ezeulu seeks to preserve the past and contain the future.)

The effect of this temporal movement of the narrative is on the one hand to prevent the reader from being 'carried unreflecting on the stream of events', and on the other to insist on reflections about cause and effect, with particular regard to Okonkwo's success and failure in his attempt to control his future. For Joyce Cary one of the fundamental constants facing all human beings, and of intense concern to novelists, is the conflict between human nature and material facts, between freedom and necessity, so that 'we have a reality consisting of permanent and highly obstinate facts, and permanent and highly obstinate human nature'.[11] One might see that conflict voiced differently in the recurring reference in *Things Fall Apart* to the relationship between a man and his *chi* and the contrasting sayings concerning it: 'When a man says yes, his *chi* says yes also' (p. 19) and 'A man could not rise beyond the destiny of his *chi*' (p. 92) or 'He had a bad *chi*' (p. 13). Cary turns Johnson's attempt to create and control his destiny into a comedy or farce whose outcome affects only Johnson and Rudbeck; Okonkwo's attempt and failure is turned into tragedy which involves the fate not just of an individual but of a whole community. Historical awareness of the ultimate fate of Okonkwo's proudly self-contained community combined with respect for Okonkwo's determination to preserve all that he values in that community, nudges the reader into frequent reflection on the question of what values and events will either allow that community to survive or contribute to its distintegration. Such reflection is directed also by prophecies of doom, such as that of the oracle of Abame about the coming of the whites, and Uchendu's lamentation about the consequences of that visitation:

'But I fear for you young people because you do not understand how strong is the bond of kinship. You do not know what it is to speak with one voice. And what is the result? An abominable religion has settled among you. A man can now leave his father and his brothers. He can curse the gods of his fathers and his ancestors, like a hunter's dog that suddenly goes mad and turns on his master. I fear for you; I fear for the clan.' He turned again to Okonkwo and said, 'Thank you for calling us together.'

(p. 118)

Uchendu's lamentation ends part 2 of the novel and acts as a summary of the events dramatized in that section, where we have seen both the value of kinship in the material and spiritual assistance given the banished Okonkwo, and the inroads made by the new religion with its blessing on those 'who leave their father and mother' for Christ's sake. In these lines, the reader is asked to consider the wider significance of Okonkwo's story and of Nwoye's choice. Similarly, part 1 ends with a reflection and a series of questions:

Obierika was a man who thought about things. When the will of the goddess had been done, he sat down in his *obi* and mourned his friend's calamity. Why should a man suffer so grievously for an offence he had committed inadvertently? But although he thought for a long time he found no answer. He was merely led into greater complexities. He remembered his wife's twin children, whom he had thrown away. What crime had they committed? The Earth had decreed that they were an offence on the land and must be destroyed. And if the clan did not exact punishment for an offence against the great goddess, her wrath was loosed on all the land and not just on the offender. As the elders said, if one finger brought oil it soiled the others.

(p. 87)

Obierika's reflection prods the reader to ask similar questions – not only about the injustice of Okonkwo's banishment and the suffering of innocent twins and their mothers, but also about the inadequacy of Obierika's recourse to the formulas of the clan. One becomes aware here of a way in which language can become an evasion of intuitive understanding. The proverbs which so potently create for the European reader another world and culture can prevent creative change. Obierika feels that the twins and Okonkwo have committed no crime; inner feeling, however, is soon suppressed by the prefabricated declaration: 'The earth had decreed . . .' And the final proverb closes off all further questions for Obierika, but not for the reader.

The questions of Nwoye and of the women who have lost their twins are less easily silenced by the formulas of the elders. They are searching for a new language which will close the gap between their inner feeling of what should be and the language the culture has developed to justify what is. And above all it is 'the poetry of the new religion' which appeals to Nwoye when the Christians first bring their message:

But there was a young lad who had been captivated. His name was Nwoye, Okonkwo's first son. It was not the mad logic of the Trinity which captivated him. He did not understand it. It was the poetry of the new religion, something felt in the marrow. The hymn about brothers who sat in darkness and in fear seemed to answer a vague and persistent question that haunted his young soul – the question of the twins crying in the bush and the question of Ikemefuna who was killed. He felt a relief within as the hymn poured into his parched soul. The words of the hymn were like drops of frozen rain melting on the dry palate of the panting earth. Nwoye's callow mind was greatly puzzled. (pp. 103–4)

The simile of words like drops of rain on the dry palate of

the parched earth recalls 'the kind of story Nwoye loved' as a child, the story of how Earth and Sky quarrelled and Sky withheld rain for seven years. Vulture was sent to soften Sky with a song 'of the suffering of the sons of men. Whenever Nwoye's mother sang that song he felt carried away to the distant scene of the sky where Vulture, Earth's emissary, sang for mercy. At last Sky was moved to pity, and he gave to Vulture rain wrapped in leaves of coco-yam. But as he flew home his long talon pierced the leaves and the rain fell as it had never fallen before' (p. 38). Okonkwo has taught Nwoye that such stories are for 'foolish women and children', and to please his father Nwoye pretends to despise 'women's stories', listening instead to his father's accounts of tribal wars and his exploits as a warrior. Thus the deliberate link between these two scenes suggests that it is not specifically the words of the new religion that stir Nwoye, but the songs of suffering and poetry in general. In denying the fictional tales as womanish and insisting on stories which are factual and historical, Okonkwo has denied the poetic world, which in both contexts quoted is closely related to the world of myth. His rejection of the poetic is also related to his suppression of what he 'inwardly knows', or intuition, and for Nwoye poetry is equivalent to 'something felt in the marrow'. For Nwoye, then, the appeal of the new religion is its seeming recognition of that inner, unverbalized world, where the vague and persistent questions are felt in terms of situations, not understood on a verbal level. The 'poetry of the new religion' is at its most powerful for Nwoye and other Igbo when received through imagery and music: we are told that the rollicking hymn tunes pluck 'at silent and dusty chords in the heart' (p. 103), and that Nwoye is affected by the image of 'brothers who sat in darkness' and the image of the lost sheep. The 'dusty chords' again pick up the connection between the songs of suffering and the rain and the parched earth and are a subtle reminder of Unoka, who was a musician, an expert with the flute and a man of great feeling, constantly vacillating between extremes of joy and grief. He is called *agbala*. But the Oracle is also called Agbala, and symbolizes the power of the word at its highest

40

level, and the word which is mysterious and enigmatic.
Poetry, myth and fiction are all associated with the
spiritual, the sacred, the feminine and, paradoxically, with
the inner, unspoken word. All are linked with the powerful
figures of Chielo, priestess of the Oracle, whose voice when
possessed is described as unearthly. When Okonkwo pleads
with her not to carry off Ezinma, she responds, 'Beware
Okonkwo! . . . Beware of exchanging words with Agbala.
Does a man speak when a god speaks? Beware!' (p. 71)

   In the series of lectures published as *Art and Reality*, Joyce
Cary discusses the gap between intuition and expression:
'A cold thought has to deal with a warm feeling. I said that
intuitions are evanescent. Wordsworth's intuitions die not
only for the man, they fade very quickly for the child. But
the conceptual thought cannot only destroy them, it can
bar them out.'[12] The conflict between cold thought and
warm feeling is dramatized in *Mister Johnson*. But although
Cary stresses in his essays the need for both artists and
political thinkers to resolve that conflict, there is no
coherent resolution in his African novels. For Achebe, the
problem of artistic expression and the problem of social
change are inextricable, for language is central to both.
The reader's task is to be aware of the limits of language,
to be alert to the ways in which words, formulas and
rhetoric can obscure understanding. He is not allowed to
separate feeling and judgement, to swim unreflecting
before emerging on the shore to look back and criticize, but
must continually combine criticism and sympathy. The
concern with the problem of language and the demand that
the reader learn to examine language critically take different forms in Achebe's later novels, but remain crucial to
all of them.

3

'The best lack all conviction': *No Longer at Ease*

Men in general think badly: in disjuncture from their personal
lives, claiming objectivity where the most irrational passions
seethe, losing . . . their senses in the pursuit of professionalism.
— Adrienne Rich

THINGS FALL APART begins with one kind of certainty
and ends with another. The assured tone of the pre-
colonial Igbo village elder is replaced by the equally
assured and unquestioning tone of the British District
Commissioner. For the reader, the real significance of the
novel lies in the gap between those two certainties. *No Longer
at Ease*, on the other hand, begins and ends with questions,
and the fact that we begin with Obi Okonkwo's trial means
that the reader is concerned not with *what* happens, but *why*
'a young man of [Obi's] education and brilliant promise
could have done this'.[1] Although the judge's question is
chiefly a rhetorical formula and he is not seriously seeking an
answer, Obi's emotion interests the reader in him and the
reason for his downfall, while allowing, through the cracks in
Obi's self-image of himself as a cynical and realistic man of
the world, a glimpse of some of the clues to that answer.
Those small clues – the 'treacherous tears', as well as the
oddity of his telling himself that his mother's death and
Clara's departure were 'merciful' – alert the reader and
make him wary of the easy answers proposed by Mr. Green
at the European Club or by members of the Umuofian Progressive Union. The reader should also be wary of the easy
answers that Obi gives himself.

Like *Mister Johnson*, *No Longer at Ease* is the story of a
young man who, educated by the British, attracted by
much of what British civilization has to offer, employed by
the British, seeks to live up to a new inflated image created
by his position, falls into debt, takes bribes, is caught, tried
and convicted. Cary's additional melodrama of murder

and execution is omitted (although a drama of execution, assassination of the messenger and suicide is included in *Things Fall Apart*). That omission is part of Achebe's response to Cary's assertion that novels set in Africa demand coarseness of detail and melodramatic plots. Obi's self-conscious and introspective nature is another response – making him, and hence the whole tone and quality of his story, quite unlike Mister Johnson. However, Mr. Green may be assumed to speak for Cary, and also Conrad, in his assertion that education is wasted on Africans, that 'the African is corrupt through and through', and the African climate has 'sapped [him] mentally and physically'. Later in the novel, Green is linked to Conrad and Kurtz, and his name links him also to Graham Greene, whose *Heart of the Matter* is much admired by Obi and whose protagonist, Scobie, is as much ridden by duty as is Mr. Green. Of course, Green's attitude is a crude summary of Cary's, as Achebe reads him, but the melodramatic endings of three of Cary's African novels, particularly *The African Witch* with its regression of another university-educated African, give sufficient grounds to make the caricature recognizable.

For Green and the other members of the British club, Obi and all Africans belong to a race apart, whose psychology and mentality is permanently alien. Mr. Green's attitude is juxtaposed with that of the Umuofia Progressive Union, for whom Obi is permanently a kinsman, a brother against whom anger 'was felt in the flesh, not in the bone' (p. 4). For the Union, Obi's crime is clearly individual, rather than generic ('He was without doubt, a very foolish and self-willed young man') whose main fault is the lack of experience which caused him to get caught. Thus, the Umuofians, although contrasted to the British in attitude, language and ceremony, at first sight seem merely to modify Mr. Green's assertion that 'They are all corrupt.'

The reader may at first take the worlds of the British Club and the Umuofia Progressive Union to be two mutually and deliberately exclusive worlds, each equally alien in the urban African environment of Lagos, each a defensive enclave against it. The juxtaposition of those two worlds is a means not only of posing two responses to Obi Okonkwo's trail, but also of suggesting two traditions, two cultures, which Obi was intended to bridge, and whose expectations he has failed in both cases. To Obi the demands of the two worlds seem irreconcilable, his western education has made him 'beast of no nation', as an outraged patient cries when Obi pushes past him into the doctor's surgery following Clara's abortion.

A number of critics have accepted Obi's passive view of himself as an inevitable victim of the cultural conflict and corruption which characterize modern Nigeria. But from the first chapter we are given hints that the problem may not be simply the difficulty of a traditional value system unable to adjust acceptably to an urban world, far less the supposedly corrupt nature of Africans, or the impossibility of reconciling Igbo and western values. It is Obi's *perception* of himself and the situation which may be the real problem, and insofar as the novel is addressed to readers who are rather like Obi – the young educated elite, new graduates of British and Nigerian universities and high schools, the Nigerians who might be expected to read novels like *No Longer at Ease* and recognize the literary allusions as well as the worlds portrayed – it seeks to enlarge their understanding of the limitations and blind spots in Obi's perception of his predicament and Nigeria's. Obi's concern with self-image and his lack of self-knowledge are suggested in the trial scene discussed above. The cracks in the legal world, in the exclusivity of the British Club, or of the Umuofia Progressive Union are revealed with deftly ironic details: the fraudulently obtained doctor's certificates, the discreet presence of the African stewards in the British Club, the blending of Christian prayer formula and Igbo proverb and ritual at the Umuofia Progressive Union meeting (pp. 5–6). It is clear that the separate cultures of *Things Fall Apart* have come together in a variety of modes, and because this passage is so reminiscent of the rituals and idioms characteristic of the earlier novel, it is a forceful reminder of the changes that are taking place. It is also clear that the love of debate and oratory and the lively oral culture of traditional Umuofia remain alive. The three opening scenes also bring to the foreground three of the most important areas in which the question of cultural combination must be raised: the legal and political world of the courtroom; the social, class and racial divisions of the club and European suburb of Ikoyi; and the religious and social world of the Umuofians. Obi will confront and be overcome by cultural conflict in all three areas.

From the contrasting and opposing attitudes of the British Club and the Umuofia Progressive Union, Achebe takes us back in time to Obi's departure and to a group of people for whom the combination of cultures seems to present no problem. For the Christian pastor, Mr. Ikedi, Obi's trip to England represents not a step into a different culture and set of values, but a new form of fulfilling traditional expectations:

'In times past,' he told [Obi], 'Umuofia would have required of you to fight in her wars and bring home human heads. But these were days of darkness from which we have been delivered by the blood of the Lamb of God. Today we send you to bring knowledge. Remember that the fear of the Lord is the beginning of wisdom. I have heard of young men from other towns who went to the white man's country, but instead of facing their studies they went after the sweet things of the flesh. Some of them even married white women.' The crowd murmured its strong disapproval of such behaviour. 'A man who does that is lost to his people. He is like rain wasted in the forest. I would have suggested getting you a wife before you leave. But the time is too short now. Anyway, I know that we have no fear where you are concerned. We are sending you to learn book. Enjoyment can wait. Do not be in a hurry to rush into the pleasures of the world like the young antelope who danced herself lame when the main dance was yet to come.'   (pp. 9–10)

It is ironic that the sacrificial Christian imagery should be used to express the disapproval of another kind of bloodletting, and it is also ironic that the pastor's message should be enclosed in so-called 'heathen' wisdom beginning with a reference to past expectations and ending with an Igbo fable. And despite the fact that the warning is also 'coloured' by Christian puritanism, the emphasis on marrying a wife approved by his family and returning to the clan is solidly traditional. Here, as in the earlier meeting, the concern is with the welfare of the clan, the community, to which individual desires must always be subordinate.

The first chapter begins with the trial for bribery; it ends with the description of the gifts freely given by the people of Umuofia – gifts of money also, but given for Obi's benefit not the individual giver's:

They pressed their presents into his palm, to buy a pencil with, or an exercise book, or a loaf of bread for the journey, a shilling there and a penny there – substantial presents in a village where money was so rare, where men and women toiled from year to year to wrest a meagre living from an unwilling and exhausted soil. (p. 10)

Chapter 2 immerses Obi in other kinds of worlds – the English academic world and the urban world of Lagos. The narrator's comment on England's contribution is particularly ironic: 'It was in England that Nigeria first became more than just a name to him. That was the first great thing that England did for him.' But, like Celia's romanticized image of Africa in *Mister Johnson*, the nostalgic and romantic picture which Obi associates with Nigeria when he is distant from it has little to do with the complexity of the 'real' Nigeria or, specifically, the 'real' Lagos, one which in some aspects parallels the 'real' African town of Fada, described by Cary – with its slums, and putrid smells, and dirt. In Achebe's work, however, the slums are presented as a consequence of colonial intervention, not as preceding it.[2]

Chapter 2, by virtue of its placement after the Igbo scenes of chapter 1, emphasizes the degree to which Obi has become immersed in the English literary tradition and academic culture. While in England, his view of Nigeria is enclosed in the romantic form of the Georgian pastoral poets – a kind of debased Tennyson, with a touch of Shelley's neo-platonism:

Here was Lagos, thought Obi, the real Lagos he hadn't imagined existed until now. During his first winter in England he had written a callow, nostalgic poem about Nigeria. It wasn't about Lagos in particular, but Lagos was part of the Nigeria he had in mind.

> 'How sweet it is to lie beneath a tree
> At eventime and share the ecstasy
> Of jocund birds and flimsy butterflies;
> How sweet to leave our earthbound body in its mud,
> And rise towards the music of the spheres,
> Descending soft with the wind,
> And the tender glow of the fading sun.'

He recalled this poem and then turned and look at the rotting dog in the storm drain and smiled. 'I have tasted putrid flesh in the spoon,' he said through clenched teeth. 'Far more apt.'

(pp. 14–15)

Obi's second formulation is as 'English' as his first romantic one, though it belongs to a more recent tradition – the alienated and world-weary vision of the post-World War I poets, typified by T. S. Eliot, whose 'Journey of the Magi' gives this novel its title.[3] Eliot's influence also is seen ironically when Obi tells Clara that her simple and candid insistence that she would rather not 'meet people that I don't want to meet' is 'pure T. S. Eliot' (p. 17). The Eliot echoes contrast in turn with the comparison of Lagos to a palm-nut: 'It always reminded him of twin kernels separated by a thin wall in a palm-nut shell. Sometimes one kernel was shiny-black and alive, the other powdery-white and dead' (p. 16).

That image and that division are perhaps also images of Obi's consciousness, of a kind of schizophrenia arising from his inability to integrate the two cultures of which he is a product. Although he describes the white section, Ikoyi, as 'like a graveyard', that is where he chooses to live. Obi does not appear to see the contradiction between his European description of the slums with its allusions to Eliot, and his African description drawing on the image of the palm-nut, but the reader should. Here, as in other sections of the novel, Obi is satisfied with making phrases; he does not seek answers, and the phrases allow him to escape from deeper, perhaps uncomfortable answers. He does not seriously expect a reply to the comment he addresses to

47

Clara, 'I can't understand why you should choose your dressmaker from the slums'. The reader is left to consider the difference between the extremes of Obi's detached literary view and Clara's wordless acceptance of and involvement with this area, and what it has to offer.

The last paragraphs of this chapter again focus on the gap between rhetorical formulations and actual understanding in the debate on the cures for bribery. We are told that this is a recurring debate, that: '*Whichever* line Obi took, Christopher had to take the opposite'. We are already aware of Obi's fall and are so alert to the irony that all this discussion of bribery does not prevent Obi himself from taking bribes. Hence we are more likely to notice that it is pleasure in the debate itself rather than the pursuit of truth which motivates the discussion. The debate ends not with agreement on a course of action or a general principle, but with admiration for style: 'Very well put', conceded Christopher (p. 18).

The second chapter of the novel has contrasted Obi's perception of Lagos before and after his trip to England, revealing the difference between the excitement of Lagos city life glimpsed by a young man from the country, his wonder and slight unease at the life led by his 'countryman' Joseph Okeke, and the more complex world which he articulates in a variety of idioms, but nevertheless fails to make coherent sense of as a sophisticated 'been-to' who has experienced London. From Lagos now, the story shifts back in time again, to the trip 'home' from England. In contrast to the complexity and bustle of Lagos life, with its variety of idioms and life styles, the ship (and perhaps student life in London) provides an artificial world, abstracted from the demands of family and society, in which interracial friendships or romance are unaffected by financial concern or social prejudice. Only the natural world is at odds with man, and it can be controlled on the one hand by Obi's reflections on its likeness to a vast aerodrome or by Clara's even-handed dispensation of pills.

That idyllic journey comes to an abrupt end with the boat's arrival in Lagos and 'reality'. Obi immediately encounters corrupt customs officials and characteristically responds with a formula which is both sentimental and cynical, and certainly inappropriate: 'Dear old Nigeria'. Three more scenes quickly disabuse Obi and the reader of any expectation that he will easily and comfortably fit into the New Nigeria. His informality of dress and language emphasize his inability or unwillingness to meet the expectations of the Umuofians. At this point the reader is likely to sympathize with Obi, since the speech appreciated by the Umuofians is absurdly inflated in its prediction that Obi will allow Umuofia to 'join the comity of other towns in their march towards political irredentism, social equality and economic emancipation' (p. 28). Then there is the vividly drawn image of the slovenly old British woman and her parrot at The Palm Grove, which despite its name, specializes in mixed grills, boiled potatoes and a British ambience. Finally, it appears that Obi will have to compete with the rich, handsome and popular Sam Okoli for Clara. Against these disconcerting encounters, however, one becomes aware of the genuine pleasure and hospitality of Joseph's welcome to Obi.

So far, the problem of selecting from the two cultures, although more complex than Obi may have realized, seems to him a soluble one. The demand for bribes at customs may cause inconvenience if ignored, but no more. The consequences of refusing to use inflated rhetoric or uncomfortable formal dress are minor ones – a faint coolness on both sides, perhaps, but Joseph's welcome remains warm. Boiled potatoes and British seediness can be avoided. The reader may smile slightly at Obi's youthful determination to establish a sensible, if not always sensitive, median way, but he is likely to approve of Obi's choices. Similarly, Obi seems well in control as the next chapter opens with his Public Service Commission interview, where he impresses the English chairman of the board (and obviously and ironically the Englishman is the man he needs to impress). In discussing English literature and literary theory, Obi is fluent and articulate, alluding tellingly to Greene, Auden, Waugh, and even to an elder from his village. Much has been made of Obi's definition of tragedy and its appropriateness to the novel in which he is a character:

49

'You think that suicide ruins a tragedy,' said the Chairman.

'Yes. Real tragedy is never resolved. It goes on hopelessly forever. Conventional tragedy is too easy. The hero dies and we feel a purging of the emotions. A real tragedy takes place in a corner, in an untidy spot, to quote W. H. Auden. The rest of the world is unaware of it. Like that man in *A Handful of Dust* who reads Dickens to Mr Todd. There is no release for him. When the story ends he is still reading. There is no purging of the emotions for us because we are not there.' (p. 36)

It is true that Obi's definition applies more readily to this novel, although his dismissal of the 'happy ending' of *The Heart of the Matter* has to be seen as clever rather than profound. Yet the alert reader may also reflect that Obi's rejection of suicide as a proper ending for tragedy involves a rejection of *Things Fall Apart* as a tragic novel, and is perhaps Achebe's means of reminding the reader of the separation between the novelist and the character he creates. That reminder of difference is emphasized by the literary models Obi frequently refers to (Eliot, Housman, Auden, Conrad, Greene), and also by his thoughts about the kind of novel *he* would write 'about the Greens of this century', contrasted with the novel *Achebe* has previously written, not about Europeans but about Africans.[4]

Obi's story, though set chiefly in Lagos, is structured around a series of journeys, each of which takes him and the reader to a deeper and more complex understanding of the culture which has formed Obi as well as the degree to which he has grown away from it. The first is his journey from Umuofia to Lagos; the second the voyage back from England to Lagos. The third and fourth journeys are the most significant – the two trips back to Umuofia – for the difference between these two trips marks the change that takes place in Obi. On the first trip he starts from the room and friendship shared with Joseph, travels in a crowded mammy wagon, where he must be continually aware of the driver's state of alertness, the body of the young mother next to him, the comments and songs of the traders crowded into the back. Again he comes face to face with bribery, and is forced to realize that the simple refusal to co-operate is not enough; by refusing to look away he has cost the

driver ten shillings rather than two and he is attacked by
driver and passengers for being one of those 'book' people
and 'too-know' young men. Obi's reaction is characteristic: he retreats into haughty and bookish disdain,
dissociating himself from the people with whom he is
travelling, and reflecting on the problems much as Mr.
Green might:

'What an Augean stable!' He muttered to himself, 'Where does
one begin? With the masses? Educate the masses?' He shook his
head. 'Not a chance there. It would take centuries. A handful of
men at the top. Or even one man with vision – an enlightened
dictator. People are scared of the word nowadays. But what kind
of democracy can exist side by side with so much corruption and
ignorance? Perhaps a half-way house – a sort of compromise.'
When Obi's reasoning reached this point he reminded himself
that England had been as corrupt not so very long ago. He was
not really in the mood for consecutive reasoning. His mind was
impatient to roam in a more pleasant landscape.   (p. 40)

Characteristically, Obi stops when he comes to the difficult
question; he is 'not really in the mood for consecutive
reasoning', and turns to sensual pleasures. The *reader* is left
with the question, 'But what kind of democracy can exist
side by side with so much corruption and ignorance?'
   Nor does Obi follow through the implications of his ex-
egesis of the traders' song. True, his realization that his
critical powers can also be turned to Igbo songs as well as
European poetry and fiction is a desirable progression, but
he stops short of applying the implications of kinship, the
speaking of English, the reversal of the old order to himself.
Instead the subject remains an academic one; he looks for
other songs 'that could be given the same treatment', until
the bawdiness of the traders' songs once again removes him
from the realm of abstract intellectual reflection. The
incident is treated with light humour, although characteristically Obi is much quicker to smile at others than
himself.
   As Obi draws closer to home, the intermingling of
western and Igbo cultures takes on different forms and proportions. Two scenes at the Onitsha market are singled
out, scenes which foreshadow the long description in

chapter 13 of his father's room filled with printed paper and his mother's room 'full of mundane things' and recycled utensils:

The first thing that claimed his attention was an open jeep which blared out local music from a set of loudspeakers. Two men in the car swayed to the music as did many others in the crowd that had gathered round it. Obi was wondering what it was all about when the music suddenly stopped. One of the men held up a bottle for all to see. It contained Long Life Mixture, he said, and began to tell the crowd all about it. Or rather he told them a few things about it, for it was impossible to enumerate all its wonderful virtues. The other man brought out a sheaf of hand-bills and distributed them to the crowd, most of whom appeared to be illiterate. 'This paper will speak to you about Long Life Mixture,' he announced. It was quite clear that if there was something on paper about it, then it must be true. Obi secured one of the bills and read the list of diseases. The first three were: 'Rheumatism, Yellow feaver, dog-bight.'
On the other side of the road, close to the water-front, a row of women sat selling *garri* from big white enamel bowls. A beggar appeared. He must have been well known because many people called him by name. Perhaps he was a little mad too. His name was One Way. He had an enamel basin and began a tour of the row. The women beat out a rhythm with empty cigarette cups and One Way danced along the row, receiving a handful of *garri* in his basin from each of them in turn. When he got to the end of the row he had received enough *garri* for two heavy meals.
(p. 43)

In the first scene, local music and western technology (loudspeakers and printing) combine to make language deceptive, promising 'long life' from the patent medicine. Since the audience is illiterate, it is the *form* of the message, the fact that it is printed, that convinces. In the second scene, western cigarette cups and white enamel bowls are transformed into instruments of local music, which accompany the genuinely life-giving and generous gifts of *garri*. Significantly, the first is associated with men, the second with women. Here for the first time one sees the male–female associations which are so significant in *Things Fall Apart*, and which will become increasingly dominant in this novel.

52

Now as an adult he stumbles again, and then lies to his father, pretending that he has maintained his faith and his bible reading. He wonders why Clara doesn't want his parents to know about her, remembers his mother's telling him that she only waits for his first child, and thinks with compassion of his youngest sister's loss of her child: 'It must be dreadful to lose one's first child' (p. 56). For the time being these hints seem of little consequence in a chapter whose predominant tone is one of genuine family feeling and unity, where past and present seem to come together as familiar relationships are resumed. The chapter closes with Obi falling asleep, thinking in terms of traditional seasonal myth as the rains pour down and he rests contentedly in his old home.

The middle third of the novel is set in Lagos, moving within each chapter from the office to varied scenes of city life as Obi visits Clara, Joseph, Christopher, Sam Okoli, the Irish girls, Christopher's girls, and returns to the isolation of his flat in Ikoyi. This third of the novel begins with two main events and is concerned with their deepening consequences: Obi's acquisition of a car and Clara's revelation that she is an *osu*. The first event is one of the chief causes of Obi's financial difficulties, since he has to pay not only for the car, but also for a driver and insurance. The second results in Obi's increasing alienation from members of his clan and his family. Obi's thoughts about the two betray the confusion and self-deception in his thinking. He assures himself that he cannot give up the car because that would be letting down the clan. The incongruity of his comparison with inappropriate responses from a masked spirit emphasizes the confusion in Obi's thinking and values concerning material and spiritual status:

Obi admitted that his people had a sizeable point. What they did not know was that, having laboured in sweat and tears to enrol their kinsman among the shining elite, they had to keep him there. Having made him a member of an exclusive club whose members greet one another with 'How's the car behaving?' did they expect him to turn round and answer: 'I'm sorry, but my

Now as an adult he stumbles again, and then lies to his father, pretending that he has maintained his faith and his bible reading. He wonders why Clara doesn't want his parents to know about her, remembers his mother's telling him that she only waits for his first child, and thinks with compassion of his youngest sister's loss of her child: 'It must be dreadful to lose one's first child' (p. 56). For the time being these hints seem of little consequence in a chapter whose predominant tone is one of genuine family feeling and unity, where past and present seem to come together as familiar relationships are resumed. The chapter closes with Obi falling asleep, thinking in terms of traditional seasonal myth as the rains pour down and he rests contentedly in his old home.

The middle third of the novel is set in Lagos, moving within each chapter from the office to varied scenes of city life as Obi visits Clara, Joseph, Christopher, Sam Okoli, the Irish girls, Christopher's girls, and returns to the isolation of his flat in Ikoyi. This third of the novel begins with two main events and is concerned with their deepening consequences: Obi's acquisition of a car and Clara's revelation that she is an *osu*. The first event is one of the chief causes of Obi's financial difficulties, since he has to pay not only for the car, but also for a driver and insurance. The second results in Obi's increasing alienation from members of his clan and his family. Obi's thoughts about the two betray the confusion and self-deception in his thinking. He assures himself that he cannot give up the car because that would be letting down the clan. The incongruity of his comparison with inappropriate responses from a masked spirit emphasizes the confusion in Obi's thinking and values concerning material and spiritual status:

Obi admitted that his people had a sizeable point. What they did not know was that, having laboured in sweat and tears to enrol their kinsman among the shining elite, they had to keep him there. Having made him a member of an exclusive club whose members greet one another with 'How's the car behaving?' did they expect him to turn round and answer: 'I'm sorry, but my

The welcome from his home village of Iguedo again illustrates a mixture of forms, media and convictions: the brass bands, the tunes from evangelical hymns and 'Old Calabar' bring memories of mission school rivalries and Empire Day; the dispute about whether a rainmaker should be called in and which god has protected Iguedo from thunder; questions about the use of kola in a Christian household. It is interesting to compare the account in chapter 2 of Obi's sea voyage home – which uses metaphors of tarmac and aerodromes – with his narration in Igbo to the villagers – which uses metaphors of snakes on grass and voyages to the land of the spirits. Once again the problem of translating one culture into the language of another is brought to the fore. There is also the difference between the literary, introspective consciousness typical of Obi on his own, and the demand for direct, concrete description, the interplay between audience and speaker produced by an oral situation. The contrast here is also with the formal and fairly meaningless speeches 'for show' appreciated by the members of the Umuofia Progressive Union in Lagos. David Carroll sees these disputes as an index of the decline and trivialization of Igbo culture since the days of *Things Fall Apart*, but it seems to me the disputes are lively, yet settled amicably, and that there is tolerance, especially among the traditional believers, which allows for a fairly friendly compromise.[5] Ogbuefu Odogwo's ceremonial use of the kola suggests a dignified and meaningful blending of the two cultures, and with Odogwo's speech about the return of Okonkwo and the continuity of the greatness of the past, we are truly back in the world of *Things Fall Apart*. Obi is home.

However, being home and becoming part of his family again involve more than passive enjoyment of a hero's welcome. Obi on this first trip quickly recognizes and takes on his responsibilities as a son and brother. Nevertheless, there are hints that all is not quite well, and these hints will gain increasing significance as the novel progresses and as Obi's second visit home is contrasted with this one. He remembers how as a child he stumbled over the verses of the Bible (as well as over the telling of traditional stories).

car is off the road. You see I couldn't pay my insurance premium'? That would be letting the side down in a way that was quite unthinkable. Almost as unthinkable as a masked spirit in the old Ibo society answering another's esoteric salutation; 'I'm sorry, my friend, but I don't understand your strange language. I'm but a human being wearing a mask.' No, these things could not be. (p. 90)

On the other hand, he will not give up Clara, because in his view the clan has no right to interfere in his affairs. The contradiction in his attitudes is ironically underlined in his second visit to the Umuofia Progressive Union, with first the jubilant celebration of his arrival in the car, and then his appeal in Igbo words and idioms to the traditional value of community – a speech which moves towards English as he asks for four months' grace before he begins repaying his loan. His affirmation of the right to make his own choices without interference is shouted in English, suggesting the degree to which the belief in individual fulfilment and romance derives from western culture. The point is not that the reader should not sympathize with Obi's dilemma and his refusal to give up Clara because she is *osu*, but that Obi does not face the issues honestly and clearly, and has no consistent set of values or convictions on which to stand firm. Nor does he examine his own reactions deeply enough. His silence when Clara tells him of her origins betrays a prejudice within him as well as in his society. He evades a full discussion with Joseph, and also evades the recognition that intellectual conviction and argument may not go to the heart. Again and again, Obi underestimates his own vulnerability while also underestimating the depth of conviction and strength of others. Hence his characteristic assurance that he will be able to manage others. Again and again he, and also Clara, avoid thinking through the problem, finding refuge in sex, social activity, and literature (as Obi turns at crucial moments to Housman).

'Four years in England had filled Obi with a longing to be back in Umuofia' (p. 45). One year in Lagos has filled him with reluctance. The family feeling which prompted him to take on responsibilities readily and to feel pleasure in their company has been replaced by his sense of them as a financial burden, and opposition to be overcome (or 'managed'), an opposition which he has refused to face, and which he and Clara refuse to face on the eve of his departure. This time it is not erotic thoughts or bawdy songs but the real Clara in his bed offering an escape from serious discussion.

The images from scenes in the Onitsha market which prefaced his first visit with the printed handouts and the dance rhythms beaten out on cups and bowls to accompany the giving of food are paralleled and given much fuller treatment in the description of his parents' two rooms and of the band of young women who welcome him. I will quote this passage in full because it dramatizes so effectively the two worlds which pull at Obi:

Mother's room was the most distinctive in the whole house, except perhaps for Father's. The difficulty in deciding arose from the fact that one could not compare incomparable things. Mr. Okonkwo believed utterly and completely in the things of the white man. And the symbol of the white man's power was the written word, or better still, the printed word. Once before he went to England, Obi heard his father speak with deep feeling about the mystery of the written word to an illiterate kinsman:

'Our women made black patterns on their bodies with the juice of the *uli* tree. It was beautiful, but it soon faded. If it lasted two market weeks it lasted a long time. But sometimes our elders spoke about *uli* that never faded, although no one had ever seen it. We see it today in the writing of the white man. If you go to the native court and look at the books which clerks wrote twenty years ago or more, they are still as they wrote them. They do not say one thing today and another tomorrow, or one thing this year and another next year. Okoye in the book today cannot become Okonkwo tomorrow. In the Bible Pilate said:"What is written is written." It is Uli that never fades.'

The kinsman had nodded his head in approval and snapped his fingers.

The result of Okonkwo's mystic regard for the written word was that his room was full of old books and papers – from Blackie's *Arithmetic*, which he used in 1908, to Obi's Durrell, from obsolete cockroach eaten translations of the Bible into the Onitsha dialect to yellowed Scripture Union Cards of 1920 and earlier. Okonkwo never destroyed a piece of paper. He had two boxes full of them. The rest were preserved on top of his enormous cupboard, on tables, on boxes and on one corner of the floor.

Mother's room, on the other hand, was full of mundane things. She had her box of clothes on a stool. On the other side of the room were pots of solid palm-oil with which she made black soap. The palm-oil was separated from the clothes by the whole length of the room, because, as she always said, clothes and oil were not kinsmen, and just as it was the duty of clothes to try and avoid oil it was the duty of the oil to do everything to avoid clothes.

Apart from these two, Mother's room also had such things as last year's coco yams, kola nuts preserved with banana leaves in empty oil pots, palm-ash preserved in an old cylindrical vessel which, as the older children told Obi, had once contained biscuits. In the second stage of its life it had served as a water vessel until it sprang about five leaks which had to be carefully covered with paper before it got its present job. . .

Later that evening a band of young women who had been making music at a funeral was passing by Okonkwo's house when they heard of Obi's return, and decided to go in and salute him.

Obi's father was up in arms. He wanted to drive them away, but Obi persuaded him that they could do no harm. It was ominous the way he gave in without a fight and went and shut himself up in his room. Obi's mother came out to the *pieze* and sat on a high chair by the window. She liked music even when it was heathen music. Obi stood in the main door, smiling at the singers who had formed themselves on the clean-swept ground outside. As if from a signal the colorful and noisy weaver birds on the tall palm tree flew away in a body deserting temporarily their scores of brown nests, which looked like giant bootees. . . . The leader . . . had a strong piercing voice that cut the air with a sharp edge. She sang a long recitative before the others joined in. They called it 'The Song of the Heart.'

> A letter came to me the other day.
> I said to Mosisi: 'Read my letter for me.'
> Mosisi said to me: 'I do not know how to read.'
> I went to Innocenti and asked him to read my letter.
> Innocenti said to me: 'I do not know how to read.'
> I asked Simonu to read for me. Simonu said:
> 'This is what the letter has asked me to tell you:
> *He that has a brother must hold him to his heart,*
> *For a kinsman cannot be bought in the market,*

Neither is a brother bought with money.'
Is everyone here?
(*Hele ee he ee he*)
Are you all here?
(*Hele ee he ee he*)
The letter said
That money cannot buy a kinsman,
(*hele ee he ee he*)
That he who has brothers
Has more than riches can buy.
(*Hele ee he ee he*)   (pp. 114–17)

The father's room represents the written culture brought
by the Europeans. Mr. Okonkwo's reverence, one might
say fetish, for the printed word is explained in his own
words, but it is also undercut by them. His use of Pilate's
words is indeed ironic, for they represent Pilate's use of the
written word to evade personal responsibility, much as
Rudbeck insists on following the official orders to the letter
in the trial and hanging of Mister Johnson. The implication of the gospel account is clearly that what was written
should have been unwritten in that particular case.

Similarly, the collection of printed matter that crowds
Isaac Okonkwo's room implies an ironic comment on his
reverence. The Durrell, the *Arithmetic*, the cockroach-eaten
translations, the Union cards are all equated, and they are
all equally useless to him. They are obsolete and have
become meaningless. They are of no further personal use.
On the other hand, the *uli* which lasts no more than eight
days is associated with beauty and personal significance.
Although it fades, it never as long as it lasts becomes
dissociated from the women whom it ornaments and
enhances.

In contrast to the unfading *uli* associated with Pilate, the
elders, Isaac Okonkwo, the male world, the woman's *uli* is
associated with the personal, the immediately useful or
meaningful, the female. And so the mother's room is filled
with things that are edible, organic, personal and adap-
table. In contrast to the father's stacks of papers, Obi's
mother's world and what she represents is symbolized by
the 'old cylindrical vessel' which now contains palm-ash

but has been earlier a biscuit container and then a water vessel. And the contrast is emphasized by the mother's use of paper to patch that water vessel, to help provide for the immediate physical needs of her family, while Mr Okonkwo's biblical tracts feed only cockroaches.

The transformation of the biscuit container parallels the song of the village band. The singers are women and Obi's mother is a lover of music, whether Christian or heathen. While Mr Okonkwo shuts himself away, the mother listens. Once again, we find the contrast suggested in *Things Fall Apart* between statement or doctrine represented by the printed word and the poetry which can bridge cultures. The song is a mixture of Igbo and European elements, suggesting the successful mingling of the two worlds. It is traditional in form, but speaks of the new cultural form, the letter. Unlike Isaac Okonkwo's documents, however, the letter represents a personal communication, and the message it brings grows out of traditional Igbo values regarding the importance of kin and brotherhood over material riches. As such it speaks for and to a whole group of people. Yet it is particularly significant for Obi, for whom the song is sung, for he is torn between the expectations of his family and those of Clara, as well as being caught in the demands and pleasures of a form of life which emphasizes his need for money.

Despite the dissimilarity between the two rooms and between the personalities of Isaac and Hannah Okonkwo, Obi's parents are united in their opposition to his proposed marriage with Clara. Given Obi's admission to the reader on his previous visit that he no longer believed, there is something of the devil quoting the scriptures to his own use in Obi's attempt to demonstrate that opposition to marriage with an *osu* is unchristian. Isaac is prepared to acknowledge the rationality of his argument, although he is also gravely concerned about the social consequences to Obi and his children. But it is the depth and feeling of his mother's response which shakes Obi; he can give no rational response to her chilling dream vision of white termites eating away the bed and mat beneath her nor to her threat to kill herself. Isaac Okonkwo's faith and understanding is strong and profound, tested by bitter experience, and it reveals the shallowness of Obi's convictions and understanding of his father, himself and his society. But it is an understanding which can be discussed intellectually. To Hannah's dream, conveying so starkly the power of her inner feeling, the only reply can be equal depth of feeling, and this is what Obi lacks. The discovery that this is so devastates him:

He was amazed at the irrelevant thoughts that passed through his mind at this the greatest crisis in his life. He waited for his father to speak that he might put up another fight to justify himself. His mind was troubled not only by what had happened but also by the discovery that there was nothing in him with which to challenge it honestly. All day he had striven to rouse his anger and his conviction, but he was honest enough with himself to realize that the response he got, no matter how violent it sometimes appeared, was not genuine. It came from the periphery, and not the centre, like the jerk in the leg of a dead frog when a current is applied to it. But he could not accept the present state of his mind as final, so he searched desperately for something that would trigger off the inevitable reaction. Perhaps another argument with his father, more violent than the first; for it was true what the Ibos say, that when a coward sees a man he can beat he becomes hungry for a fight. He had discovered he could beat his father. (p. 124)

It is a moment of self-discovery which might have been a turning point for Obi, but characteristically he retreats and shuts himself away from his family and from the community, knowing full well that his behaviour is hurtful, and rushes back to Lagos entirely on his own, in his haste nearly bringing about his destruction in his car. Before he leaves, his father tries again to communicate, and reveals for the first time the suffering caused by his decision to become a Christian and his own father's curse. Although Obi feels pity for his father, he misses the point: he fails to see the analogy with his own situation and assumes that the story is 'not about the thing that was on their minds'. Similarly the 'sad story of Ikemefuna' remains simply a story that everybody knew. Obi will learn neither from Isaac's account of the suffering caused by his break with his family, nor from Isaac's refusal to attend Okonkwo's funeral, nor from the elders 'who said it was a great wrong that a man should raise his hands against a child who called him father' (p. 126).

The implications of that sad story, and of the reflection on his first visit about Agnes' loss of her first child, are quite forgotten by Obi the moment he returns to Lagos and discovers that Clara is pregnant. Neither Obi nor Clara considers the *morality* of abortion, and until it is too late, no other considerations than the cost and possible dangers to Clara are brought to the surface of Obi's consciousness. The question of morality and illegality is raised by both doctors, but Obi does not reflect upon it. Such reflection is left to the reader. Western education is used to destroy life rather than save it. Neither Christian nor Igbo morality troubles Obi's mind. Clara's abortion and Obi's failure to stop it are followed immediately by Obi's return to 'the pessimism of A. E. Housman' and his tossing away of the idealistic poem 'Nigeria'. The reader has encountered Housman and this poem before, just after Obi's first financial difficulties and quarrel with Clara, but on that occasion 'Obi smiled, put the piece of paper back where he found it and began to read his favourite poem, "Easter Hymn".' With the destruction of the piece of paper, Obi's fashionable but surface pessimism is replaced by a deeper cynicism. The ideal of forming a new united nation, however embryonic, is also aborted. The point is emphasized by the epithet hurled at him by an angry patient in the waiting room of the doctor who performed the abortion:

'Foolish man. He tink say because him get car so derefore he can do as he like. Beast of no nation!'

The novel now draws quickly to its close – or rather, to the point at which it began. The previous chapters have indicated the answer to the final question: 'Everybody wondered why . . .' The remaining chapters elaborate and detail Obi's sins. His reaction when Clara turns away from him is one of embarrassment and hurt pride – despite the surface acknowledgement that she has a right to be angry.

That has been characteristic of their relationship in the past, and it has generally been Clara who has made the move towards reconciliation – including the major and practical one of finding him £50 to pay off his overdraft. He rationalizes his discovery 'that there was nothing in him to challenge his father's conviction honestly' (p. 124) and creates a new self-image as one who has done away with all 'humbug' and illusions. In terms of the male/female symbolism of the novel it is significant that the loss of Clara and the death of his mother coincide with his acceptance of his new hard-headed realism. It is clear to the reader that what Obi terms realism and 'seeing the situation in its true light' (p. 141) is rationalization to justify whatever is convenient to him and preserves his self-image. 'Family commitments' become the rationalization for stopping the payments of his loan from the Union, although he evades the family commitment to attend his mother's funeral by telling himself it is better to send money. The disapproving reaction of the members of the Union to Obi's failure to go home must be endorsed by the reader, and one is touched by their insistence on holding a wake in his apartment. Yet the comparison of his action with his father's refusal to attend Okonkwo's funeral is an ironic one, for the reader has heard Isaac's version and knows that his refusal sprang from deep and painful conviction and feeling, whereas Obi's refusal comes from lack of conviction, numbness of feeling, and his characteristic impulse to cut himself off from others and retreat from difficulty. The contrast between the world of *Things Fall Apart* and the world of *No Longer at Ease* is again suggested in the final page of the latter novel:

'Are you Mr Okonkwo?' asked the stranger. Obi said yes in a voice he could hardly have recognised. The room began to swim round and round. The stranger was saying something but it sounded distant – as things sound to a man in a fever. He then searched Obi and found the marked notes. He began to say some more things, invoking the name of the Queen, like a District Officer in the bush reading the Riot Act to an uncomprehending and delirious mob. Meanwhile the other man used the telephone outside Obi's door to summon a police van. (p. 154)

One recalls the District Commissioner speaking of peace and justice to the uncomprehending village elders and invoking an earlier queen. But their crime had been one of active rebellion, based on religious conviction and righteous anger. Obi has passively drifted into crime 'lacking all conviction' and also lacking 'passionate intensity'. Yet Obi shares with his grandfather pride and concern for self-image which overrides inner knowledge and feeling, the female principle within, and so leads to the destruction and loss of those people and values he most cares for.

In a lecture delivered at Harvard in 1972, 'Africa and Her Writers', Achebe was particularly critical of Ayi Kwei Armah for adopting the fashionable pessimism of the 'human condition' syndrome associated with Sartre and other European writers, and for portraying Ghana through the eyes of an alienated native whose perceptions are those of a British administrator. Achebe compares Armah's description of Accra with Joyce Cary's description of Fada and he is scornfully dismissive of Armah's 'pale, passive' hero.[6]

With some modification, this description of Armah's hero might well be applied to Obi Okonkwo, with the crucial distinction that what *saves* 'the Man', Armah's unnamed protagonist, from joining the ranks of the corrupt – his detachment and alienation from his family and community – is what *causes* Obi to crumble. For Achebe, writers like Armah and young 'been-to's' like Obi who adopt the 'fashionable pessimism' of the west are the problem.[7] The reader who learns this may begin to move towards answers other than those given with such assurance by Mr. Green, Joyce Cary, the Umuofia Progressive Union, or Obi Okonkwo himself.

4

Religion and power in Africa: *Arrow of God*

> What can be more fascinating than the work of the religious
> imagination, for good or evil, on men's minds and so upon
> history . . . ?   Joyce Cary, Preface to *The African Witch*

> Wherever something stands, there also Something else will stand.
>   Igbo proverb cited by Achebe

PUBLISHED IN 1964, *Arrow of God* tells the story of a
priest, Ezeulu, who declines an appointment as warrant
chief during the years when District Officers were attempting to apply Lugard's policy of indirect rule to Eastern
Nigeria. He is imprisoned for several weeks, and so is
unable to announce the appearance of the new moon in his
village. As a result the feast of the New Yam is delayed, the
villagers suffer from hunger as their old supplies of yams
run out, and some begin to turn to the harvest festival of
the Christian god as an alternative. The novel's closing
pages show Ezeulu isolated in his madness following the
death of his favourite son. Achebe has based his novel on an
actual incident, recorded by Simon Nnolim in *The History
of Umuchu*, in which a priest called Ezeagu rejected a chief-
tancy in 1913, was imprisoned and refused to roast the
sacred yams for the months missed.[1]

Insofar as it is the story of the interaction between colonists and colonized, *Arrow of God* can be seen as yet
another response by Achebe to *Mister Johnson* and the
literary and historical perspective it represents, a response
which, as Robert Wren has argued, illustrates complexities
of cause and effect barely guessed at by Joyce Cary and his
colonial administrators.[2] *Arrow of God* is set in the second
decade of this century, at about the same time as *Mister
Johnson*, and it provides a whole group of mission-educated
Igbo who, like Johnson, see the white man's civilization as
the wave of the future. In both works, the building of a

road is a significant event, becoming in each novel the cause as well as the symbol of the disruption of the ordinary, everyday world of the indigenous society.

Indeed, although the building of a road is a common ingredient in novels of the colonial period as well as oral stories, the similarity between the situations and attitudes of Achebe's Mr. Wright and Cary's Mr. Rudbeck is so close that it is sometimes possible to read Achebe's version as a parody as well as an implicit comment upon Cary. Like Rudbeck, Wright must overcome the fact that the vote for capital works is already overspent. In each case, that problem is solved by simply going to the village authorities and 'persuading' them to provide a gang of unpaid labourers. Achebe and Cary both send these labourers to work the day after a festival, some of them suffering from hangovers. Like Rudbeck, Mr. Wright develops a certain affection for the leaders of his gang:

In fact he had got very much attached to this gang and knew their leaders by name now. Many of them were, of course, bone lazy and could only respond to severe handling. But once you got used to them they could be quite amusing. They were as loyal as pet dogs and their ability to improvise songs was incredible. As soon as they were signed on the first day and told how much they would be paid they devised a work song. Their leader sang: 'Lebula toro toro' and all the others replied: 'A day,' at the same time swinging their matchets or wielding their hoes. It was a most effective work-song and they sang it for many days:

Lebula toro toro

A day

Lebula toro toro

A day

And they sang it in English too!   (pp. 75–6)

Achebe's tone is unmistakably parodic here with his mimicking of the Englishman's patronizing language and complacency, the colonialist's peculiar idiom, and the comparison with pet dogs, recalling Celia Rudbeck's amusement at their 'Wog' and the recurring comparisons of Africans to animals in *Mister Johnson*, or Marlowe's comparison of the African fireman on the steamer in *Heart of*

Darkness to 'a dog in a parody of breeches and a feather hat, walking on his hind legs'.[3] The brief little song whose sarcasm is lost on the overseer contrasts strongly with the elaborate compositions Cary ascribes to Johnson and his happy labourers, songs concerning the challenge of men to the lordly trees in the forest and their joyful creation of a road on which 'the sun and the moon are walking'.[4]

The difference between Cary's road-building songs in which the labourers, led by Johnson, rejoice in the glory of the task British civilization has assigned to them, and the sardonic little chant set up by Achebe's conscripts points the reader towards a series of contrasts in these two versions of the building of a road as well as the wider stories of the reception of British culture by Nigerians. One can also contrast the fulsome and sentimental prisoner's song Cary gives Johnson with the epigrammatic and egalitarian little verse which irritates Winterbottom as the prisoners work on Government Hill:

> When I cut grass and you cut
> What's your right to call me names?   (p. 55)

Within the novel itself, the presence of the prisoners and their chant form an ironic counterpoint to the substance and inflated style of the Lieutenant Governor's memorandum concerning indirect rule, a concept which is clearly circumscribed by the British Administration's power to enforce its law and imprison natives or, in Achebe's convincing representation of officialese, the colonial government's 'endeavour to purge the native system of its abuses' (p. 56).

Achebe challenges Cary's presentation of the road-building as an enterprise at first greeted suspiciously by the natives, who are then sent out by corrupt and power-hungry chiefs after being promised a £5 'prize' if their villagers clear more bush than other groups, and who quickly come to rejoice in the opportunity the road-building brings to take 'the first essential step out of the world of the tribe into the world of men'. In fact, in addition to Wright's view quoted above, Achebe gives us two other views of the road-building, one through Winter-

bottom's eyes, and the other from the point of view of the
Umuaroans. First, Winterbottom recalls how three years
previously he had been made, under Lugard's policy of indirect rule, 'to appoint a Warrant Chief of Okperi against
his better judgement'. The man appointed, James Ikedi,
had behaved scandalously, exploiting the villages, and
Winterbottom had suspended him. His decision was over-
turned by the Senior Resident and Ikedi was reinstated,
only to go on to further extortion:

There was at that time a big programme of road and drainage
construction following a smallpox epidemic. Chief James Ikedi
teamed up with a notorious and drunken road overseer who had
earned the title of Destroyer of Compounds from the natives.
The plans for the roads and drains had long been completed and
approved by Captain Winterbottom himself and as far as possible did not interfere with people's homesteads. But this overseer
went around intimidating the villagers and telling them that
unless they gave him money the new road would pass through
the middle of their compound. When some of them reported the
matter to their chief he told them there was nothing he could do;
that the overseer was carrying out the orders of the white man
and anyone who had no money to give should borrow from his
neighbour or sell his goats or yams. The overseer took his toll
and moved on to another compound, choosing only the wealthy
villagers. And to convince them that he meant business he
actually demolished the compounds of three people who were
slow in paying, although no road or drain was planned within
half a mile of their homes. Needless to say, Chief Ikedi took a
big slice of this illegal tax.

Thinking of this incident Captain Winterbottom could find
some excuse for the overseer. He was a man from another clan;
in the eyes of the native, a foreigner. But what excuse could one
offer for a man who was their blood brother and chief? Captain
Winterbottom could only put it down to cruelty of a kind which
Africa alone produced. It was this elemental cruelty in the
psychological make-up of the native that the starry-eyed European found so difficult to understand.   (pp. 57–8)

Like Johnson, the drunken and corrupt overseer is 'a
man from another clan; in the eyes of the native, a
foreigner', and this might offer some explanation for his
behaviour. It is not an explanation that Cary offers or finds

necessary, and the seriousness with which Winterbottom views the matter may be seen as a subtle rebuke on Achebe's part for the lightheartedness with which Cary treats Johnson's antics. Other similarities in detail further emphasize the comparison and contrast between the Cary and Achebe versions: as Ikedi is reinstated after the Senior Resident comes back from leave, so Johnson has been reinstated by Rudbeck in spite of his dismissal by Tring and Blore. Both Johnson and the overseer impose an illegal road tax.

However it is not Ikedi and his overseer but Wright and Moses Unachukwu who 'persuade' the Umuaroans to contribute their labour. Like Rudbeck, Wright is obsessed with getting the road finished before the rainy season, not for idealistic reasons but so that he can 'get away from this hole of a place'. Achebe does not allow his road-builder and Senior Officer Rudbeck's excuse of ignorance of what is going on, since it is Wright who decides he must use unpaid labour, and Winterbottom who agrees that the circumstances (presumably Wright's desire to 'get away') justify 'an exception to the aphorism that the labourer is worthy of his hire'. (Incidentally, Achebe's paid workers receive three pence a day rather than Cary's nine pence.) Whereas Cary's village chiefs were bribed to send volunteers, who clearly play no part in the decision, 'the leaders of Umuaro were *told* to provide the necessary labour for the white man's new, wide road' (my italics), and after a meeting 'offer the services of the two latest groups to be admitted into full manhood' (p. 76). As part of the labour gangs, the Umuaroans do not 'step into the world of men' but out of it. They are treated as children, whipped unjustly, forbidden to ask questions, prevented from fighting back man to man.

While Cary seems either blind to the indignities suffered by native conscripts or unable to conceive that the natives are capable of feeling indignity any more than pet dogs or monkeys might, Achebe portrays in detail the consequences of Wright's attitudes and actions, and also goes on to show why the colonial administrators might not have been forced to hear complaints of unjust treatment. Achebe describes not a group of workers gradually and proudly coming 'to believe that they are engaged in some important and glorious enterprise',[5] but *conscripts* using the sound of hoes and matchets to cover their planning of a meeting to discuss the problem. At that meeting, the reader encounters a series of eloquent, sometimes fiery, sometimes pragmatic, sometimes stoical speeches concerning possible responses to the white man and his road (pp. 84–6).

The length of the discussion (occupying three pages of the novel) is in itself a response to Cary's portrayal of the villagers as inarticulate, sullen, unthinking, not wanting roads because these 'poorer, more cut-off people . . . have not enough energy or imagination to break out from their poverty'.[6] And, of course, the discussion makes it clear that the young men do not, as Cary would have it, go home to 'talk about their road and come to believe that they are engaged in some important and glorious enterprise'. Nor do they 'smile at the road, because they have made it and sung of it, but . . . have no idea of its beginning or end . . . like men brought up on a forgotten island far from ship routes, to whom the rest of the world is as much a mystery, a blank inhabited by monsters as to their ancestors of the old Stone Age'.[7]

But above all, this passage is one of several in the novel which are concerned with the reasons for Africans joining in the white man's enterprise, and the long speech by Moses Unachukwu, whose function as spokesman and organizer for the white man makes him Mister Johnson's counterpart, is especially significant in presenting an alternative reason for acceptance of the white man's culture. For Johnson the white man brings romance, the promise of a richer and 'more glorious destiny';[8] for Moses Unachukwu the white man represents suffering, from which there is no escape. British power has been manifested in the terrible destruction of Abame, and it is clearly the devastating power, not the glory or the richness of European culture which has converted Moses. ('The white man, the new religion, the soldiers, the new road – they are all part of the same thing. The white man has a gun, a matchet, a bow and carried fire in his mouth. He does not fight with one weapon alone.' p. 85)

For others, the white man's power is not yet adequate reason for conversion to his god, but it provides a pragmatic reason for acting prudently, and it is Nweke Ukpaka, with his counsel of caution, who gains the assent of his age group; 'I know that many of us want to fight the white man. But only a foolish man can go after a leopard with his bare hands. The white man is like hot soup and we must take him slowly-slowly from the edges of the bowl.' Particularly telling, in the face of Cary's clownlike and foolish native characters, is Ukpaka's further counsel: 'But in dealing with a man who thinks you a fool it is good sometimes to remind him that you know what he knows but have chosen to appear foolish for the sake of peace.'

One could explore the contrasts between *Mister Johnson* and *Arrow of God* in greater detail, for example, the contrast between the drunken village orgies described by Cary (pp. 196–7) preventing the languid and hungover young men from being alert enough to imagine the importance of the road for them, and Achebe's elaborate account of the Festival of the New Pumpkin Leaves, not a secular and sensual orgy, but a religious rite or purification, in which every action has significance. Obika's heavy drinking and hangover afterwards is portrayed not as the norm, but as an understandable, though irresponsible, incident which dismays his family and friends and angers his father. Ezeulu's amazement and his family's grief over Obika's whipping, which emphasize the ties between each individual, his family and his clan, contrast with the absence of such ties in *Mister Johnson* where what happens to the clerk or to the labourers seems to have no impact on anyone else – unless, as in the case of Bamu, there's money involved. And just as Cary leaves out of his novel any suggestion of whippings or other injustice to native labourers, so Tony Clarke's report discounts the possibility. The offhand written report will outweigh the oral accounts as far as British officialdom and the historical records are concerned.

While the episode of the road can be read as a Nigerian version of the road-building in *Mister Johnson* and many other colonial novels, it is *The African Witch* with its themes

of religious, political and personal rivalry and power, and
its interest in the conflict between rational and irrational
forces, which provides a fuller comparison with both *Arrow
of God* and its successor, *A Man of the People*; the latter taking
up the theme of intertwined sexual and political antagonism which Cary explores in the relationships between
the characters in his novel. One of the main differences between *Arrow of God* and *Things Fall Apart* is the stress on
complex relationships and rivalries, the jealous concern for
status which influences almost every social contact in *Arrow
of God*. Okonkwo, although a product of his society's high
valuation of material achievement, is seen as an extremist
in an otherwise harmonious and almost placid community.
But Ezeulu is surrounded by a whole web of conflicts and
rivalries: his eldest son, Edogo, is troubled by his father's
preference for Obika and Nwafo; his two wives are constantly quarrelling and jealously guarding the rights of
their children; the children are also seen more often than
not quarrelling, and in one rare peaceful scene, they are
telling one another a chant of vengeance, 'and who will
Punish Water for Me?' There is rivalry between Nwaka
and Ezeulu, and between Ezidemili and Ezeulu, as well as
between the different villages, so that at the time of the
story 'few people from the one village would touch palm
wine or kolanut which had passed through the hands of a
man from the other' (p. 38).

Another mark of the difference between *Things Fall Apart*
and *Arrow of God* is in the narrative point of view. The
predominant voice in the earlier novel is the collective one,
distinct from but in tune with the voices of Obierika,
Uchendu, Okonkwo and others, resulting in a fairly
unified perspective which makes the shock of the District
Commissioner's differing perspective in the final pages all
the more effective. In *Arrow of God* the voices are much more
various. Not only are we given the contrasting cultural
perspectives of Igbo and British communities, but also a
series of contrasting views and voices within each community.
On Government Hill, Wright is excluded from the bleak
social gatherings of Winterbottom and Clarke; Clarke sees
Winterbottom as smug and old fashioned; Winterbottom is

bitterly opposed to the Lieutenant Governor's directives concerning indirect rule. And in Umuchu, there are a number of quite different views – not only those representing the conflict between generations, and between Christians and traditional believers, but also the opposing views and statements of Ezeulu and Ezidemili concerning the founding of Umuchu and the status of their gods, between Ezeulu and Nwaka concerning the farmland claimed by Okperi, and between Akuebue and Ofoka concerning the motives for Ezeulu's actions. As Nwaka says, 'Wisdom is like a goatskin bag; every man carries his own' (p. 16). An important difference between the disputes on Government Hill and those in Umuchu, however, is that in the Igbo community views are spoken freely and fully, and it is for the males as a whole to decide. In the British community Clarke is promptly silenced by Winterbottom, and similarly the hierarchical structure means that Winterbottom's objections to Indirect Rule will not get a hearing. In the dispute between Nwaka and Ezeulu, however, the reader is given no indication which version is correct, and it is Nwaka's rhetorical skill, together with his insinuations concerning Ezeulu's bias towards his mother's home village, that sways the assembly. Of course, the reader may have his own personal bias in Ezeulu's favour, and like Ezeulu, he may feel that the outcome proves Ezeulu right, whether we see in it the hand of Ulu or some other form of Providence!

This variety of perspectives (and their lack of resolution) is fundamental to the theme of the novel in three ways: first, in comparison with *Things Fall Apart* it provides a much more convincing and complex portrayal of a traditional community and the tensions and rivalries which make it active and vital; secondly, this varied community becomes both the background and the most stringent test for traditional Igbo forms of policy making and leadership, for the balancing and reconciling of rival claims, and for raising issues concerning individual and communal authority; thirdly, these opposing perspectives are concerned with what seems to me the central theme of the novel, the problem of 'knowing', a problem with which Ezeulu wrestles in the first chapter of the novel, as his mind 'never content with shallow satisfactions' creeps to 'the brinks of knowing' (p. 4). To put it another way, *Arrow of God* is 'about' the problem of authority and the related questions of whom or what to believe and follow; and if, as David Carroll complains, 'the author is unwilling to commit himself finally on the precise relationship between inner and outer, between Ezeulu's need for power and the god he worships, between Winterbottom's aggressiveness and the rituals of power he practices',[9] it may be because Achebe wishes to leave the reader involved in the problem of 'knowing'. Moreover, this problem is inextricably bound up with questions of language (or languages), with 'naming' and the power to manipulate words, and with the refusal to name.

Together with the problem of knowledge, the interrelationship between power and naming is introduced in the first chapter of the novel:

Whenever Ezeulu considered the immensity of his power over the year and the crops and, therefore, over the people he wondered if it was real. It was true he named the day for the feast of the Pumpkin Leaves and for the New Yam feast; but he did not choose it. He was merely a watchman. His power was no more than the power of a child over a goat that was said to be his. As long as the goat was alive it could be his; he would find it food and take care of it. But the day it was slaughtered he would know soon enough who the real owner was. No! the Chief Priest of Ulu was more than that, must be more than that. If he should refuse to name the day there would be no festival – no planting and no reaping. But could he refuse? No Chief Priest had ever refused. So it could not be done. He would not dare.

Ezeulu was stung to anger by this as though his enemy had spoken it.

'Take away that word *dare*,' he replied to this enemy. 'Yes I say take it away. No man in all Umuaro can stand up and say that I dare not. The woman who will bear the man who will say it has not been born yet.'

But this rebuke brought only momentary satisfaction. His mind never content with shallow satisfactions crept again to the brinks of knowing. What kind of power was it if it would never be used? Better to say that it was not there, that it was no more than the power in the anus of the proud dog who sought to put out a

73

furnace with his puny fart . . . He turned the yam with a stick.

(pp. 3–4)

This passage follows the introductory paragraphs which establish not only Ezeulu's priestly role and character, but also the forces which limit and contest his power: the forces of nature, the moon and rains which obscure the moon, and also the internal ravages of nature – his failing sight, his growing age, and his unwillingness to acknowledge such limitations, evidenced in his delight in making young men wince from the power of his grip. Ezeulu records the months and the seasons, but in turn the months and the seasons gradually rob him of his strength and sight. It is within this context that we see Ezeulu questioning his power and the nature of power and knowledge, and, of course, by the end of the novel we find that the question has been brought to the test: Ezeulu does refuse to name. The answer to his question is partially suggested in the example he himself uses of the child and the goat, for like the goat, Ulu will be destroyed by his real owner – in this case, the community which needs to survive.

The responsibility to name what is, to confirm what, in effect, the community should know, does not extend to the power to name what will be; 'no one would be so rash as to say openly that Ulu would do this or do that'. (p. 4) Here again we are reminded of the limitations of power and knowledge. Although Edogo suspects that in sending Oduche to the Christians, Ezeulu is attempting to influence the choice of his successor, we are reminded here and at the end of the book of the inability of humans to control the future.

Nevertheless, Ezeulu is not restrained from foretelling the future when his hurt pride sees in it a vindication. Hence he sees the white man's 'coming to tell the villagers the truth they knew but hated to hear. It was an augury of the world's ruin.' (p. 8) For Ezeulu, his priestly role involves speaking the truth he knows for 'how could a man who held the holy staff of Ulu know that a thing was a lie and speak it? How could he fail to tell the story as he had heard it from his own fathers?' (p. 7) For the reader, the intensity and all-inclusiveness of his view, 'it was an augury of the world's ruin', is an indication of the limitation of his knowledge and the anger which clouds his vision. Like many others, he assumes *his* world is *the* world.

The analogy of the goat is again taken up in the next chapter when Ezeulu warns his community of the consequences of fighting an unjust war: 'When an adult is in the house the she-goat is not left to suffer the pains of parturition on its tether . . . If in truth the farmland is ours, Ulu will fight on our side. But if it is not, we shall know soon enough. I would not have spoken again today if I had not seen adults in the house neglecting their duty. Ogbuefi Egonwanne, as one of the three oldest men in Umuaro, should have reminded us that our fathers did not fight a war of blame' (p. 18).

But the issue of speaking the truth is complicated by the problem of knowing what the truth is. Ezeulu is utterly convinced that his version is the authoritative one, because he got it from his father, who was also a priest of Ulu. But as Nwaka says, 'We know that a father does not speak falsely to his son. But we also know that the lore of the land is beyond the knowledge of many fathers . . . Ezeulu . . . speaks about events which are older than Umuaro itself . . . My father told me a different story' (p. 16).

The issue of which story is 'true' is left unresolved, although the community chooses Nwaka's as the most likely one. Later, yet another version is given by Winterbottom, who is also quite certain of his facts. Winterbottom's account differs not so much in the facts, but in the emphasis, understanding and attitude. He omits the whole history of the founding of the gods, of the rivalries between the community leaders, of the village debate, of the complex personal histories and relationships of the individuals involved. His language is that of the anthropologist and outsider; the ikenga is for him a 'fetish'; Ezeulu's truthful testimony the result of 'some pretty fierce tabu'. Winterbottom's approach is secular and pragmatic; his authority is human, the Lieutenant Governor or the King, and so he fails to understand a culture which is profoundly religious in its orientation, or a man like Ezeulu whose ultimate authority is his god.

At one level Ezeulu and Winterbottom believe they share the 'truth', and they do not differ significantly concerning the bare facts of the case. But what Achebe leads the reader to understand through the three contrasting versions of the Okperi war is that the mere recovery of the facts is not enough – even if it is possible (and the differing versions of the war, as well as of the beatings on the road must lead us to doubt what we have been given as facts, whether through written or oral history). Coming to Winterbottom's version after the Igbo ones, the reader is better equipped to question the Englishman's attitude and language, and will be struck particularly by the differences between Ezeulu's understanding of his action and his subsequent relationship with Winterbottom (his friend), and Winterbottom's patronizing view.

Chapter 2 deals not only with the responsibility to speak what is or was, insofar as one can know it, but also with the power of language to *create*. We are told that to protect themselves from the raids of the Abame, six villages banded together and 'hired a strong team of medicine-men to install a common deity for them. This deity which the fathers of the six villages made was called Ulu . . . The six villages then took the name of Umuaro, and the priest of Ulu became their chief Priest' (p. 15). The making and allocating of gods by man is further emphasized in Ezeulu's story of how the villagers of Okperi gave the Umuaroans their deities – their Udo and their Ogwugwu – and insisted that they call the deities 'not Udo but the son of Udo, and not Ogwugwu but the son of Ogwugwu'. (The final sentence in the novel perhaps gains greater resonance from this early linking of gods and sons.) And again in this same chapter, Akukalia tells of the creation of gods to oversee particular markets.

What is the status of gods created by men? What authority can they or their priests maintain? Such questions cannot be allowed to trouble the surface of Ezeulu's mind, but they do haunt his dreams:

That night Ezeulu saw in a dream a big assembly of Umuaro elders, the same people he had spoken to a few days earlier. But instead of himself it was his grandfather who rose up to speak

76

to them. They refused to listen. They shouted together: *He shall not speak*; *We will not listen to him*. The Chief Priest raised his voice and pleaded with them to listen but they refused saying that they must bale the water while it was still only ankle-deep. 'Why should we rely on him to tell us the season of the year?' asked Nwaka. 'Is there anybody here who cannot see the moon in his own compound? And anyhow what is the power of Ulu today? He saved our fathers from the warriors of Abam but he cannot save us from the white man. Let us drive him away as our neighbours of Aninta drove out and burnt Ogba when he left what he was called to do and did other things, when he turned round to kill the people of Aninta instead of their enemies.' Then the people seized the Chief Priest who had changed from Ezeulu's grandfather to himself and began to push him from one group to another. Some spat on his face and called him the priest of a dead god. (p. 159)

Nwaka's challenge is crucial, and he raises questions which lie at the core of the novel. If man can create gods, why should he not destroy them? To what extent should the gods be the servants of the men who created them? And since every man can see the moon for himself and record the seasons, what need is there for gods or priests? Nwaka's view is essentially a secular and a pragmatic one.

To attempt to respond to this challenge, one can turn again to the story of the creation of Ulu, as it is told in mythical form during the Festival of the Pumpkin Leaves:

'At that time when lizards were still in ones and twos, the whole people assembled and chose me to carry their new deity. I said to them:
' "Who am I to carry this fire on my bare head? A man who knows that his anus is small does not swallow an udala seed."
'They said to me:
' "Fear not. The man who sends a child to catch a shrew will also give him water to wash his hands."
'I said:"So be it."
'And we set to work. That day was Eke: we worked into Oye and then into Afo. As the day broke on Nkwo and the sun carried its sacrifice I carried my Alusi and, with all the people behind me, set out on that journey. A man sang with the flute on my right and another replied on my left. From behind the heavy tread of all the people gave me strength.' (p. 71)

And so the first priest of Ulu goes ahead of his people and in time, marked by the four days, encounters and clears the way of evil and danger for his people. As their leader, he recognizes and names the forces that he encounters, he makes sacrifices and he is purified by the rain, until he emerges triumphant. He carries the deity for the people, a deity made by them, and it is the flute players on either side of him with 'the heavy tread of all the people' behind him that give him strength. Ezeulu's role as carrier of the *communal* spirit, both as leader and scapegoat, is, of course, the role emphasized in the Festival of the Pumpkin Leaves. The leaves represent the evils and transgressions of each household, and they are hurled at Ezeulu, who must then lead the village in burying them and trampling them underfoot. The community is not an abstract thing, as Ugoye's individual prayer and concern about Oduche's defilement of the python reminds us, but nevertheless the community is greater than each individual, and it is perhaps *this* that Ulu represents, the spirit of the community, and the power of the community. In this light, Nwaka's threat implied in the question, 'Is there anybody who cannot see the moon in his own compound?' is particularly significant, for what he is proclaiming is the supremacy of each individual over or at least equal to the communal representative.

The mythical journey related during the Festival of the Pumpkin Leaves forms a counterpoint to the journey that Ezeulu makes towards the end of the novel as he returns from Okperi. In this case he travels almost alone, having refused to wait for Obika or other representatives of his community to accompany him, and the rain which drenches him serves not to purify and cleanse Ezeulu and Umuaro of their transgressions, but rather to soak them in. As they trudge among the red swamp that the new government road has become, Ezeulu feels 'a certain elation', as the rain pours down upon him. 'But Ezeulu's elation had an edge of bitterness to it. This rain was part of the suffering to which he had been exposed and for which he must exact the fullest redress. The more he suffered now the greater would be the joy of revenge. His mind sought out new grievances to pile upon all the others' (p. 182). Thus, not only is Ezeulu alone except for the outsider, John Nwodika, but his role as scapegoat carrying away evil from his community is reversed, for he piles on transgressions and grievances to bring to his community, and it is his personal and individual pride that he seeks to avenge. In later passages, it becomes clear that he has made the mistake of abstracting and separating Ulu from the communal spirit he serves. Once Ezeulu sets himself and Ulu apart from and against his community, both lose their primary role and meaning.

There is a point after his return when Ezeulu begins to acknowledge his responsibility and his failure. Softened by the welcomes and renewed respect of many of the people, he can no longer think of the community as abstraction, 'as one hostile entity'. And after the visit of the forthright Ofoka who perhaps speaks most nearly for the authorial perspective and who reminds Ezeulu that it was his duty to 'wrestle' with the white man, Ezeulu concludes that 'it was right that the Chief Priest should go ahead and confront danger before it reached his people', and he recalls the mythical journey of the first priest of Ulu (p. 189). Unfortunately for Ezeulu and Umuaro, however, this thought 'became too intense for Ezeulu and he put it aside to cool'.

One might compare this moment with the one at the end of part 1 of *Things Fall Apart* when Obierika reflects on his friend's banishment. In that passage traditional wisdom in the form of proverb acts as a formula, suppressing thought and the possibility of change. In this episode from *Arrow of God*, Ezeulu's *failure* to follow through the implications of traditional wisdom in the form of myth has tragic consequences. In Obierika's case, the reader is left to move outside the proverbial network in order to pass judgement on the failure of the community; when Ezeulu 'puts aside his thought to cool', the reader must take up the train of thought and continue the reference to the mythical journey in order to pass judgement on the failure of Ezeulu, and to respond to the 'voice' of Ulu. Given the immediately preceding reminder that Ulu is a creation of man, one must see Ezeulu's submission to Ulu's authority as if he were a mere arrow in the bow of god, as a violation of the concept

79

of the god as originally created. Ezeulu's delight in finding a single pattern, a single explanation for all that has happened, and his abdication of all responsibility ought to make us suspicious, since the novel has insisted continually on the variety of perspectives, the necessity of considering all possibilities, the constant demand to judge and the difficulty of making decisions. Ezeulu's abrogation of responsibility at this point is comparable to Winterbottom's, when despite what he *believes* to be his better knowledge, he decides not to protest against the Lieutenant Governor's directive for implementation of Indirect Rule. Such attempts to take action without taking responsibility are foreshadowed in that early episode where Oduche shuts the python in a box, hoping that it will die without his actually being guilty of killing it. That episode also foreshadows the shutting up of Ezeulu in prison by the British Administration. At one level, Tony Clarke knows that the concretely expressed reasons, 'refusing to be a chief' or 'making an ass of the Administration', are inadequate; the more abstract phrase 'refusing to cooperate with the Administration' supplied from above fills him with a delight not unlike Ezeulu's, for it allows him to justify what he has done and wants to continue to do without feeling guilty.

Like *The African Witch*, *Arrow of God* may be read as an exploration of 'the work of the religious imagination, for good or evil, on men's minds and so upon history', as well as an inquiry into the interaction of rational and irrational motives and desires affecting the actions of men and women, one of those desires being the will to power. *Arrow of God* provides a profound and complex response to Cary's depiction of religion in Africa, setting a theological and philosophical perspective against Cary's portrayal of ju-ju, fear and superstition as the dominating instruments. Although neither Cary nor Achebe condone the abdication of responsibility for one's actions or the wilful ignorance of one's own motive or of the society one seeks to shape or lead, Achebe suggests that a 'true' understanding of either is very difficult, and perhaps impossible. The implication of *The African Witch* is that disinterested knowledge *is* attainable through the maintenance of a firm hold on the rational, through a refusal to abstract and oversimplify, through self-understanding and self-discipline, and that through such knowledge the right choices may be made; the political leader like the artist may control his material. This view is endorsed by the objective and authoritative tone of the omniscient narrator. Neither the narrator nor the structure of *Arrow of God*, with its variety of perspectives, tones and kinds of language, leaves the reader with the implication of a single and final understanding, and one of the constant ironies of the novel is that Ezeulu and Winterbottom act, or would act, most admirably and responsibly on what the reader knows to be misunderstandings. Moreover, man's necessary attempt to control his own destiny is frequently overthrown by forces outside his control, by change, by nature, and by events and peoples of which he can have no knowledge. Nor must man rely on rational knowledge alone: Ezeulu's dream visions, the mythical telling of the creation of Ulu and the role of his priest, the folk tales and songs all are sources of a significant and valid understanding.

The more complex and diversified world and vision of *Arrow of God* moves away from the dichotomies suggested in *Things Fall Apart* between intuitive, felt knowledge and prosaic expression, and between art and action. In Achebe's first novel, the artist is an outcast, and myths and tales are relegated by both Okonkwo and the novel to the realm of women (though the novel also suggests that this need not be the case). In *Arrow of God*, Edogo the carver of masks, though more introspective and less impulsive than his brother, Obika, is also a responsible member of the community and a successful farmer. The mask he carves in the shrine 'in full communion with his ancestors', although carved in isolation, can only be judged in action, and the response of the villagers is important. Myth and ritual become central to the novel's plot and meaning, since the Festival of the Pumpkin Leaves and the Feast of the New Yam embody the meaning of Ulu, the role of the priest and community leader, and the question of power to 'refuse to name'. Music also plays a much more prominent part in this novel. (One may note, in contrast, the lack of any

81

music, fiction or poetry in the British enclave – a lack which contributes to the reader's sense of its dreary lifelessness.)

In one of his most eloquent speeches, addressed to Umuaro after the death of Akukalia in Okperi, Ezeulu reminds his audience of the story of the wrestler who challenged the whole world, the spirits, and finally (despite the pleas of his flute player) his *chi*, which 'seized him with one hand and smashed him on the stony earth . . . This,' concludes Ezeulu, 'is what our kinsman did – he challenged his *chi*. We were his flute player, but we did not plead with him to come away from death' (p. 27). Like Unoka, Achebe in *Things Fall Apart* found solace in his flute and in remembering the past. In *Arrow of God*, written when the political rivalries in newly independent Nigeria made the question of responsible leadership an urgent one, the novelist has become the flute player whose duty is to entreat his community to 'come away from death'.

5

Courting the voters: *A Man of the People*

ARROW OF GOD had been concerned with the nature of Igbo religious belief and believers, portraying not fetishes and ju-ju, 'so crude and stupid', as Louis Aladai describes Rimi civilization in *The African Witch*, but a metaphysic, constructed and questioned by Igbo intellectuals and leaders, a system of beliefs fashioned to respond to and balance the demands of individual and communal well-being and to acknowledge the limits of human knowledge and power. With *A Man of the People*, Achebe takes up some of the other themes significant in Cary's novels, and especially *The African Witch*: these are the themes of inter-linked political and sexual jealousy, of the young western-ized idealist and would-be leader of his people, of political demagoguery, and of political abuse in a situation where African and European forms of political leadership and participation each have a particular kind of appeal and function.

Odili, the narrator and chief protagonist of *A Man of the People*, is like Louis Aladai a nationalist who has nothing but contempt for the traditions of his nation. He does not 'care too much for our women's dancing'[1], he speaks as any foreigner might of the members of the hunters' guild as 'these people', 'bush' is the nastiest epithet he can think of, and he scornfully dismisses the people with whom he works and whose children he teaches:

Here were silly ignorant villagers dancing themselves lame and waiting to blow off their gunpowder in honour of one of those who had started the country off down the slopes of inflation. I wished for a miracle, for a voice of thunder, to hush this ridiculous festival and tell the poor contemptible people one or two truths. But of course it would be quite useless. They were not only ignorant but cynical. Tell them that this man had used his position to enrich himself and they would ask you – as my father did – if you thought that a sensible man would spit out the juicy morsel that good fortune placed in his mouth.   (p. 2)

Rereading this passage, one wonders how early reviewers and critics of this novel could ever have identified Achebe with Odili.[2] The gap between Achebe's attitude toward the people of the villages, manifested in all three of his previous novels, and Odili's dismissal of them is enormous. Nor would a novelist who has so clearly demonstrated his careful and self-conscious use of English be found using a mixed and tired metaphor like 'down the slopes of inflation' in his own right.

Like Louis Aladai, Odili will eventually discover that he too is *of* the people, but the significance of that discovery will have very different consequences for the heroes and readers of each novel. For whereas the irrational prejudices and jealousies of the European community become forces which drive Louis back into the African community and hence into even worse irrationality and barbarism, it is Odili's own prejudices, and especially those acquired through western influence, which cut him off from his community and therefore make him *less* capable of enlightened self-knowledge and leadership.

The whole question of just what it means to be 'of the people' is, of course, central to the novel and is focused by the title. It is introduced in the first paragraph:

No one can deny that Chief the Honourable M. A. Nanga M.P., was the most approachable politician in the country. Whether you asked in the city or in his home village, Anata, they would tell you he was a man of the people. I have to admit this from the onset or else the story I'm going to tell will make no sense.

As with the opening paragraphs in Achebe's other novels, this one will take on increasing significance as the story progresses. Nanga's 'approachability' as well as his appellation, 'a man of the people', take on a double meaning, referring both to his affability and to his willingness to listen to those who offer bribes. And it does make a difference 'whether you ask in the city or in his home village', for different kinds of expectations and relationships belong to each world. The problem of bridging the worlds of city and village is as central to this novel as it was to *No Longer at Ease*.

In addition to introducing the narrator and his attitudes, the opening paragraph and chapter introduce the man of the city and the man of the village, as well as the people of the city and village and Odili's responses to them. The contrast at first seems absolute: on the one hand we have the spectacle of Nanga 'yapping and snarling' shamelessly and viciously 'for the meaty prize' of a ministerial seat, leading the 'pack of back-bench hounds,' sharing in the derisive laughter of the 'hungry hyena', a Nanga who behaves like a mere animal. The Nanga of the village, on the other hand, is all human, responding warmly and genuinely to the pupil he has not seen for over fifteen years, delighting and seeming delighted by the villagers, and emphasizing that a minister is a servant, whose earnings are lavished on parties and donations for the benefit of the people.

The division between the two worlds is further marked by language. The language of the capital, parliament and the newspapers is parodied and heavily satirized by Achebe:

Let us now and for all time extract from our body-politic as a dentist extracts a stinking tooth all those decadent stooges versed in text-book economics and aping the white man's mannerisms and way of speaking. We are proud to be Africans. Our true leaders are not those intoxicated with their Oxford, Cambridge or Harvard degrees but those who speak the language of the people. Away with the damnable and expensive university education which only alienates an African from his rich and ancient culture and puts him above his people. (p. 4)

The prime minister uses language very like that of the newspaper editorial Odili has quoted:

He said that the Miscreant Gang had been caught 'red-handed in a nefarious plot to overthrow the Government of the people by the people and for the people with the help of enemies abroad.' . . . 'From today we must watch and guard our hard-won freedom jealously. Never again must we trust our destiny and the destiny of Africa to the hybrid class of Western-educated and snobbish

85

intellectuals who will not hesitate to sell their mothers for a mess of pottage.' (pp. 5–6)

Rightly perceiving himself to be one of the 'hybrid class of Western-educated and snobbish intellectuals' under attack, Odili also begins to perceive the glaring faults of Nanga and the leaders of the People's Organization Party. What he fails to perceive, however, is the irony that this call for Africanization is couched in a language, metaphors and clichés that are entirely western: 'Government of the people by the people and for the people', 'a mess of pottage', 'caught red-handed', 'decadent stooges'. And nothing could be less like 'the language of the people' than the mannered syntax and diction of the sentence which immediately follows the newspaper editorial's advocacy of its use. There is the further irony that despite this noisy rejection of *earned* degrees, Nanga is inordinately proud of the honorary doctorate he is to be awarded in the United States. Odili's failure to note these ironies stems from the fact that his own language, though somewhat less formal, is dangerously close to that of the editorial and speech writers, and never more so than when he is defensively rationalizing an attitude:

Somehow I found myself admiring the man for his lack of modesty. For what is modesty but inverted pride? We all think we are first-class people. Modesty forbids us from saying so ourselves though, presumably, not from wanting to hear it from others. Perhaps it was their impatience with this kind of hypocrisy that made men like Nanga successful politicians while starry-eyed idealists strove vaingloriously to bring into politics niceties and delicate refinements that belonged elsewhere. (p. 12)

While Odili is not *all* wrong, he is, as usual, only partly right. The speeches quoted above are not the speeches of men 'impatient with . . . hypocrisy' of any kind, while Nanga's behaviour as a snarling backbencher simply does not belong to the category in which one thinks of 'niceties and delicate refinements'. Odili has not managed to separate ethical judgements from aesthetic ones, morals from manners, form from content. And indeed, the pomposity of his description of himself as one of those 'starry-eyed idealists [who] strove vaingloriously to bring into politics niceties and delicate refinements that belong elsewhere' is matched only by its banality and emptiness. 'Starry-eyed idealists' was also one of Winterbottom's favourite dismissive phrases.

Throughout this chapter and throughout the novel, the English language is used to deceive rather than to communicate, and it can be used in this way because for most of the hearers, the *form* of language used conveys more than the content. Clichés from the metropolitan language (the language of the city, the language of the 'mother country') pour forth and submerge the judgement of the listeners, who are not concerned with the precise meaning of statements that 'teaching is a noble profession', that they make up 'a mammoth crowd . . . unprecedented in the annals of Anata', or that 'they must press for their fair share of the national cake'. What they *do* understand is that Nanga commands 'the white man's language' and that he is 'Owner of book!' It is a command which is as hollow as the honorary doctorate, but the people are equally impressed and equally bemused by both, as Andrew overreacts to being called 'Sir' by a white man. Odili may be less deceived by the doctrate, but he is in his own way as much deceived by the trappings of language as is the crowd. And because it is the language of his own consciousness, it is himself he most bemuses and deceives. One sees the self-deception again in the next chapter where Odili informs the reader that 'one reason why I took this teaching job in a bush, private school instead of a smart civil service job in the city with car, free housing, etc., was to give myself a certain amount of autonomy' (p. 19). After what we have already seen of Odili, his life in and attitude to the village, his relationship with the headmaster, his 'autonomy' seems non-existent, although the word does have an impressive ring to it.

The first chapter begins with a series of public statements in formal and hollow English; it ends with a series of conversations in the informal and more personal language of pidgin. But just as it is the formality of the earlier statements which gives them their real significance and which actually undermines the content, the informality of pidgin is its real message. Nanga uses pidgin to express what is meant to be taken as genuine and private feeling:

'If some person come to you and say, "I wan' make you Minister" make you run like blazes comot. Na true word I tell you. To God who made me.' He showed the tip of his tongue to the sky to confirm the oath. 'Minister de sweet for eye but too much katakata de for inside. Believe me yours sincerely.'

(p.16)

We have seen how strenuously Nanga has striven to become minister , and we have seen how he delights in his position. He protests too much, and the form of language used to convey the depth of his sincerity becomes merely an additional deception. The effect is similar when the very wealthy Mrs. John bewails the trouble of the rich:

'When you done experience rich man's trouble you no fit talk like that again. My people get one proverb: they say that when poor man done see with him own eye how to make big man e go beg make e carry him poverty de go je-je.'   (p. 16)

The use of pidgin in these situations is analogous to Nanga's proposed use of 'bush law and custom' to marry a second 'parlour' wife because the first is too 'bush'. In other words, Nanga draws upon native tradition only to enhance his 'city' life, whether he is seeking votes or a more glamorous wife.

The role of women is of great importance in the novel, for what we see of the men's relation and attitudes towards them serves not only to give us a greater understanding of the characters of Nanga and Odili, but also parallels the relationships between the politicians and the electorate. The parallel is detailed and I might have judged it almost heavyhanded had not other critics failed to comment on it. Elsie, Edna and Mrs. Nanga, and to a lesser extent Eunice, Jean and Mrs. John – all can be seen as signifying particular elements of the electorate or influential bodies that the politicians either court or take for granted.

Apart from brief and intriguing glimpses of Edna, the woman first introduced to the reader is Elsie, a young modern woman, who belongs to the city, and who has settled for the 'good life', the city ethic, which seeks only physical fulfilment, and for whom loyalties to fiancés or former lovers are of little significance. But while Elsie is no innocent and like Jean, seduces rather than succumbs to Odili, Odili's attitude to her nevertheless leads the reader to judge him harshly and question his values. For Odili's values are pretty much the same as Elsie's; he is not as monstrous as the notorious 'Irre', but he does admire him, and like him seeks sexual fulfilment and conquest without responsibility. Elsie appeals to him as 'a beautiful, happy girl' who makes 'no demands whatever' (p. 28). Given Elsie's attitude, and Odili's to her, it should be no surprise to anyone that Elsie is won by the man who seems to offer all the most glamorous ingredients of the good life – a Cadillac, a 'princely seven bathroom mansion' with its seven gleaming, silent action water-closets, a chauffeur and a ministerial flag, and a man with a great deal more physical vitality and charisma than Odili. And in the political arena, the voter seduced by luxury, what Armah's narrator in *The Beautyful Ones* refers to as 'the gleam', is most likely to be seduced by the politician who shares the view that nothing is as important as a material heaven on earth. Odili should have been forewarned by Elsie's enthusiasm when she first views the Cadillac:

'Ah! This na the famous Cadillac? I no think say I done see am before.' She was full of girlish excitement. 'Na tough car! Eje-je-je! You think say these people go go another heaven after this?'
(p. 65)

Odili might have been forewarned also by his own re-action, on his first night in Nanga's mansion:

The first thing critics tell you about our ministers' official residences is that each has seven bedrooms and seven bathrooms, one for every day of the week. All I can say is that on that first night there was no room in my mind for criticism. I was simply hypnotized by the luxury of the great suite assigned to me. When I lay down in the double bed that seemed to ride on a cushion of air, and switched on that reading lamp and saw all the beautiful furniture anew from the lying down position and looked beyond the door to the gleaming bathroom and the towels as large as a *lappa* I had to confess that if I were at that moment made a minister I would be most anxious to remain one for ever.

89

And maybe I should have thanked God that I wasn't. We ignore
man's basic nature if we say, as some critics do, that because a
man like Nanga had risen overnight from poverty and insignificance to his present opulence he could be persuaded
without much trouble to give it up again and return to his
original state.

A man who has just come in from the rain and dried his body
and put on dry clothes is more reluctant to go out again than
another who has been indoors all the time. The trouble with our
new nation – as I saw it then lying on that bed – was that none
of us had been indoors long enough to be able to say 'To hell
with it'. We had all been in the rain together until yesterday.
Then a handful of us – the smart and the lucky and hardly ever
the best – had scrambled for the one shelter our former rulers
left, and had taken it over and barricaded themselves in. And
from within they sought to persuade the rest through numerous
loudspeakers, that the first phase of the struggle had been won
and that the next phase – the extension of our house – was
even more important and called for new and original tactics; it
required that all argument should cease and the whole people
speak with one voice and that any more dissent and argument
outside the door of the shelter would subvert and bring down the
whole house.

Needless to say I did not spend the entire night on these
elevated thoughts. Most of the time my mind was on Elsie, so
much so in fact that I had had to wake up in the middle of the
night and change my pyjama trousers.   (pp. 41–2)

The language in which Odili here expresses these
thoughts carries a new authority, a conviction and clarity
lacking in his earlier comments and self-justifications. One
feels that Odili has learned from experience, and his experience has humbled him; he has seen that he too is
vulnerable, and because at this point his interests are not
at stake, he can afford to imaginatively comprehend Nanga
and those like him. But this tolerance quickly dissipates
when Nanga's position interferes with his personal life.
The problem is that they can't *both* have Nanga's position
or Nanga's mansion, and they can't both have Elsie.
Moreover, Nanga's easy conquest of Elsie forces Odili to
realize that it is not merely material comfort which is
important to *him*; when his pride is attacked, he can easily
give up Nanga's mansion. And in revenge he will strike not

at Nanga's material possessions but at his self-esteem, first insulting him as just 'bush', and then determining to rob him of his bride.

But before the loss of Elsie, Odili has come into contact with Nanga's world in other ways, and together with Odili, the reader learns something about 'the corridors of power', and how things are done by those who inhabit them. There is the farcical episode in which the minister unwittingly drinks the 'home made' coffee his party has so vociferously exhorted the electors to buy, and believes himself poisoned, wherein Odili learns not only a further lesson in the hypocrisy of those in power, but also a new lesson about the fear of those who know they have abused their power, and who desperately hang on to it:

I was saying within myself that in spite of his present bravado Chief Nanga had been terribly scared himself, witness his ill-tempered, loud-mouthed panic at the telephone. And I don't think his fear had been for Chief Koko's safety either. I suspect he felt personally threatened. Our people have a saying that when one slave sees another cast into a shallow grave he should know that when the time comes he will go the same way.

(p. 40)

Odili has also begun to recognize the evasive language of corruption, as he overhears Nanga's phone conversation with the Minister of Construction and is told, with no apparent unease on Nanga's part, of the buses Nanga is to get on 'never-never' loan from British Amalgamated. He fails, however, to scrutinize the implication of his own visit with Nanga to the Hon. S. Koko, Minister for Overseas Training, to see 'whether there was anything doing' (p. 20). He learns that Nanga will accept from whites the kind of behaviour which would have 'made him go rampaging mad' if it had come from Odili or any of his own people. Here again there is welcome self-irony, as Odili recognizes his own willingness to become 'partly Americanized' and allow relative strangers to call him by his first name (p. 50). And he also begins to learn at Jean's party that he knows more about some things, especially African art and culture, than the Europeans do, and begins to resent the superficial and detached knowledge of those who wish to 'show' him

91

Lagos and 'take up' the food and dancing of his culture.

Odili's willingness to learn – his curiosity and alert interest in the world around him – is perhaps his most likeable trait. It is a characteristic which is important, for the novel is concerned with learning – Odili's *and* the reader's. We accompany Odili on his tour of the city, his visit to those in power, we see what he learns, and just as significantly, we see what and how he fails to learn. The reader is also concerned with making judgements: Odili's very failure to pass judgement on Nanga's behaviour leaves a space for the reader to do so. The reader becomes not a passive onlooker, as Odili is at times, but a participant in the novel, making the connections that Odili has failed to make. At the same time, we rarely question what Odili reports – the brittle, empty and condescending party-talk at Jean's house, the lively and exuberant welcome given Nanga and his response to it. It is the very sharpness of his perception and communication of these events that allows us to feel the fuzziness of his understanding of himself and his responses.

That fuzziness is apparent in his attitude to Mrs. Nanga, who is almost everything Elsie is not – homely, plain, motherly and, above all, loyal. While Elsie (like Nanga) speaks either pidgin or English, Mrs. Nanga generally speaks 'our language'. While Elsie delights in the city parties and all the material things it has to offer, Mrs. Nanga is unconcerned with them, characterizing 'going to all these embassy parties and meeting all the big guns' as 'nine pence talk and three pence food. "Hallo, hawa you. Nice to see you again." All na lie lie' (p. 41). While Elsie and Odili coyly pretend or provoke jealousy by referring to other partners, Mrs. Nanga's answer concerning Edna's status is simple and direct: 'She is our wife . . . We are getting a second wife to help me.' (p. 41) Mrs. Nanga is most at ease in Anata, the Nangas' home village, to which she insists that the children return at least once a year lest they become 'English people'. If Elsie represents the urbanized generation of electors, Mrs. Nanga represents that older generation of electors firmly tied to traditional customs and to traditional values. And Odili's attitude to Mrs. Nanga is

similar to his attitude toward the villagers – a mixture of
contempt, admiration, sympathy and awe, combined with
a willingness to use them for his own ends, as he does
shamelessly on his return to Anata.

But before returning to the country, Odili has another
kind of encounter with the world of the city – this time the
world represented by Kulmax (whose name suggests Karl
Marx), leader of the Common People's Convention,
which, as Odili is quick to point out, entirely lacks
representation from the common people. That it is a Common People's Convention in name only does not worry
Max and his group in the least, and Max's contempt for
these common people is suggested in his criticism of
Nanga: ' "That's all they care for," he said with a solemn
face. "Women, cars, landed property. But what else can
you expect when intelligent people leave politics to il-
literates like Chief Nanga?" ' (p. 87) Nanga is advised by
Americans; Max and his group are befriended, advised,
and financed by the comrade from Eastern Europe. It
would seem clear that Achebe shares the attitude of Edna's
mother towards both parties: 'They are both white man's
people.' (p. 119) And while Max's party is most likely to
win the allegiance not of the common people but of the
western-educated and highly idealistic younger generation
represented by Eunice, those like Odili who actually run
for political positions seem to be doing so for negative
reasons and personal ends. Indeed, Odili's participation
seems to be mostly a case of sour grapes which is then ra-
tionalized by the kind of sentimental and vague idealism
suggested by Max's ode to the 'Earth-Mother', in which
Achebe parodies Senghor:[3]

I will return home to her – many centuries have I wandered –
And I will make my offering at the feet of my lovely Mother:
I will rebuild her house, the holy places they raped and
plundered,
And I will make it fine with black wood, bronzes and terra-cotta.
(p. 91)

The vague and sentimental idealism of the young,
western-educated professional classes to which Max and

Eunice belong, and which Odili still admires even at the end of the novel, contrasts strongly with the village ethic seen at work immediately following Odili's visit to Max and the city. As many critics have pointed out, and David Carroll has demonstrated most lucidly and at the greatest length,[4] the episode in which Josiah brings about his own ruin provides one of the novel's central parables and morals:

Josiah called Azoge to his shop and gave him rice to eat and plenty of palm-wine. Azoge thought he had met a kind man and began to eat and drink. While he was eating and drinking Josiah took away his stick – have you ever heard such abomination? – and put a new stick like the old one in its place thinking that Azoge would not notice. But if a blind man does not know his own stick, tell me what else would he know? So when Azoge prepared to go he reached for his stick and found that a strange one was in its place, and so he began to shout . . .

'I still don't understand. What does Josiah want to do with his stick?'

'How are you asking such a question, teacher? To make medicine for trade, of course.'

'That is terrible,' I said, still very much in the dark but not caring to make it known.

'What money will do in this land wears a hat; I have said it.'

(p. 96)

That Josiah's deed bears a general resemblance to the dishonesty and corruption of politicians like Nanga and Koko who in Timothy's words, later reiterated by Odili's father, have 'taken away enough for the owner to notice', has been demonstrated by others, but less attention has been paid to the particular relevance of Josiah's action. The behaviour of Nanga and others who appeal to the traditions of the country, the traditions which in the past have allowed the people to find their way through a world full of unforeseeable elements, in order to deceive and blind others, giving back to the people a false, though superficially similar Africa, parallels Josiah's substitution of the false stick. It is significant too that Odili, like the blind man – or those whom Josiah seeks to blind – remains 'in the dark', for Odili is not yet capable of distinguishing the false wares from the true. However, he does ponder and begin to realize the implications of the saying about the owner beginning to notice. The episode is important not only as a parallel to the affairs of the nation, but as a counterweight to Odili's repeated comments on the apathy, ignorance and cynicism of the people. We are made aware that there *are* occasions on which the community can be roused to effective action, and that the apparent cynicism is balanced by a deeply felt set of values and standards which Josiah's action has outraged.

Although Odili remains even at the end of the story an admirer of Max, and can maintain the view that the crowd is 'contemptible' and that those like Edna who lack his standard of education are to be despised; although he feels that city men in their Italian-type shoes and tight trousers, city girls with their lipstick and pressed hair bring 'an air of well-dressed sophistication' and raise 'the general tone of the village', there are significant ways in which he has become less blind. One is his recognition of the existence and importance of certain values, as distinct from customs, belonging to the village, some of which he rejects, and others which he begins to respect and see himself a part of. He still cannot accept the 'wisdom' of his elders, represented by his father, Edna's father and Nanga, who constantly urge him to take the money Nanga offers him and live in comfort. Nor can he accept the appeal to village loyalties that Max makes on his behalf and which is eloquently expounded by an old man in the audience. The father figures all endorse the masculine ethic espoused by Okonkwo, the materialism which Achebe has elsewhere declared a significant part of the Igbo ethic, and which the coming of the white man has reinforced.[5]

But what of the feminine and spiritual side? Has it been completely destroyed or repressed? It is significant that Odili's mother died at his birth, and that he grows up both alienated from and a destroyer of the traditional world which produced him. Yet the same father/son conflict which led Nwoye to reject his father also leads Odili to reject his father's materialism and to turn instead to the idealism which Eunice represents.

The reactions to his father, to Nanga, to Odo, have all led

95

Odili away from self-interested detachment and aloof 'autonomy' towards involvement – both personal and political. It is this involvement which brings him into contact with the feminine ethic, this time demanding genuine concern and feeling rather than the superficial and vague sentiment of Max's 'Dance-Offering to the Earth Mother'. That involvement, the breaking down of the armour of detachment, must also come after a little humbling, the realization of his own vulnerability at Nanga's, the deflation of his pride by Nanga as a sexual rival with Elsie and as a political rival at the farcical Anata meeting at which Odili becomes a mere figure of fun. So too his genuine involvement with Edna can be realized after the humiliation of the bicycle accident, another incident in which Odili's own feelings and perceptions are revealed partly to himself and more fully to the reader. Odili revels in Edna's admiration of his physical strength as he cycles up a steep hill, with her as passenger on the handlebars:

'I haven't seen any hill yet,' I replied, getting back some of my breath as I pedalled freely down the small, friendly descent that followed. These words were hardly out of my mouth when a stupid sheep and her four or five lambs rushed out of the roadside on my left. I braked sharply. Unfortunately Edna's back was resting on my left arm and prevented me from applying the brake on that side effectively. So only the brake on the front wheel performed fully. The bicycle pitched forward and crashed on the road. Just before the impact Edna had cried out something like 'My father!' She was thrown farther up the road and as soon as I got up, I rushed to help her to her feet again. Then I turned to gaze at the foofoo and soup in the sandy road. I could have wept. I just stood looking at it and biting my lip. Then Edna burst into nervous laughter which completed my humiliation. I didn't want to look at her. Without taking my eyes from the food I murmured that I was very sorry.

'It was not your fault,' she said, 'it was the stupid sheep.'

Then I noticed with the corner of my eyes that she was bending down. I turned then and saw where she had grazed her knee on the road.

'Oh dear!' I said, 'Edna, I am sorry.'

She left her frock which she had held up a little at the knee and came to dust my shoulder where my new white shirt carried a thick patch of indelible red-earth. Then she bent down and picked up the travelling-can and began to wipe away the sand, and the spilt soup with green leaves. To my surprise she was crying and saying something like 'My mother will die of hunger today.' Actually I think her crying was probably due to hurt pride because the food lying on the road showed how poor her family was. But I may be wrong. At the time, however, I was greatly upset.

'Can she manage bread and corned beef?' I asked. 'We could buy some outside the hospital.'

'I haven't brought any money,' said Edna.

'I have some money,' I said, feeling the first breath of relief since the accident happened. 'And we could get some disinfectant for your knee. I'm terribly sorry, my dear.' (pp. 105–6)

What is particularly noteworthy in this incident is Odili's interpretation of Edna's distress, his assumption that she must be humiliated by this revelation of her 'poverty', and that foo-foo soup is a sign of great deprivation. Nor can he believe that she could cry for anyone but herself. While the reader must feel that this interpretation reveals more about Odili's character than Edna's, he can also perceive that Odili has for once forgotten about himself and *his* humiliation and is genuinely concerned about Edna's physical and emotional well-being. It is an important emotional step for Odili, one that he only later realizes he has taken, and which will lead him to fight for Edna for her own sake, not just to use her as a tool in his fight against Nanga. This personal involvement parallels the one he will take later when, thinking he has lost Edna, he realizes that he wishes to continue with the political work anyway. And in this case, his very involvement, whatever the original motives, gradually leads him to a fuller and deeper understanding of the community he seeks to win from Nanga.

As Odili campaigns, one senses an increasing respect on his part for the people. He learns to see his father in a new light, and the growing understanding between father and son, like Odili's decision to return to his village to start a school, indicates a new understanding and appreciation of the world of the village. In particular, his father's refusal to recant and dissociate himself from his son causes Odili to re-examine his assumptions:

He was silent for a while, then he said:
'You may be right. But our people have said that a man of worth
never gets up to unsay what he said yesterday. I received your
friends in my house and I am not going to deny it.'

I thought to myself: You do not belong to this age, old man.
Men of worth nowadays simply forget what they said yesterday.
Then I realized I had never really been close enough to my father
to understand him . . . Anyway, this was no time to begin a new
assessment; it was better left to the tax people.   (pp. 152–3)

Like his father, Odili has felt it was wrong to 'unsay what
he said yesterday'. He was particularly dismayed by Max's
taking of the money from Koko, dismissing the paper he
had signed as having 'no legal force'. Odili insists that it
still has moral force, and he also insists that it is only by
strict adherence to such morality that he and his party
could oppose Nanga.

Odili's concern with the debasement of language, his
scorn for those who 'unsay what they said yesterday',
reflects one of Achebe's main concerns in this novel.
Throughout the story politicians have used words and
gestures to deceive; a relationship between the corruption
of language and the corruption of tradition is implicit. The
problem is, however, a complex one, for it concerns those
who like Max and Nanga deliberately deceive (and very effectively use folk parable and proverbs to win the people),
as well as those who do not care whether the language they
use is accurate – as in the case of the Common People's
Convention, or Elsie's delirious calling of her ex-partners'
names. Yet again, there is language which is self-deceptive,
as is so often the case with Odili's language which allows
him to evade the truth rather than confront it. There is,
finally, the problem of finding an adequate language, and
Edna's letter, both touching and banal, brings this problem to the fore. For Edna's problem, like that of most of
the villagers with regard to the English language, is not
that she has little to say or wishes to avoid communicating
fully, but that she has little mastery of English, and so must
resort to the clichés manufactured by others. One thing
that the reader may observe as Odili's story progresses is
the increasing effectiveness of the language he uses, the

increasing authority of his voice. That authority comes largely from his move away from the clichés of chapter 1, the newspaper and boy scout jargon which infects his style, and which is both a symptom and a cause of his near acceptance of Nanga and his world. In the last chapters, Odili's consciousness and style have been influenced increasingly by the language of 'our people', a language organically connected with the life of the village. Of course, the change is not complete, and it is clear that Odili still has far to go. Odili and the reader are left at the end of the novel to sort out and make a new beginning out of the variety of political attitudes, possible actions and languages manifested in the final paragraphs of the novel.[6]

But their most touching gesture as far as I was concerned was to release Eunice from jail and pronounce Max a Hero of the Revolution. (For I must point out that my severe criticism of his one fatal error notwithstanding, Max was indeed a hero and martyr; and I propose to found a school – a new type of school, I hasten to add – in my village to his memory.) What I found distasteful however was the sudden, unashamed change of front among the very people who had stood by and watched him die.

Overnight everyone began to shake their heads at the excesses of the last regime, at its graft, oppression and corrupt government: newspapers, the radio, the hitherto silent intellectuals and civil servants – everybody said what a terrible lot; and it became public opinion the next morning. And these were the same people that only the other day had owned a thousand names of adulation, whom praise-singers followed with song and talking-drum wherever they went. Chief Koko in particular became a thief and a murderer, while the people who had led him on – in my opinion the real culprits – took the legendary bath of the Hornbill and donned innocence.

'Koko had taken enough for the owner to see,' said my father to me. It was the day I had gone to visit Eunice and was telling him on my return how the girl had showed no interest in anything – including whether she stayed in jail or out of it. My father's words struck me because they were the very same words the villagers of Anata had spoken of Josiah, the abominated trader. Only in their case the words had meaning. The owner was the village, and the village had a mind; it could say no to sacrilege. But in the affairs of the nation there was no owner, the laws of the village became powerless. Max was avenged not by

99

the people's collective will but by one solitary woman who loved him. Had his spirit waited for the people to demand redress it would have been waiting still, in the rain and out in the sun. But he was lucky. And I don't mean it to shock or to sound clever. For I do honestly believe that in the fat-dripping, gummy, eat-and-let-eat regime just ended – a regime which inspired the common saying that a man could only be sure of what he had put away safely in his gut or, in language ever more suited to the times: 'you chop, me self I chop, palaver finish'; a regime in which you saw a fellow cursed in the morning for stealing a blind man's stick and later in the evening saw him again mounting the altar of the new shrine in the presence of all the people to whisper into the ear of the chief celebrant – in such a regime, I say, you died a good death if your life had inspired someone to come forward and shoot your murderer in the chest – without asking to be paid. (pp. 166–7)

Odili has not lost his idealism, despite the experiences he and his country have undergone, and despite the biting indictment with which the novel ends. More importantly, his idealism, though the reader may judge it still too submerged in the wave of emotion left by Max's death and Eunice's revenge, is now directed toward realistic action – the founding of a new type of school in his own village. Now the earlier claim to 'autonomy' gains substance, but it is an independence of action tied to a new-found relationship to his father, to Edna, and to his home community. He has also moved beyond his earlier tendency to see people and events in terms of simple good or evil, when Nanga and his father had to be either hero or villain, friend or foe. Odili is now able to condemn his friend's fault – Max's acceptance of money in bad faith – while maintaining his admiration for his attempt to change the country. Similarly his rueful condemnation of the fickleness of public opinion lacks the extreme contempt for the populace expressed at the beginning of his story.

Odili's use of language has also become much more critical and self-conscious. Whereas his father has accepted without question the relevance of the saying, 'Koko had taken enough for the owner to see', Odili reflects on the saying and sees that its meaning cannot be stretched to cover national affairs. In that reflection, his voice takes on a new clarity and authority. He has also learned to judge and make telling use of another concrete Nigerian language, pidgin. But the flight of rhetoric which ends the novel suggests the danger of letting oneself be carried away by the language one is using. It is an emotive and stirring final sentence idealizing individual action as an end in itself, however futile its consequences for the community. Odili, telling his story in retrospect, has begun the process of judging critically the insufficiencies of language and its speakers. It is now the reader's task to continue that process.

6

The novelist as critic: politics and criticism, 1960–1988

ACHEBE'S FIRST FOUR NOVELS were written while he worked for the Nigerian Broadcasting Corporation from 1954 as a Talks Producer and later as Director of External Broadcasting. As Nigeria moved towards independence in 1960, the role of the NBC in helping to create a sense of national identity, ensuring that the electorate was politically well informed, and linking new technology to the continuation of traditional cultures and forms was an exciting and important one. Achebe's work took him to various parts of Nigeria to research topics and interview his fellow Nigerians, and might well have contributed to his keen ear for nuances in language and varieties of dialogue, as well as to the sense his novels convey of awareness of an immediate audience. In 1961, the year he married Christie Chinwe Okoli, he was appointed Director of External Broadcasting for the Nigerian Broadcasting Corporation. His two first novels had by this time brought him considerable fame, and in 1962 he was asked to become founding editor of the influential African Writers Series which had been started by Alan Hill and Van Milne of Heinemann Educational Books, with *Things Fall Apart* as the first in the series. In just over twenty years, this series of inexpensive paperback editions made available to African, European and American readers the works of some hundred and fifty writers from all over the African continent.

This enterprise marked Achebe's emergence as a critic of and spokesman for African literature. As Talks Producer for NBC he had visited East Africa on a Rockefeller Scholarship in 1961, and reported on a conference of

African Writers he had attended in Makere.[1] He had written about Amos Tutuola for the *Radio Times* (Lagos),[2] and reviewed collections of poetry by Okigbo and Rabearivelo for *Spear*.[3] And in 1962 he published in *Nigeria Magazine* 'Where Angels Fear to Tread', an admonition to European critics and writers who made dogmatic pronouncements about Nigerian (or African) literature.[4] In these essays Achebe questions the assumption that African literature must follow the patterns established by European writers and that the same aesthetic criteria should apply to both. Referring to an anonymous critic who had berated African writers for concentrating 'too much on society and not sufficiently on individual characters', thus failing to create ' "true" aesthetic proportions', Achebe commented:

I wondered when this *truth* became so self-evident and who decided that (unlike the other self-evident truth) this one should apply to black as well as white.
It is all this cock-sureness which I find so very annoying.[5]

Here we see the opposition to single-minded dogmatism, whether theological, political, social or literary, which is so much a feature of the novels. And going on to express his irritation at European critics who so readily claim to be able to distinguish 'real' Nigerians in fiction from 'unreal' ones, or the truly rural from the truly urban, Achebe links their ignorance with their monolinguism – a recurring motif in the novels:

But theories and bogeys are no substitute for insight. No man can understand another whose language he does not speak (and 'language' here does not mean simply words, but a man's entire world view). How many Europeans and Americans have our language? I do not know of any, certainly among our writers and critics.[6]

Achebe began writing novels partly in reaction to the 'superficiality' of outsiders' stories about Nigeria. In 1962, the 'superficiality' of criticism by outsiders likewise spurred him to write and to encourage others to begin writing criticism from the inside, and to seek to take into their own hands the control of publication and establishing of criteria

for African literature. The essays and lectures written between 1962 and 1966 can frequently be seen as attempts to
oppose dominant European (or rather British) assumptions
about literary worth – the doctrines of universalism, the
consequent divorce of art from politics, the emphasis on
formal qualities rather than social concerns – in order to
clear space for the creation of a literature which reflects
African values and concerns.

Two of the key critical pieces in this enterprise, and the
ones which are still most likely to be quoted with reference
to Achebe's critical stance, are 'The Role of the Writer in
the New Nation,' first published in Nigeria in 1964,[7] and
'The Novelist as Teacher', first published in England in
1965.[8] 'The Role of the Writer in the New Nation' is
more specifically concerned with writers in new African
nations, and draws upon the kind of analysis Frantz Fanon
has made of the psychological impact of colonialism upon
the colonized. Like Fanon he defends the role of the writer
(and intellectual) as cultural nationalist, restoring the
picture of the African past so crudely distorted by the
colonialists, and thus restoring to Africans their belief in
their own humanity:

as far as I am concerned the fundamental theme must first be
disposed of. This theme – put quite simply – is that African
peoples did not hear of culture for the first time from Europeans;
that their societies were not mindless but frequently had a
philosophy of great depth and beauty, that they had poetry and,
above all, they had dignity. It is this dignity that many African
peoples all but lost in the colonial period, and it is this dignity
that they must now regain . . . The writer's duty is to help them
regain it by showing them in human terms what happened to
them, what they lost.[9]

Written in the same year, 'The Novelist as Teacher' begins
by challenging the posited assumptions of Achebe's audience
in Leeds that art and social education are incompatible,
that the writer and his society must always be at odds, and
that African writers appeal (intentionally or not) mainly to
European readers. Achebe then restates his position concerning the role of the African writer in more personal and
impassioned terms, taking a position closer to Fanon's

than Senghor's with regard to Négritude as a necessary antithesis in the struggle to combat racism and its consequences:

Here then is an adequate revolution for me to espouse – to help my society regain belief in itself and put away the complexes of the years of denigration and self-abasement. And it is essentially a question of education, in the best sense of that word. Here, I think, my aims and the deepest aspirations of my society meet. For no thinking African can escape the pain of the wound in our soul. You have all heard of the African Personality; of African democracy, of the African way to socialism, of négritude, and so on. They are all props we have fashioned at different times to help us get on our feet again. Once we are up we shan't need any of them any more. But for the moment it is in the nature of things that we may need to counter racism with what Jean-Paul Sartre has called anti-racist racism, to announce that we are not just as good as the next man but that we are much better.

The writer cannot expect to be excused from the task of re-education and regeneration that must be done.[10]

One of the issues that has been central to discussion in Africa about the nature of African literature has been that of social and political commitment (the two are often confused). Indeed, the majority of African critics and writers have accepted Leopold Senghor's pronouncement that African art differs from European in that it is 'functional, collective and committed', and in recent years this view has been strongly endorsed by influential writers such as Ngugi wa Thiong'o and critics such as Chinweizu.[11] Like these, Achebe has not refrained from classifying European literature and aesthetics in terms of recent though influential modernist works and critical attitudes, ignoring a much longer tradition in the west of concern for the relationship between literature and society. Language has been the other recurring issue, on which a number of African writers and critics including Senghor and Ngugi wa Thiong'o have taken sides – this time opposing ones. Senghor argued that French was a beautiful, clear and universal language, and hence the language he *chose* to write in. Ngugi, however, has argued that English, like any other European language, carries with it the values and world view of the colonizer, and, more significantly, prevents communication with the common people in his own country, Kenya. After publishing four novels and two plays in English, Ngugi has now begun writing in Gikuyu, his mother tongue. His recent book, *Decolonising the Mind: The Politics of Language in African Literature*, argues the case for the use of African rather than European languages in fiction, poetry and drama.

Achebe's position in this debate has not been rigid; it is an issue which he has returned to on several occasions, sometimes with second thoughts. In general, however, he stands somewhere between the lines drawn by Senghor and Ngugi, seeing English not so much as a chosen language, but one that has been imposed, and which must be wrestled with and transformed before it can be used to 'carry the weight of [his] African experience'.[12] In a lecture given in 1964 at the University of Ghana, he argued that African literature in English could take its place among other African literature in indigenous languages, such as Igbo, Yoruba or Hausa, but asserted that it had the additional merit of providing a *national* tongue, without which different writers from different communities in Nigeria would be unable to communicate with one another or with a national audience.[13] He cited the works of Equiano, Tutuola, Okigbo and John Pepper Clark as proof that English *could* be used creatively and in new ways to express non-European experience, and so sought to refute the argument made by Obi Wali the previous year in his *Transition* article, 'The Dead End of African Literature,' that 'until these writers and their Western midwives accept the fact that any true African literature must be written in African languages, they would be merely pursuing a dead end, which can only lead to sterility, uncreativity and frustration'.[14]

Though always tempered by his acute sense of the complexities and intractabilities of the social/political world in which changes must take place, the views Achebe expresses in these talks given prior to 1965 about the possibilities of change, the writer's role in helping to direct it, and the creation of a national community, are comparatively optimistic. Indeed, they suggest a view of history and 'progress' which differs from the more tragic and ironic temper of his first three novels – a 'will to change' which many of his fictional characters share and his plots resist. Increasingly, events in Nigeria were to make that optimism difficult to sustain.

After independence in 1960, regional tensions, which had often been exacerbated by colonial policy and pre-independence jockeying for power, had not dissipated. The first serious crisis came with the Western Nigeria Emergency, which resulted from a rift between Chief Awolowo, leader of the mainly Yoruba Action Group, and the premier of the Western Region, Chief Akintola. The disorder and violence in the Western House led to a declaration of a state of emergency by the Federal Government and the sending of Federal troops to Ibadan to restore order. The Emergency lasted for six months, but after that the situation continued to stir trouble, with the treason trials in 1963 of Chief Enahoro, Chief Awolowo and 18 others, who were convicted of treasonable felony and illegally importing arms into Nigeria. The 1964 census results also caused much controversy, particularly in the east and mid-west where it was felt that the figures from the north were greatly inflated. In late 1964, during the run up to the federal elections, political campaigning was marked by violence and thuggery of the kind portrayed in *A Man of the People*, which Achebe completed in these months and handed to his publisher in February 1965.[15] One of the worst episodes of violence during the election campaign involved a riot in the Tiv region, which the army put down at a reported cost of 700 lives.[16] When the United Progressive Grand Alliance decided to boycott the elections, President Azikiwe declared the election invalid, and at first refused to recognize the new government of Prime Minister Balewa. However, a compromise was reached in January 1965, and it was announced that Balewa would proceed to form a 'broadly-based national government'. After further violence and claims of fraud in the Western Region elections in late 1965, the Nigerian army intervened (perhaps following an example already set in Togo). A *coup d'état* involving many Igbo as well as other army officers on 15 January 1966 ended the First Nigerian Republic and established a military government with General Ironsi at its head. Its declared aim was to bring stability to the country and end corruption, an aim welcomed by many Nigerians. In May, the federal system was abolished and replaced by a unitary state. This led to demonstrations and protests in the northern areas, and attacks upon Igbos living in the north. A second coup in July 1966, led by military officers from the north, seized General Ironsi, installed General Gowon in his place, and restored the federal system. One of Achebe's cousins was among the many Igbo officers assassinated in this coup.

This second coup increased rather than diminished tension between ethnic groups both in the north and south. The following months saw widespread riots in the north. Hundreds of Igbos were massacred in Kano and Kaduna, and thousands were repatriated to the south. Others abandoned their property and positions in industry or the civil service and fled. In Lagos, soldiers went to Achebe's office at the Nigerian Broadcasting Corporation to search for him. A telephone call to Achebe's house from his staff alerted him to the danger, and Achebe took his family into hiding at the home of a friend in Lagos for more than two weeks. Achebe then reluctantly accepted that he could no longer live in Lagos and took his wife and two young children to the safety of his home region.

Fearing northern intentions towards the Igbos, the military governor of the Eastern Region, Lieutenant Colonel Ojukwu, boycotted the constitutional talks held in October 1966, and finally, on 30 May 1967, declared the secession of the Eastern Region. The terrible and traumatic conflict that followed, known to most people as the Biafran War or the Nigerian Civil War, lasted until January 1970. Arms and money were supplied to both sides, but chiefly to the federal armies, by outside governments who sought to retain some stake in Nigerian oil deposits recently discovered in considerable quantity in the south. Biafran forces fought bravely and with initial success, but with the fall of Port Harcourt in 1968, Biafra lost its chief supply link to the outside, and the war went increasingly in favour of the federal forces. Biafran casualties, both civilian and military, were very high. Thousands died of starvation.

Many of Nigeria's leading writers took sides or attempted to intervene in the conflict. Wole Soyinka was imprisoned for two years, an experience eloquently recorded in his autobiographical account, *The Man Died*, and the prison poems, *A Shuttle in the Crypt*. The last sections of Christopher Okigbo's poetic sequence, *Labyrinths*, speaks out powerfully although obliquely against the events preceding and beginning the war. A major in the Biafran army, Okigbo died in battle near Nsukka in 1967. Achebe put his skill as a writer to use responding to the distortions and arguments of commentators such as Tai Solarin and Margery Perham,[17] and, together with other writers such as Cyprian Ekwensi, Gabriel Okara and Flora Nwapa, made several visits to other African countries, Europe and America to speak on behalf of the Biafran cause. In a speech at Makere University in 1968, he asserted the necessity and justice of the Biafran struggle, and of the involvement of writers in it:

Biafra stands in opposition to the murder and rape of Africa by whites and blacks alike because she has tasted both and found them equally bitter. No government, black or white, has the right to stigmatise and destroy groups of its own citizens without undermining the basis of its own existence. The government of Nigeria failed to protect the fourteen million people of its former Eastern Nigeria from wanton destruction and rightly lost their allegiance.

Secondly Biafra stands for true independence in Africa, for an end to the 400 years of shame and humiliation which we have suffered in our association with Europe. Britain knows this and is using Nigeria to destroy Biafra.

. . . Biafran writers are committed to the revolutionary struggle of their people for justice and true independence. Gabriel Okara, Cyprian Ekwensi, Onuora Nzekwu, Nkem Nwankwo, John Munonye, V. C. Ike, Flora Nwapa are all working actively in the cause for which Christopher Okigbo died. I believe our cause is right and just. And this is what literature in Africa should be about today – right and just causes.[18]

After completing *A Man of the People*, Achebe had begun a new novel, some of whose characters were eventually to appear in *Anthills of the Savannah*.[19] Under the conditions of the war, he found it impossible to continue novel writing, and turned to shorter works, particularly poems, but also short stories. Many of the poems published in *Beware Soul Brother* were composed during or just after the war, commemorating specific events and scenes from the conflict.

When the war finally ended in 1970, Achebe joined in the arduous task of reconstruction. Many homes had to be rebuilt, cities had been badly damaged, and what had become known as the University of Biafra looted and bombed. (Its original name, the University of Nigeria in Nsukka, has since been resumed.) Achebe's own home had been destroyed in a bombing raid in 1967. As a Senior Research Fellow at the University of Nigeria, Nsukka, Achebe with his fellow intellectuals set about salvaging and restoring some of the ideals which for them had always been involved in the Biafran struggle, and which are expressed in the speech quoted above. He edited the university journal, *Nsukkascope*, and in 1971 founded *Okike: A Nigerian Journal of New Writing*, whose stated aim was to provide a forum for writing by Africans, to establish standards, and to debate the criteria by which African writing should be judged. The first issue contained three poems by the South African writer Dennis Brutus, as well as contributions from Nigerian writers such as Soyinka, Ekwensi, Okara, Obiechina and Achebe himself. It also contained advertisements for a group of new publications from Nwamife Books (Enugu), including a collection of stories, the first edition of *Beware Soul Brother*, Flora Nwapa's *This Is Lagos and Other Stories*, and Emmanuel Obiechina's important study of Onitsha Market Literature, *Literature for the Masses*. It was as if writers and intellectuals were determined to demonstrate clearly that creativity in the eastern region was alive and well, and that the Igbo spirit was not to be quenched even by war and military defeat.

Okike has been one of a handful of African literary journals to survive beyond the first few issues, and is still being published It celebrated its twentieth issue in 1981 with two anthologies culled from contributions to the magazine: *Rhythms of Creation: A Decade of Okike Poetry*, edited by Donatus Nwoga; and *African Creations: Stories from Okike*, edited by E. N. Obiechina. In later years, the 'Nigerian' subtitle was changed to 'African', reflecting its wide range of contributions from the African continent, the Caribbean and black America. It was also to publish a number of substantial critical works, including a two-part study of Afro-American literature by the South African novelist and critic, Ezekiel Mphahlele, and it serialized the first version of *Towards the Decolonization of African Literature* by Chinweizu, Onwuchekwa Jemie and Ihechukwu Madubuike.[20]

In 1972, Achebe was offered and accepted a Visiting Professorship at the University of Massachusetts in Amherst, in the United States of America, where he taught African literature and continued to edit *Okike*. It was to be four years before he returned to Nsukka.

During his three years at the University of Massachusetts and one year as University Professor at the University of Connecticut, Achebe was invited to be the keynote speaker at a number of universities and conferences. Several of these lectures are published in *Morning Yet On Creation Day* and *Hopes and Impediments*. Some, such as 'Africa and Her Writers', given at Harvard University in 1972, 'Language and the Destiny of Man', given at Dartford College in 1972 and 'Thoughts on the African Novel', given at a conference on African Literature at Dalhousie University, Halifax, Canada, in 1973, continue the themes and concerns of the pre-1965 lectures, although they are presented with greater elaboration and complexity, and with keen awareness of the assumptions and blind spots in his North American audiences. Thus 'Africa and Her Writers' stresses the desirability of art firmly rooted in and responsible to its community, taking the *mbari* ceremony of the Owerri Igbo as a model.[21] The aesthetic ideals underlying *mbari* particularly stressed by Achebe were the involvement of 'ordinary members of society', not a particular caste or secret society, and the insistence, despite its acknowledgement of the importance of master artists and craftsmen, that: '*There is no rigid barrier between makers of culture and its consumers. Art belongs to all, and is a "function" of society.*' (Achebe's italics; *MYCD*, p. 22). He contrasts with the 'unbridled republicanism' of Igbo society the aristocratic and oligarchic conditions under which the European aesthetic developed, a culture in which 'kings and their nobilities in the past cultivated a taste different from the common appetite'. Speaking in Boston, the birthplace of American republicanism, Achebe's inclusion of American writers and critics in an essentially aristocratic European culture and his example of Igbo culture as democratic model, might well have come as a calculated surprise to his American audience. Many among them might have been aware of Walt Whitman's similar rejection one hundred and twenty years earlier of European models as too rarefied, decadent and essentially hierarchical for an American democratic republic. Achebe returns to the example of the *mbari* ceremony in a later lecture titled 'The Writer and His Community' given at the University of California in Los Angeles in 1984. Here he stresses its rejection of individualism, and of the notion of individual proprietorship of a work of art (*HI*, pp. 32–3). In the same year, in his foreword to the superbly illustrated *Igbo Arts: Community and Cosmos*, edited by Herbert Cole and Chike Aniakor, he emphasizes the importance given by *mbari* to art as process rather than product (*HI*, pp. 42–61)

Throughout all the lectures delivered in North America and Europe runs a desire, sometimes explicit, sometimes implicit, to unsettle the complacency of westerners who assume that their political and cultural institutions and products are to be models for the rest of the world, a complacency which Achebe continually encountered in the media as well as among his students and colleagues in the United States. In these lectures he again and more fully takes up the criteria of 'universality', which all too often is equated by westerners with their own values, customs and conventions. He takes to task the Ghanaian writer, Ayi Kwei Armah, for imposing western 'existentialism' upon his portrayal of modern Ghana (in his novel, *The Beautyful*

Ones Are Not Yet Born), and in his anxiety to escape being labelled as 'merely an African writer', attempting to write of the 'human condition' as conceived by contemporary European novelists. In 'Thoughts on the African Novel' he again takes to task African writers and critics who distinguish between 'African' or 'Nigerian' situations, characters or audiences and 'universal' situations, characters or audiences. By offering a critique of such African writers, and in the process often contrasting them with others such as Senghor and Okigbo as well as with traditional Igbo artists, Achebe indirectly but effectively undermines the shared assumptions of western critics and members of his audiences. However, his criticism is much more direct in a lecture delivered to an international conference on Commonwealth Literature at Makere University in January 1974. Titled 'Colonialist Criticism', the lecture takes up and illustrates in much greater detail and variety the case against European critics of African literature argued twelve years earlier in 'Where Angels Fear to Tread'. But here the critics are seen not merely as fools, whose rush to judgement is a cause for irritation, but rather as giving cause for concern and anger. One of the grim lessons of the Biafran war, and the continuing lesson of the western media surrounding Achebe in the United States, had been the importance of control of information and dissemination of knowledge. Such lessons had already been acknowledged in *Things Fall Apart* in the weight of the final paragraph and in *A Man of the People* where newspaper editorials change their tune as politicians gain or lose power. But here the global control held by western media and western academic institutions and publications becomes a significant issue. Despite the independence of African nation states, he sees a continuation of colonialist attitudes linked to the desire to maintain control of 'the natives':

To the colonialist mind it was always of the utmost importance to be able to say: *I know my natives*, a claim which implied two things at once: (a) that the native was really quite simple and (b) that understanding him and controlling him went hand in hand – understanding being a pre-condition for control and control constituting adequate proof of understanding. Thus in the hey-day of colonialism any serious incident of native unrest, carrying as it did disquieting intimations of slipping control, was an occasion not only for pacification by the soldiers but also (afterwards) for a royal commission of enquiry – a grand name for yet another perfunctory study of native psychology and institutions. [Achebe's italics]   (*MYCD*, p. 5)

Among the consequences of colonialist criticism are the selection and encouragement of writers who flatter the prejudices of their critics, or at the very least avoid troubling them, and the misreading of particular writers such as Amos Tutuola who are, wrongly in Achebe's view, praised for revealing a lack of 'awareness of cultural, national, and racial affinities'. Here, and in a later essay on Tutuola, Achebe goes on to read Tutuola as a much more serious writer than the naive story teller he is often taken to be, demonstrating how *The Palmwine Drinkard* repeatedly reinforces the lesson of social responsibility, and also offers a sharply critical comment on the behaviour of colonists.[22] Both consequences are part of the west's desire to discourage those, including writers, who seek 'to change the world' and who are 'too earnest' in their endeavour to do so. With sharply pointed sarcasm, Achebe proceeds to speak of 'the importance of being earnest', while acknowledging the preference of others for peace, quiet and 'self-indulgent levity':

Perhaps they have already accomplished the right amount of change to ensure their own comfort . . . Even the evangelist, once so earnest and certain, now sits back in contemplation of his church, its foundation well and truly laid, its edifice rising majestically where once was jungle; the colonial governor who once brought his provinces so ruthlessly to heel prefers now to speak of the benefits of peace and orderly government. Certainly they would rather have easy-going natives under their jurisdiction than earnest ones – unless of course the earnestness be the perverse kind that turns in against itself.   (*MYCD*, p. 14)

In this lecture, Achebe spoke chiefly about the criticism of African literature and its encouragement of particular tendencies for implicitly political reasons. The following year, his controversial lecture on Conrad's *Heart of Darkness* to faculty and students at the University of Massachusetts extended his argument to literature by non-Africans and the powerful influence of English Departments in North American and British universities in perpetuating and reinforcing racist stereotypes through their high valuation of Conrad.[23] As Achebe pointed out, *Heart of Darkness* was the single most frequently taught novel in English courses at the University of Massachusetts, and he went on to argue that, however well-written, a novel which – as his detailed analysis sought to demonstrate – consigned Africans to the category of the subhuman, could not be regarded as 'great literature' and did not deserve the status accorded it by so many Professors of English.[24] His 1979 address to the Berlin Festival of African Arts extended his critique to Naipaul, whose elevation along with Conrad by western critics seemed to him one of the impediments to a dialogue between north and south, for neither writer accepted the full humanity of Africans, and no genuine dialogue could take place without unreserved acceptance of human equality on both sides.[25]

In 1976, Achebe and his family returned to Nsukka, where he resumed his position as Professor of Literature at the University of Nigeria, and the following year he became head of the English Department. Christie, his wife, having obtained her doctorate in Education at the University of Massachusetts, took up a lectureship at the University of Nsukka. Back on its home base, *Okike* continued to grow, and began to publish, in addition to the journal itself, which had special editions on South Africa and East Africa and Angostinho Neto, an educational supplement for teachers and students in secondary schools. Achebe's concern for the literary education of the younger generation had also been manifested in his stories for children. Before the war, he and Christopher Okigbo had set up the Citadel Press in Enugu, one of whose aims would be to produce for African children stories which did not, like the stories in Chike's primary school reader, view Africans as exotics and primitives. The plan foundered with the Civil War and Okigbo's death, but Achebe had already written one children's novella, dedicated to his daughter Chinelo.

Published in 1966 by Cambridge University Press, *Chike and the River* is set near Onitsha and is a story full of adventure, humour and vivid evocation of local scenes and characters seen through the eyes of an eleven-year-old boy. In 1972, Achebe and John Iroaganachi wrote for younger children *How the Leopard Got His Claws*, an animal fable whose tragic power and eloquence must have come in part from the recent experience of the war.[26] More recent retellings of traditional tales for younger children include *The Drum* and *The Flute*.[27]

The year preceding Achebe's return to Nigeria had seen a third military coup exactly nine years to the day after the coup which brought General Gowon to power. So, on 29 July 1975, Murtala Muhammed was installed in his place, and promptly announced a five-stage programme for return to civilian rule, a return which Gowon had decided in 1974 to postpone. The following February, Murtala Muhammed was assassinated in an abortive coup, but his programme was carried on by the Obansanjo regime, which also introduced universal primary education and greatly expanded tertiary education. Other reforms included constitutional changes, such as the redivision of Nigeria into nineteen states instead of twelve, an attempt to reform the traditional land tenure system to encourage larger scale farming, and reformation of the trades unions. The regime's energetic and decisive action, its firm commitment to returning civilian rule, its intolerance of corruption and laxity, its rejection of the controversial 1973 census results, its emphasis on education as a right for all children, brought new life and new hope to Nigerians in all sections of the country, and many foresaw 1 October 1979, the date set for the installation of the civilian government, as a new beginning for the Nigerian nation.

But it was not to be. Instead of a new beginning, Nigerians saw a replay of the first unhappy years of independence. Like James Joyce's Stephen Dedalus, Nigerians found themselves unable to awake from 'the nightmare of history', in which all too familiar characters and patterns recurred in grotesque and inflated forms. Achebe described the nightmare thus in *The Trouble With*

Nigeria, a book addressed to voters in the 1983 elections:

A crop of newcomers in Nigerian politics emerged in 1979 whose manifest mission should have been to inaugurate a new philosophy and a new practice of politics devoid of narrowness and opportunism, and capable of preparing Nigeria in the twenty-odd years left of this century for the grim challenges of the Third Millenium. But they chose instead to become rivivalists of a bankrupt and totally unusable tradition of political manoeuvering, tribal expediency and consummate selfishness. And they are valiantly fostering this diseased tradition among the masses of their followers by a soft-headed and patently dishonest adulation of a couple of tired old men who apparently see the Nigerian Presidency in the 1980's as a pension and gratuity for certain services they think they rendered to the nation thirty years ago.

Surely the electorate should find the courage to tell them that in as much as they have the right to dream their dreams of the past, they must not be allowed to block our vision of the present, or mortgage our children's chances of success in the twenty-first century.[28]

Achebe is referring here to the entry into the election campaign of those veteran politicians, Chief Awolowo and Dr. Azikiwe, around whom were gathered respectively mainly Yoruba and Igbo opposition to Shehu Shagari, who was a northerner.

Shagari was elected in 1979 and installed as President of Nigeria's Second Republic on 1 October 1979. He was unable or unwilling to control the rampant corruption that was a feature of his regime. Despite its oil wealth, Nigeria suffered rapid economic decline. Prices rose steeply, even for basic goods, and the gap between rich and poor increased dramatically. At the same time services declined, and the movement towards education freely available to all was reversed. Not surprisingly, crime rates rose and tension between different groups increased. There were riots in the north led by Muslim fundamentalists and at various times universities were closed as students protested the cuts which affected them most.

It was in this situation, and in the approach to elections following the government's first four-year term of office, that Achebe was persuaded to become involved in politics.

He declared in *The Trouble With Nigeria* that Nigeria's educated elite had 'stood too long on the sidelines' and must address itself to the task of informing the electorate and educating it to treat with scepticism the ethnic appeals and religious appeals made by politicians. Now, he went on to say:

All those enlightened and thoughtful Nigerians who wring their hands in daily anguish on account of our wretched performance as a nation must bestir themselves to the patriotic action of proselytising for decent and civilized political values.

(*TWN*, p. 53)

The Trouble With Nigeria is just such an attempt to 'proselytise for decent and civilized political values'. Unlike African Marxist writers such as Ngugi wa Thiong'o or Sembene Ousman, who would argue that such values can only be the product of a radically changed and socialist economic structure created by a worker/peasant revolution, Achebe appeals for change in leadership and in an enlightened elite. His position is stated very firmly in the opening sentences of the book:

The trouble with Nigeria is simply and squarely a failure of leadership. There is nothing basically wrong with the Nigerian character. There is nothing wrong with the Nigerian land or climate or water or air or anything else. The Nigerian problem is the unwillingness or inability of its leaders to rise to the responsibility, to the challenge of personal example which are the hallmarks of true leadership. (*TWN*, p. 1)

He cites several leaders who have met that challenge and proved responsible. Murtala Mahammed is one; Ghandi another. In particular, he holds up as a shining example the late Mallam Aminu Kano, leader of the People's Redemption Party. Indeed it was Aminu Kano's death in 1983 and the tragic gap left by it which persuaded Achebe to accept nomination and election as Deputy National President of the People's Redemption Party and to campaign on behalf of the party, thus himself setting an example of the refusal to jump on the bandwagon of appeal to regional rather than national interests. Chief among those national interests, Achebe believes, are peace and social justice, each dependent upon the other. His book bitterly and sharply attacks those leaders and politicians, together with the privileged elite, who have served only their own interests and have blatantly ignored the poverty and injustice suffered by a majority of Nigerians. In an eloquent passage, Achebe speaks of the misery of the poorest of all, those who live below even the minimum basic wage:

the peasant scratching out a living in the deteriorating rural environment, the petty trader with all his wares on his head, the beggar under the fly-over and millions and millions that you cannot even categorize. Twenty of these would be glad any day to share *one* minimum wage packet!

These are the real victims of our callous system, the wretched of the earth. They are largely silent and invisible. They don't appear on front pages; they do not initiate industrial actions. They drink bad water and suffer from all kinds of preventable diseases. There are no hospitals within reach of them; but even if there were they couldn't afford to attend. There may be a school of sorts which their children go to when there is 'free education' and withdraw from when 'levies' are demanded.

The politician may pay them a siren visit once in four years and promise to *give* them this and that and the other. He never says that what he *gives* is theirs in the first place. [Achebe's italics]   (*TWN*, p. 24)

Shagari was re-elected in 1983. Three months after his reinstallation, Nigeria's fourth military coup removed him on New Year's Eve, 1983. Few mourned the demise of the Shagari government and the coup met with general approbation from a majority of Nigerians, although some, like Achebe, were concerned that the almost automatic resort to military coups as a cure for Nigeria's ills made the future of democracy all the more uncertain. General Buhari's regime made well-publicized attempts to end corruption and 'indiscipline', with trails of many major and minor officials and businessmen, public executions of criminals and drug dealers, and his unremitting 'War Against Indiscipline'. In effect, corruption continued, the economic situation worsened, and Buhari met with increasing opposition, which did not cease when he tried to silence Nigeria's traditionally outspoken press. A fifth coup in 1985 replaced General Buhari with Major General Babangida as Head of State.

It was against this background that Achebe returned to the writing of the novel he had set aside during the Civil War and which he finally completed in 1986. *Anthills of the Savannah* was published in 1987 in Britain, where it was one of the finalists for the prestigious Booker-McConnell Prize for fiction that year. Achebe had by this time retired from teaching in order to devote more time to writing, but had been elected Emeritus Professor at the University of Nigeria, Nsukka, where he retained an office in the Institute of African Studies and continued to edit *Okike*. He also inaugurated a new publication dedicated to the exploration and preservation of Igbo culture, the bilingual journal *Uwa ndi Igbo: A Journal of Igbo Life and Culture*, and coedited an anthology of Igbo 'egwu' verse, *Aka Weta*. In addition to his writing of poetry and fiction in English, Achebe had also begun to experiment with the composition of Igbo poetry, often created for oral performance.

7

Marginal lives: *Girls at War and Other Stories*

BETWEEN THE PUBLICATION OF *Things Fall Apart* and *No Longer At Ease,* Achebe published two shorter pieces of fiction, 'The Sacrificial Egg' in 1959 and 'Chike's School Days' in 1960. The latter at first sight may seem to be in part an elaboration of some of the autobiographical reminiscences in the essay, 'Named for Victoria, Queen of England', but most of the details given about Chike's family differ from Achebe's. The sketch also includes some of the details which will later be either elaborated or alluded to in the novel which was to be written twenty-five years later, *Anthills of the Savannah.* One such detail is the amused memory of the half-understood counting rhyme, 'Ten Green Bottles', which Chike and his fellow primary school puils sing with great vigour; another is the English proverb so much loved by Chike's teacher and by Beatrice's schoolmaster father, 'Procrastination is a lazy man's apology'. Like many of the stories, it provides the opportunity for a variation or another perspective on a theme or story which Achebe will deal with elsewhere. Thus, the conflict and consequences created by marriage to an *osu,* given a contemporary setting in *No Longer At Ease,* is here, in a two-page flashback within the six-page sketch, placed in the first decades of the century, and focused on Chike's parents, two early Christian converts supported by the missionary, Mr. Brown. In this case the marriage is also bitterly opposed by the mother of the young man, but Chike's father neither wavers (as Obi does in the face of this opposition) nor effects a reconciliation through the next generation (as Nnaemeka does in 'Marriage Is A Private Affair'). Here the mother reacts by renouncing Christianity and returning to 'the faith of her people'. The whole episode

121

concerning the marriage of Chike's parents is told in the voice and from the perspective of non-Christian villagers, and acts as a counterpoint to the rigid certainty of the Christian father and schoolteacher as well as the innocent pleasure which Chike experiences in his discovery of English language and storytelling – those 'jaw-breaking words from [the] *Chambers Etymological Dictionary*'; his delight in the sound of English words often conveying 'no meaning at all'; the first sentences in his *New Africa Reader* 'like a window through which he saw in the distance a strange, magical new world'. Those seemingly innocent first sentences have from the adult reader's perspective particularly ironic implications: 'Once there was a wizard. He lived in Africa. He went to China to get a lamp.' (*GW*, p. 40). The tale for European children, plucked from its Arabic origins, takes for granted the exoticism of both Africa and China, and the unreality and unsavouriness of wizards. For Chike, these European cultural assumptions and perspectives mingle happily with the fantasy and magic evoked by what to the English reader are 'homely' words such as 'periwinkle' and more literary and latinate ones such as 'constellation'.

These final sentences and Chike's delight in half-understood English words have a peculiar impact on the reader because the sketch has already introduced us to two 'wizards'. One is the missionary Mr. Brown, chiefly respected by the villagers 'not because of his sermons, but because of the dispensary he ran in one of his rooms' from which Amos, Chike's father, had emerged 'greatly fortified' (*GW*, p. 36); the other is the diviner, consulted by Elizabeth, Chike's grandmother, whom the villagers knew to be 'a man of great power and wisdom'. Her visit to the diviner who, like Mr. Brown, combines spiritual concern and the knowledge of healing, is described in considerable detail, which subverts the assumptions by which such men have been dismissively termed 'witch-doctors' and 'wizards' in European myth and colonial discourse.

'Chike's School Days' is deceptively simple in appearance, seemingly a rambling sketch, to whose random nature even the narrator draws attention when he declares after that two page 'digression' about the marriage of Chike's parents that 'we have wandered from our main story'. The fact that it has been ignored by most critics, even when discussing the other stories in the same collection, suggests that it has been taken at face value. But with the first two novels in mind, readers should by now have learned to look twice at such declarations by the fictive narrator. Second and third readings reveal that this is a carefully constructed and closely packed piece which explores and sets off reverberations in the reader's mind from a multiplicity of conflicts and contrasts, from the suggested but unforeseen consequences concerning the colonial encounter, and from the innocent youngster's delighted discovery of an exotic English language and literature, whose cultural assumptions he is not yet able to question, although the reader has already seen the power with which the teacher, notorious for his floggings, and the father, unwavering in his Christian certitude, will impose them.

'The Sacrificial Egg' is one of the many stories in this collection which focus on people, periods and perspectives which are more marginal in the four novels published by 1966. Whereas the novels have told the stories of those who aspired to be central to their communities or their nation, these stories dwell on the perspectives and situations of those who have never seen themselves as holders of power – for the most part they are concerned with physical and psychological survival, a struggle in which they generally see themselves as more or less lucky rather than good or clever. Instead of the titled men, priests, university graduates and politicians who are the focal characters in the novels, these short stories concentrate on women who become outcasts such as Akueke of the story of that name and Gladys in 'Girls At War', clerks such as Julius and Uncle Ben in rural towns like Onitsha, taxi-drivers and ex-bicycle repairers such as Jonathan Iwegbu and Rufus Okeke, eager school children such as Chike and Veronica. It is appropriate, therefore, that the story placed first in the collection, 'The Madman', should be about a character who is the greatest outsider of all, and about the movement of a man who complacently believes in his centrality to the

123

position of being an outcast. Indeed, displacement from centre to periphery might well be seen as *the* Achebe plot, the structure which informs almost all of his fiction. His primary interest is not so much in what happens when 'things fall part' as in establishing that 'the centre cannot hold'.

And like many of the other stories, 'The Sacrificial Egg' establishes an ironic tension between the reader's assumption of the desirability of a central and consistent faith or philosophy and the main character's acceptance of contradictions and inconsistencies. Unlike Okonkwo and Ezeulu, Obi and Odili, who are so concerned with distinguishing between old and new, good and bad beliefs and customs, characters like Julius Obi and Uncle Ben find no difficulty in accommodating Igbo beliefs and attitudes as well as Christian ones. Though Julius sings in the CMS Choir and is therefore approved as a suitable husband by Janet's devoutly Christian mother, all three of them accept the dreadful reality of Kitikpa, the evil god of smallpox, and of the nightmasks which swirl past Julius in the dark. Like Uncle Ben, they also accept the reality of Mami Wota, the legendary seductress who brings untold wealth but no children. Appropriately, both stories are set in Umuru, a thinly disguised Onitsha, which gathers to its market not only Igbos from the inland villages, but also different kinds of peoples from along the Niger and Anambara rivers. The traditional market place has had grafted on to it the European Palm Oil trading company 'which bought palm-kernels at its own price and sold cloth and metalware, also at its own price', and it is here that young men like Julius and Ben, with their Standard Six certificates, find work as clerks. In the case of Julius Obi, the tragic reality of Kitikpa and the abyss created first by quarantine and then death overwhelms all other divisions. For the cheerfully garrulous Uncle Ben, however, the jumble of beliefs in the baleful power of Mami Wota and the supremacy of White House Whisky have a happier outcome.

Like *A Man of the People*, published in the same year (1966), 'Uncle Ben's Choice' gains its effect from its use of a first-person narrator who is also the central character in his own story. Both, as young men, are charmingly irresponsible lovers of life and women and dangerously complacent. Odili's attempt to reconcile the traditional and 'modern' at the end of the novel is a conscious one; for Uncle Ben the question of reconciliation does not arise, since he has, despite his elevation to Senior Clerk in the Niger Trading Company, always remained 'a true son of our land' who never regrets following his kinsman's reminder: 'Our fathers never told us that a man should prefer wealth instead of wives and children.' (*GW*, p. 88)

'The Voter', first published in the important African cultural journal *Black Orpheus* in 1965, was also written about the same time as *A Man of the People*, and belongs to the same world, for it concerns the electoral proceedings of the Minister for Culture, holder of many honorary titles and doctorates, in his home village. This time the story is told from the point of view of a narrator sympathetic to one of the Minister's vote gatherers, one Rufus Okeke – Roof for short. Except perhaps for Roof's energy and lack of malice (he is just doing his job), there are no redeeming features in this election campaign – no idealistic young Odilis, no wider concern for the welfare of the nation. For the elders and the younger members of the village alike, the issue is money, and votes are sold to the highest bidder. Having committed his vote twice, Rufus has no qualms about dividing his vote, tearing the ballot paper in half and posting one half in each candidate's box. The futility of this exercise escapes him, but is for the reader merely the final example of the whole travesty of democracy which the story has unveiled, the emptiness of: 'Election morning. The great day every five years when the voters exercise their power.' (*GW*, p. 17)

As young men, Rufus and Uncle Ben have in common certain character traits: a cheerful energy and pride in 'knowing their way around', a desire for and enjoyment of the good things of life, and admiration for those who have them. But the older Uncle Ben has learned what Rufus has yet to learn and may never learn, that there are things more important than wealth, and these include above all wives and children. That lesson is learned and reiterated even more forcefully by yet another cheerfully energetic survivor, Jonathan Iwegbu, whose story is told in 'Civil Peace', which was first published in *Okike* in 1971. The reader might well view the wit, energy, compassion and muted optimism of this story in the aftermath of the civil war with something of the admiring incredulity with which he or she responds to Jonathan Iwegbu's unfailing optimism as he counts his blessings after the devastation of the war. Chief among those blessings is the survival of himself, his wife, and three of his four children. But as Jonathan reiterates, 'Nothing puzzles God' and he is delighted to recover his bicycle and then find his house still standing and only partly damaged in Enugu – and anyway, there are plenty of old bits of zinc and cardboard with which to repair it. For Jonathan, every small act of recovery – even the money earned by the hard work of his wife and himself – is *ex gratia*, an act of grace bestowed upon the lucky by the unfathomable gods. Hence when he is robbed of what he and his friends termed an *egg-rasher* (*ex gratia*) payment of twenty pounds from the federal government (in return for his hard-earned but worthless Biafran money), Jonathan does not complain:

'I count it as nothing,' he told his sympathizers, his eyes on the rope he was tying. 'What is *egg-rasher*? Did I depend on it last week? Or is it greater than other things that went with the war? I say, let *egg-rasher* perish in the flames! Let it go where everything else has gone. Nothing puzzles God.' (*GW*, p. 97)

The second half of this story, the account of the robbery, suggests that Achebe might well, if he so wished, prove a dramatist. The episode mingles fear, suspense and hilariously grim comedy as the off-stage robber leader and his chorus of thugs introduce themselves, satirically join in the cries for assistance, offer to call for the 'soja' when neither neighbours nor police respond, and reassure the frightened family:

'Awrighto. Now make we talk business. We no be bad tief. We no like for make trouble. Trouble done finish. War done finish and all the katakata wey de for inside. No Civil War again. This

time na Civil Peace. No be so?'
    'Na so!' answered the horrible chorus.   (*GW*, p. 95)

Three of the stories in this collection, including the two
longest, 'Vengeful Creditor' and the volume's title story,
focus on women and their aspirations, blighted in each case
by the society and the circumstances that surround them.
The earliest published of the three is 'Akueke', which was
first printed in 1962. Set in traditional Igbo society, this
story powerfully establishes the isolation of Akueke, surrounded by her well-meaning but uncomprehending
brothers:

Akueke lay on her sick-bed on one side of the wall of enmity that
had suddenly risen between her and her brothers. She heard
their muttering with fear. They had not yet told her what must
be done, but she knew . . . Last night Ofodile who was the eldest
had wanted to speak but had only stood and looked at her with
tears in his eyes. Who was he crying for? Let him go and eat shit.
                                                (*GW*, p. 29)

Neither Akueke nor her brothers consciously question the
laws of a society which dictates that young girls must marry
an approved suitor, and that those struck with 'the swelling
disease' must be carried out and left in the bush. Yet in each
case, Akueke's response is one of passive resistance.
Akueke longs for her mother and her mother's people in
whose presence, she believes, 'This would not have happened to her' (*GW*, p. 30), although her illness is seen by
her brothers as punishment for her pride and unwillingness
to conform to accepted patterns of female behaviour, a
judgement she has at least partially internalized. The first
half of the story ends with an appalling image of Akueke's
isolation as her sorrowing brothers follow the conventions
of society and abandon her in the bush, too exhausted to
resist any longer.

The second half of the story extends the enigma of
Akueke and her situation. Incredibly, she survives and
reappears at the house of her mother's father. How, we are
not told. Are we to believe, as the brothers at first do, that
this is the ghost of Akueke? Or perhaps the 'swelling' was
not the dreaded fatal disease at all, as the grandfather

127

implies when he demands of the shocked brothers, 'If you don't know what the swelling disease is why did you not ask those who do?' (*GW*, p. 33) Was this a psychosomatic illness, like the illnesses suffered by so many European women in the nineteenth century, as a means of resisting the intolerable demands of a patriarchal society? Can Akueke find psychological sustenance only so long as she is seen and respected as 'mother', and not as younger sister and predestined wife? Does the story reveal above all the conflicting attitudes to women in Igbo culture, both in myth and practice, so that women are on the one hand denigrated and isolated, denied control over their own lives, and on the other hand elevated as mother figures and carriers of spiritual meaning? The questions are unresolved, and we are left to contemplate the figure of Akueke, 'unsmiling and implacable' (*GW*, p. 33), readopted as Matefi and about to begin again the path of daughter and future bride, for 'When she marries', the old man concludes, 'her bride price will be mine not yours.' (*GW*, p. 34)

There could scarcely be a sharper contrast with the traditional setting and mode of 'Akueke' than 'The Vengeful Creditor', published almost a decade later in the first issue of *Okike*. Opening not in a small rural village hut but in a busy urban supermarket, and characterizing a confident, wealthy working woman who is also a wife and mother, we seem to have moved a long distance from the world of Akueke and the psychological isolation that was her lot. Nor is there the compassion and suspended judgement which hovers over the dilemma of all the characters in the earlier story, male and female alike; here the satire and judgement is directed sharply against Mrs. Emenike, along with her husband and others of their class who are so willing to sacrifice the poor and relatively helpless so that their own lives may not be discomforted. The difference between the two stories marks a more general change in Achebe's fiction from concern with those such as Unoka, Nwoye and Akueke for whom the cultural and psychological conventions and norms of their society do not allow adequate fulfilment, to an increasing recognition (seen in *A Man of the People*) of the importance of class interest as a factor in the denial of individual fulfilment.

As a means of focusing on the ways in which private and public concerns converge, Achebe uses the issue of free primary education and its abortive introduction by the Western and Eastern Regional Governments in 1955–57.[1] Mrs. Emenike, a social worker, and her civil servant husband, are quickly disillusioned with its introduction when their servants begin deserting them in order to attend school. On one of their brief and infrequent visits to Mr. Emenike's home village, they secure the services of ten-year-old Veronica for a wage of £5 a year and, more importantly as far as Veronica is concerned, the vague promise of schooling for her when their youngest child no longer needs a 'baby-nurse'. As Veronica watches the Emenike children escape each day from the world of her household duties and the moment of her own return to schooling seems ever more distant, she tries to eliminate the baby whom she sees as the obstacle to her own education, by giving him red ink to drink. Her choice of ink has been made credible by a previous warning from Mrs. Emenike, who has found her playing with it, that red ink is poisonous, but the ink is also a symbol of the education she so avidly desires. Veronica is no passive resister like Akueke, or like her tired and harassed mother, and the red ink spilt over the baby's front is a potent image of the bloody vengeance that the poor may take upon the middle classes who blindly and selfishly exploit them and frustrate their aspirations to share in those things the Emenikes so complacently take for granted as their right – bountiful food, work and good wages, and education for their children. As David Carroll points out in his discussion of this story, Mrs. Emenike's response, 'Perhaps it's from me she learnt', when Veronica's horrified mother protests that she could not have learned such things from home, is doubly ironic. For Veronica *has* learned by example from the Emenikes that the welfare and rights of others can be dispensed with if they stand in the way of her getting what she wants.[2] And the remark also epitomizes Mrs. Emenike's smug certainty that she is blameless, a blind complacency which suggests little hope of change from the top.

Although he has written a number of poems about the Civil War, 'Girls at War' is Achebe's only work of fiction which covers the Civil War period ('Civil Peace' refers back to it, but is essentially about its aftermath). Written mainly from the point of view of Reginald Nwankwo, a Biafran official from the Ministry of Justice, it records a series of meetings with a young woman called Gladys, whose changing appearance and responses to the war become for Reginald 'just a mirror reflecting a society that had gone completely rotten and maggoty at the centre', (*GW*, p. 114) But here, as so frequently in the story, Reginald's own stance is called into question by the violence of his dismissal of a society from which he considers himself detached. Nor is the reader allowed to see Gladys as 'just a mirror', and insofar as she *does* reflect her society, it is Reginald's image that stares back at us. Although Achebe here uses free indirect speech rather than first person narration, in some ways this story shares the technique so effectively used in *A Man of the People*, where the complacent young man who prides himself on his relative idealism gradually reveals the confusion and corruptibility of his own motives, especially in relation to his attitudes to women. In this short story, the circumstances and the consequences are much grimmer, and the judgement passed on Reginald is much harsher, although his attitudes and behaviour are likely to be neither more nor less damnable than those of the average male reader of a story such as this.

Reginald has encountered Gladys three times: the first is at the very beginning of the Civil War 'in the first heady days of warlike preparation when thousand of young men (and sometimes women too) were daily turned away from enlistment centres because far too many of them were coming forward burning with readiness to bear arms in defence of the exciting new nation.' (*GW*, p. 98) The parenthetical 'and sometimes women too' subtly suggests the marginal role of women in the narrator's consciousness, as well as the contrast between the role some of them would wish to play as opposed to that which they will be permitted in the war effort. Accordingly, Reginald has forgotten their first encounter, when Gladys as a schoolgirl had obtained a lift with him to go to Enugu to enrol in the militia only to be told by Reginald to go back to school and join the Red Cross.

In the beginning, Reginald has questioned neither his attitudes nor his advice, nor even his amusement at 'the girls and the women who took themselves seriously' as warriors, just like 'the kids who marched up and down the streets at the time drilling with sticks and wearing their mothers' soup bowls for steel helmets'. (*GW*, p. 100) However his second encounter with Gladys appears to chasten him as, despite his manifest annoyance, her businesslike and uncorruptible devotion to duty dampens his 'suppressed rage' at her treating him just like anybody else and awakens his 'intellectual approval' of her thoroughness. The possibility that his 'intellectual approval' and sudden new belief 'in this talk about revolution' has anything to do with his 'first real look at her, startlingly from behind . . . a beautiful girl in a breasty blue jersey, khaki jeans and canvas shoes', is not entertained by Reginald.

The third and final meeting takes up the major portion of the story, when 'things had got very bad'. As an official with the right connections, Reginald Nwankwo and his family are able to survive much more comfortably than the average Biafran citizen, and again and again, Reginald deflects his guilt and unease on to those like Gladys whom he sees as worthless goodtime girls. Nor is Gladys presented as a passive receptacle of Reginald's desires; she angrily points out the contradictions between his actions and the attitudes he expresses, contradictions which Reginald himself sometimes recognizes and rather guiltily indulges. So he collects a carload of charity food for his wife and children (and some for his driver) trying to avoid the eyes of the 'scarecrow crowd of rags and floating ribs' hanging around the depot, offers a ride to 'a very attractive girl by the roadside' and roughly dismisses a despairing old woman who is also seeking a lift. His means of avoiding embarrassment is to bury himself in a book. Yet he immediately condemns Gladys for what he assumes to be her connection with 'some well-placed gentleman' and for wearing the wig and clothing which attracted him to 'save her life' and give her a lift, and to call her 'a beauty queen'. While condemning her as a loose girl, whose ideals are lost, he plots to take her to his own house, where he lives as 'a gay bachelor'. At the 'real swinging party' to which he takes her, he silently condones the outburst of a drunken Red Cross pilot:

'These girls who come here all dolled up and smiling, what are they worth? Don't I know? A head of stockfish, that's all, or one American dollar and they are ready to tumble into bed.'

(*GW*, p. 111)

Though rejoicing as freely as his fellow party goers in the food, liquor and the luxury of 'real bread', Nwankwo salvages his conscience by priggishly refusing to dance 'as long as this war lasts', ostentatiously watching with disapproval while Gladys and others set out to enjoy themselves.

Reginald is shocked by Gladys's refusal to use euphemisms and her directness of language which fuses imagery of war and male sexual intercourse:

'You want to shell?' she asked. And without waiting for an answer said, 'Go ahead but don't pour in troops!'(*GW*, p. 113)

A paragraph follows, describing the much-used rubber condom which Reginald has ready to prevent 'pouring in troops'. The protective device, 'the real British thing', could well be an image of Reginald's own consciousness and language, ever capable of avoiding direct physical and emotional contact, and the responsibilities that might ensue. One way of avoiding such responsibility is to dismiss Gladys, and indeed all the girls of her generation, as worthless:

He had his pleasure but wrote the girl off. He might just as well have slept with a prostitute, he thought. It was clear as daylight that she was kept by some army officer. What a terrible transformation in the short period of less than two years! . . . What a terrible fate to befall a whole generation! The mothers of tomorrow! (*GW*, pp. 113–14)

The next morning, Reginald is 'feeling a little better and more generous in his judgements'. Nevertheless Gladys remains not an individual with whom he has made physical and emotional contact, but a symbol of society, and Reginald sees himself as the saviour of that society in the person of the symbolic Gladys. The ending of the story is swift and terrible, with a denouement which reveals not Reginald but Gladys as the true saviour who, as Reginald runs to save his own skin, sacrifices her own life in an attempt to rescue a crippled soldier.

Although the themes and techniques of Achebe's short stories are often closely related to those found in the novels, the characters are those who appear only in the background or in the margins of his major works. Here, in *Girls At War and Other Stories* he brings those marginalized characters into the foreground – the women, the children, the clerks, the poor traders and craftsmen – and also focuses a much harsher light on those who exploit or ignore them, the complacent middle-class professionals like Mrs. Emenike and Reginald Nwankwo. With the writing of *Anthills of the Savannah* fifteen years later, Achebe will create a novel which gives space and voice to these characters and to his concern with their fate at the hands of the privileged elite. It is a concern which he will also voice in his 1983 political tract, *The Trouble With Nigeria*.

8

Poetry and war: *Beware Soul Brother and Other Poems*

ACHEBE'S COLLECTION of short fiction and prose pieces covered a period of twenty years, tracing his development and changing preoccupations as a writer. His volume of poetry, on the other hand, spans a much shorter period and is unified by its focus on the civil war and the physical, social and psychological consequences of that war. Most of the poems were first published in Nigeria in 1971 under the title *Beware Soul Brother*[1] and were written over a period of four years during the civil war and its immediate aftermath. The first collection contained twenty-three poems; a second revised edition, containing thirty poems grouped under a series of headings, was published a year later by Heinemann Educational Books in London under the same title and won the newly established Commonwealth Poetry Prize.[2] It is this revised and restructured edition that I will discuss.

The collection is grouped under five sections which, Achebe says in his preface, 'suggested themselves to my mind': Prologue; Poems About War; Poems Not About War; Gods, Men and Others; Epilogue. Some poems are dated, others not, but it is clear that the poems are not grouped in the order in which they were written. Thus the first two poems are dated 1971, the third, 1968. As with all of Achebe's works, the placing of particular pieces is rarely unplanned; each poem and each group of poems bears some relation to the one that precedes it.

The title of the first poem, '1966', refers to the months preceding the outbreak of the civil war. Its two stanzas mirror the contrast between surface appearance, on the one hand, and the dreadful bloodshed about to disrupt that surface. Four lines in which mainly abstract and vague words suggest 'absent-minded' and 'thoughtless' 'playing' with politics, are contrasted with a second stanza of ten lines in which the imagery is compressed and concrete, and the syntax and series of short run-on lines, withholding the object of the verb, suggest the suspense as the moment of eruption is approached:

> slowly downward in remote
> subterranean shaft
> a diamond-tipped
> drillpoint crept closer
> to residual chaos to
> rare artesian hatred
> that once squirted warm
> blood in God's face
> confirming His first
> disappointment in Eden

The image of the diamond-tipped drillpoint is a particularly telling one, for the large oil deposits in Eastern Nigeria were a contributory factor to the Federal Government's determination to prevent Biafra seceding and also had much to do with the participation of the European powers who supplied arms and hoped to maintain a stake in that oil.[3] Yet like those powers at the controls, who 'play indolently' and thoughtlessly at their own political games, the reader is shocked from his own godlike stance of detached onlooker from above when what erupts is not the expected oil, but a gush of 'warm / blood in God's face'. The final, highly compressed images widen the significance of the 'subterranean shaft' and 'diamond-tipped / drillpoint' to suggest the buried instincts below the surface civility, as well as the ancient buried history common to all men – war between brothers, beginning with the murder of Abel by Cain – all tapped and brought to the surface in this particular civil war.

The following poem, 'Benin Road', takes up a related theme of the unexpected but inevitable convergence of fragile beauty or idealism and power. Here, however, the convergence is not vertical but horizontal, probing not layers of time and consciousness in an explicitly historical context as the title '1966' made clear, but the conflicting desires within each individual for power and beauty. Here the driver is identified with his car, whose speed, power and weight all equate with violence, and whose windscreen is the 'silicon / hardness' of his own vision. Against this earthbound machine and vision is balanced the fluttering lightness of the butterfly, its fragile beauty smashed against hardness of vision. In this poem also, the moment of impact is realized with an unexpected and intensely vivid image:

> and the gentle
> butterfly pops open
> in a bright yellow
> smear in the silicon
> hardness of my vision.   (*BSB*, p. 4)

Both these opening poems have included images of sky and earth, domains of the divine and the human respectively, and the conflict between them. 'Mango Seedling' inhabits a realm midway between the two, exploring the possibility of psychic survival there. The poem is dedicated to Christopher Okigbo, whom Achebe along with many others regarded as Nigeria's leading poet, and who was killed fighting for Biafra in 1967. Like Okigbo's own poetry, it draws on a mixture of Igbo and European allusions, so that its mode as well as its celebration of courage and determination against all odds make it an appropriate memorial to Okigbo. Thus the mango seedling, clinging to a ledge midway down a tall office building, is compared to 'the widow / Of infinite faith' in the Old Testament story, as well as the Tortoise of Igbo folk tale, hoping for a 'miraculous feast / On one ever recurring dot of cocoyam'.[4] In another reference to Igbo myth the seedling is described as:

> Poised in courageous impartiality
> Between the primordial quarrel of Earth
> And Sky striving bravely to sink roots
> Into objectivity, mid-air in stone.   (*BSB*, p. 5)

These lines also illustrate how skilfully Achebe is able to

use language, rhythm and syntax to heighten meaning. The final phrase, 'mid-air in stone', which might normally be placed next to 'poised', the verb it modifies, is suspended for almost four lines, so that one feels the tenuousness of the seedling's position, and the effort in its 'striving bravely to sink roots', another phrase given weight and added significance by its postponement and unexpected appearance after 'the primordial quarrel of Earth / And Sky'. And here too is the technique Achebe has used so effectively in the two previous poems of the replacement of the expected object of the verb by a noun which, because it is unexpected, suddenly recasts our whole reading of the poem so far. So the words 'chaos', 'hatred' and 'blood' in the first poem both widen the meaning and significance of the oil-drilling imagery, and also connect these consequences to the first reading. Similarly, in the second poem, the final word 'vision' instead of the expected 'windscreen' or its equivalent, revises our sense of the poem so that it is the driver rather than the car he is driving that becomes the destroyer of the butterfly and all that it symbolizes. Now, in 'Mango Seedling', roots are sunk not into earth, or even, at first, stone, but into 'objectivity', and suddenly the whole concept is brought into question. It is challenged not only as a concept in itself and in terms of the possibility of attaining it, but also in relation to Okigbo's quest in his poetry away from subjective and private allusion towards a public voice, and in relation to the varied traditions and cultural perspectives already alluded to in the poem. Nevertheless, the *struggle* towards objectivity and towards maintaining that poise midway between earth and sky – the natural material world and the spiritual – is admirable and it is a struggle that involves the reader as the poet's syntax re-enacts it. The image of the mango seedling, like Achebe's own poem, becomes an eloquent memorial to Okigbo's 'passionate courage.'

The fourth and final poem in this first group, 'The Explorer', moves into a different mode, the realm of dream and the surreal, although it too is concerned with loss. It is a strangely haunting poem, in which the dreamer discovers his own dead body, coming 'face to face suddenly / with a body I didn't even know / I lost', and the details have that clarity and sharpness, as well as that oddity and teasing inexplicability, which are typical of dreams:

All else

was perfect except the leg missing
neatly at knee-joint
even the white schoolboy dress
immaculate in the thin yellow
light; my face in particular
was good having caught nor fear
nor agony at the fatal moment   (*BSB*, p. 7)

The four poems in the prologue section have introduced the themes and concerns which will be raised subsequently, moving from the historical vision of converging forces in '1966' to the more individual voice of a particular speaker travelling his own path, caught and implicated in a moment of time in 'Benin Road'. 'Mango Seedling' records the consequences of the war in terms of personal loss or individual suffering, and like many of the subsequent poems ('Christmas in Biafra' and 'Refugee Mother and Child', for example) expresses compassion and awe for the indomitable courage of those struggling to survive and to find meaning in a world which seems to give neither physical nor spiritual sustenance. Finally, 'The Explorer,' prefacing the group called 'Poems Not About War', brings to consciousness the images of violence, loss and disorder, and the disorientation which have invaded the subconscious and which live on after the war. Each poem also brings nature imagery into conjunction with images of machines or urban buildings, sometimes showing the destruction of one by the other, sometimes their interconnection or inseparability. There is not space in this chapter to analyse all the poems and their interrelations in as much detail as I have done for this first group, but I hope that I have been able to suggest the care and skill with which each has been constructed and placed, before going on to discuss more briefly and generally the rest of the volume.

Within the seven Poems About War, the tone varies from the vehement and powerful admonition of 'Remem-

brance Day', the compassion and grim irony of 'Refugee
Mother and Child', the meditative 'First Shot', the apparently humorous but nevertheless sharply interrogative
'An If of History', to the laconic and starkly economical
snap shot of 'Air Raid'

> A man crossing the road
> to greet a friend
> is much too slow.
> His friend cut in halves
> has other worries now
> than a friendly handshake
> at noon.

The tone, style and stance of this poem contrast strongly
with the two 'mother and child' poems which precede it,
each based on an anguished comparison with the aesthetic
and religious images of madonna and child which in European art have so often sought to celebrate an idealised
family relationship and consecrate the ordinary and the
domestic. Each detail accumulated in 'Refugee Mother and
Child' – the smell of diarrhoea, the dirt, the 'blown empty
bellies' – implicitly reminds us of the absence of such misery
and squalor in the idyllic scenes and plump mothers and
babies so familiar from all the paintings. In this poem, the
point of the comparison is not to dismiss those madonna and
child images, nor the tender relationship they capture, but to
wonder at the even greater miracle that such a relationship
can survive in the midst of the dreadful misery, despair and
dislocation that the poem depicts.

'Christmas in Biafra', the title poem of the American
edition of the collected poems, takes not a series of imagined and implicit images but a particular scene, 'a fine
plastercast / scene at Bethlehem' set up near the hospital
gate by 'the good nuns'. The tone here in the description
of the crib is faintly ironic, certainly more distanced than
in the preceding poem:

> The Holy
> Family was central, serene, the Child
> Jesus plump wise-looking and rose-cheeked; one
> of the magi in keeping with legend

a black Othello in sumptuous robes. Other
figures of men and angels stood
at well-appointed distances from
the heart of the divine miracle
and the usual cattle gazed on
in holy wonder . . .   (*BSB*, p. 14)

The details are casually acknowledged, the absence of com-
mas after the second line in the lines quoted above adding
to the sense of the mere accumulation of expected attributes. The speaker's indifferent enumeration suggests in
part the irrelevance of this scene to the Biafra in which it
is incongruously placed, as well as the sense that the crib
represents even for the 'good nuns' a mere custom, set up
well-meaningly but thoughtlessly. Even the mother's devotion and her attempt to interest her child, 'flat like a dead
lizard', seem misplaced, so that the indifference of the
observer, the question whether the ideals and hope of new
life embodied in the crib scene and Christmas can have any
meaning or relevance any more, combine with and are
subsumed in the child's 'large sunken eyes / stricken past
boredom to a flat / unrecognizing glueyiness.'

Perhaps the most powerfully rhetorical poem in this
group is 'Remembrance Day'. Like 'Christmas in Biafra'
it is based on a comparison between an imported European
ritual and an African perspective. In this case the military
ceremonies and salutations to the fallen warriors which are
a feature of Remembrance Day in Europe and contemporary Nigeria are contrasted with the Igbo observance
called *Oso Nwanadi*, which Achebe explains thus in a note
to the poem: 'On the night before that day all able-bodied
men in the village took flight and went into hiding in
neighbouring villages in order to escape the fire of
Nwanadi or dead kindred killed in war.' (*BSB*, p. 64)
Although the Igbo people admire courage, Achebe goes on
to explain, they do not glorify death, and they are firmly
convinced that life is preferable to death. 'They have no
Valhalla concept; the dead hero bears the living a grudge.'
The poem builds on the gulf between living and dead, and
the anger of the dead, through a series of contrasting pro-
nouns, first an accumulation of five heavily emphasized

and accusatory 'yours' addressed to the living, followed by a series of 'theys' and 'theirs', referring to the dead. From sarcasm at the redeemable sufferings of those who survived the war to celebrate remembrance day ('your / groomed hair lost gloss, your / smooth body roundedness. Truly / you suffered much'), the poem builds to vehement anger and admonition, for it is not 'we' who will remember them, but *they* who

> will
> remember. Therefore fear them! Fear
> their malice your fallen kindred
> wronged in death. Fear their blood-feud;
> tremble for the day of their
> visit! Flee! Flee! Flee your
> gilt palaces and cities! Flee
> lest they come to ransack
> your place and find you still
> at home at the crossroad hour.   (*BSB*, p. 19)

But as David Carroll points out, 'the poem does not end on the scornful note of Wilfred Owen' (whose First World War poem 'Dulce et Decorum Est' likewise excoriates glorification of death in battle) but 'leaves open the possibility of a third ritual' and reconciliation through a future generation innocent of promoting or participating in war:[5]

> Flee! Seek
> asylum in distant places till
> a new generation of heroes rise
> in phalanges behind their purified
> child-priest to inaugurate
> a season of atonement and rescue
> from fingers calloused by heavy deeds
> the tender rites of reconciliation   (*BSB*, p. 19)

Though titled 'Not About War,' the next group of twelve poems is frequently invaded by images bred by war and violence. Thus the first of the group, 'Love Song (for Anna)' finds the would-be singer of love silenced, for the songbirds 'have hidden away their notes / wrapped up in leaves / of cocoyam' because they fear 'reprisals of middle-

141

day' and 'the air is criss-crossed / by loud omens'. His song of love is replaced by 'a choir of squatting toads' celebrating 'an infested / swamp', while in another military metaphor, the ominous vultures 'stand / sentry on the roof-top' (*BSB*, p. 25). Yet the images of birds, cocoyam leaves and vultures also carry the possibility of redemption and reconciliation, for they are a subtle reminder of the Igbo myth to which Achebe alludes in many of his works (and most significantly in *Things Fall Apart*) about Vulture's gift from Sky of rain wrapped in cocoyam leaves to take back to a drought-stricken earth. Achebe himself reminds us of this tale in his note to the poem (*BSB*, p. 65). That promise of future song and 'the return someday of our / banished dance' is made explicit in the final stanza.

In the poem titled 'Vultures', however, these birds are images of horror rather than possible emissaries of mercy, and love in association with them becomes merely grotesque. The apparent tenderness for his mate of the vulture who has just feasted upon a corpse, like that of the Nazi Commandant[6] at Belsen going home with gifts for his children 'with fumes of / human roast clinging / rebelliously to his hairy / nostrils,' may well be seen by some as grounds for praising 'bounteous / providence . . . that grants even an ogre / a tiny glow-worm / tenderness'. But the parody of Christian language, as well as the directness and finality of the closing words, gives weight to those who despairingly see such 'tenderness' as itself part of the evil for it is merely concerned with the survival of one's own kind at the cost of others:

> for in the very germ
> of that kindred love is
> lodged the perpetuity
> of evil.   (*BSB*, p. 40)

'Vulture' is the second in a group of three poems which contemplate with horror not the passive suffering of mothers in Biafra and the casualties of war, but the cruelty and savagery of those who kill and inflict pain, the murderous Cains alluded to in '1966'. All three poems intensify the horror through contrast: 'Lazarus' through

an implicit comparison with the happy outcome of the
gospel story and the dire tale based on an actual incident
in which having clubbed to death the driver who had apparently killed a pedestrian, some villagers then killed the
pedestrian 'a second time that day' when he began to show
signs of life. Rather like the old man in Yeats' *Purgatory*,
who kills his son in an attempt to put an end to the cycle
of evil and so perpetuates it, the villagers find themselves
caught up in a 'twin-headed evil' in which their intended
act of justice merely leads to monstrous injustice, and the
killing of two innocent men. 'Public Execution in Pictures'
continues this theme of 'just' execution, which perpetuates
rather than puts an end to evil. Again, the point is made
through a series of contrasts, first between the newspaper
pictures of the smartly dressed military firing squad and the
ladies in 'fine lace' for whom the execution is a gruesome
but gripping entertainment. Finally, and most tellingly, the
until now missing picture of those who have been executed
is seen through the eyes of innocently callous children, who
question not the morality of such public executions, but

> debate
> hotly why the heads of dead
> robbers always slump forwards
> or sideways. (*BSB*, p. 41)

These three poems contemplating the continuation of
evil and its breeding out of apparently tender or righteous
action, end a section which has begun in the hope of love
and redemption bred out of death and destruction. The
song of love that had been awaited in 'Love Song' is heard
and affirmed in 'Love Cycle'. The fascinated but paralysed
contemplation of individual insignificance in the eyes of an
'unamused God' and of history in 'Question' is responded
to in 'Answer', where the energetic rhythm and swift and
forceful succession of verbs enacts the speaker's decisive
break from 'terror-fringed fascination', creating his own
ladder from the past rather than hoping that like Jacob he
will be given one from heaven, and repossessing his own
house 'on whose trysting floor waited / my proud and
vibrant life'.

143

Into this now optimistic movement towards individual fulfilment and hope breaks the authoritative voice of the traditional poet. Like its equivalent poem in the preceding group, 'Remembrance', 'Beware Soul Brother' is central to this group, and indeed to the whole volume which bears its title. In similar manner to 'Remembrance' it speaks for past as well as future generations, and reminds the reader and the artist of their responsibility to the community – the necessity to think and speak in terms of 'we' rather than 'I'. Philip Rogers interprets the admonition as being addressed primarily to writers, the 'men of soul',[7] but although the poem *is* admonishing writers and other artists, it would seem unlikely in the context of the whole volume that Achebe would confine the epithet 'men of soul' to writers alone. The first poem in this group, 'Love Song', has made it clear that both the writer and his mistress/ audience are dancers, as are the men who traditionally accompany the *abia* drums beaten at the funeral of a titled Igbo man.[8] In passing references to what may be Shelleyan images of poetry linked to Christian valuation of the purely spiritual, Achebe warns of the danger of 'soporific levitation' and the necessity to remember and indeed to rejoice in the fact that we are all earthbound:

> But beware soul brother
> of the lures of ascension day
> the day of soporific levitation
> on high winds of skysong; beware
> for others there will be that day
> lying in wait leaden-footed, tone-deaf
> passionate only for the deep entrails
> of our soil . . .   (*BSB*, p. 29)

The dancer becomes for Achebe the model for all artists and indeed all members of the community, not only because as for Yeats he is an image of the integration of body and idea, creator and his creation, but because the dancer must always return to the earth 'for safety / and renewal of strength', remembering also his children:

> for they in their time will want
> a place for their feet when

they come of age and the dance
of the future is born
for them.   (*BSB*, p. 30)

In contrast with the solemn and admonitory invocation
of traditional Igbo wisdom and ritual in 'Remembrance
Day' and 'Beware Soul Brother', a number of poems view
Igbo attitudes more lightheartedly. The poetic persona
turns one of Achebe's favourite and most frequently quoted
Igbo sayings against him in 'Misunderstanding'. Here the
proverb used so effectively by the poet's 'old man' to
silence his wife – 'Wherever Something / stands, he'd say,
there also Something / Else will stand' – proves counter-
productive when tried against a wife of the present generation who is more confident of her right to answer back. Of
course, the Misunderstanding of the title is a triple one, for
the proverb is deliberately misunderstood and misused by
father, son and the son's wife to *prevent* an alternative view,
an answer, being voiced and given due attention. Behind
the humour is a serious point, one that underlies each of
the individual poems as well as the collection as a whole,
calling for a willingness to contemplate alternative perspectives, balancing one attitude against another, and insisting
on the multifaceted nature of truth, though this is not to be
seen as an excuse for remaining uninvolved, as the harshly
satiric poem 'Non-Commitment' makes clear.

Igbo tradition is also a feature of the section titled 'Gods,
Men and Others' where in two of the poems, the
metaphysical and theological questions central to *Arrow of
God*, are treated with a mixture of amused irony and in-
dulgent respect. 'Penalty of Godhead' watches men and
rats move and survive, while the household gods 'frozen in
ritual' perish in the fire which consumes the hut they all inhabited. 'Those Gods are Children' tells how villagers out-
wit the gods, or perhaps collaborate with them, by delaying
the divinely decreed hanging of a murderer until he has
spent a lifetime caring for the murdered man's orphaned
children as well as his own. The last section of this poem
invokes in an approximation of traditional praise form the
'sometimes ambivalent' attitude of Igbo people to their
gods:[9]

> They are strong and to be feared
> they make the mighty crash
> in ruin like iroko's fall
> at height of noon scattering
> nests and frantic birdsong
> in damped silence of deep
> undergrowth. Yet they are fooled
> as easily as children those deities
> their simple omnipotence
> drowsed by praise.   (*BSB*, p. 48)

This scepticism concerning theological beliefs is also directed against Christian dogma when, in 'Their Idiot Song', 'the old pagan' affirms the finality of death and declares the Christians *will* have to acknowledge its sting someday:

> Sing on, good fellows, sing
> on! Someday when it is you
> he decks out on his great
> iron-bed with cotton-wool
> for your breath, his massing odours
> mocking your pitiful makeshift defenses
> of face powder and township ladies' lascivious
> scent, these others roaming
> yet his roomy chicken-coop will
> be singing and asking still
> but YOU by then
> no longer will be
> in doubt!   (*BSB*, p. 51)

One poem in this group, 'Lament of the Sacred Python', resumes the solemn language of traditional ritual. It is, indeed, a reworking and continuation of the chant which Ezeulu hears in his dream vision towards the end of *Arrow of God* (p. 222). Even divorced from its ominous setting in the novel, the first section carries an eerie power, while the added sections provide a bitter and foreboding vision of the Christian rituals and values which replace the noble and awesome cosmology for which the Sacred Python has been a symbol:

> And great father Idemili
> That once upheld from earth foundations

146

Cloud banks of sky's endless waters
Is betrayed in his shrine by empty men
Suborned with the stranger's tawdry gifts
And taken trussed up to the altar-shrine turned
Slaughterhouse for the gory advent
Feast of an errant cannibal god
Tooth-filed to eat his fellow.   (*BSB*, p. 50)

In the Epilogue, the enigmatic poem 'Dereliction' takes up the language and mode of traditional Igbo ritual used so effectively in 'Lament of the Sacred Python' and continues and responds to that lament. 'Dereliction' has three short stanzas spoken in three voices, which Achebe in a note describes thus: 'The first is the enquirer (*onye ajuju*); the second the mediating diviner (*dibia*) who frames the enquiry in general terms and the third is the Oracle' (*BSB*, p. 67). Each stanza is an elaboration of the three related meanings of 'dereliction', defined thus in the Oxford Dictionary: '(1) abandoning, being abandoned; (2) neglect *of duty*; failure in duty; shortcoming; (3) retreat of sea exposing new land'. So, in the first stanza, the son asks how his 'quitting the carved stool' in his father's hut should be judged, since the stool was already derelict, and eaten out by termites. The diviner or mediator rephrases the question by asking what place there can be for those who failed to hand on the baton 'in a hard, merciless race'; that is, those who inadvertently failed in their duty, as well as those who more deliberately betrayed their duty, such as the priestly elder 'who barters / for the curio collector's head / of tobacco the holy staff / of his people?' (*BSB*, p. 56) To both betrayers, the inadvertent or weak and the selfishly materialistic, the oracle has the same enigmatic answer, in a stanza in which sound echoes sense:

> *Let them try the land*
> *where the sea retreats*
> *Let them try the land*
> *where the sea retreats.*

This answer has been read by both Philip Rogers and David Carroll as a harsh response, consigning the enquirer and all who have deserted their fathers' houses to 'the no man's land between the tides, which is neither sea nor land, neither the past nor the future' (Carroll); a derelict region 'where customs die rather than where cultures are born' (Rogers).[10] But while the oracle's response must include such meanings, I do not think it is limited to the merely negative ones. Many of those who have deserted their father's houses in rural Nigeria have quite literally found a new abode in what was once derelict land, for much of Lagos, centre and symbol of change from the west, is built on land reclaimed from the sea. The implications of the oracle's answer are not, of course, limited to the suggestion that the young men of Nigeria should 'go west' to Lagos, but it does suggest that the zone where the sea retreats may be one where new hybrid cultures can be built, not merely a limbo where 'customs die'.

The final poem in the collection ironically asserts the poet's difficult and often painful mission as seer and visionary, one who does not merely keep his eyes on the ground, as do most of his community, but who insists on speaking

> about trees topped with
> green and birds flying – yes actually
> flying through the air – about
> the sun and the moon and stars
> and about lizards crawling on all
> fours   (*BSB*, pp. 58–9)

Through its allusions to Oedipus, who like the 'madman blinds himself to see beyond ordinary seeing', to the healing 'crimson robe' of Christ, and the many references to Igbo and other African images and traditions, 'We Laughed At Him' brings together Greek, Christian and Igbo allusions to affirm the poet's necessary role as 'visionary missionary revolutionary / and, you know, all the other / naries that plague the peace.' With its imagery of bloody pain and suffering through which the poet may yet glimpse and proclaim 'green and birds flying', this particular poem comes as an appropriate final statement and summation for the whole collection.

In an introduction to Kofi Awoonor's novel, *This Earth, My Brother*, Achebe wrote in 1972, one year after his own collection of poetry was published:

148

Kofi Awoonor is better known for his poetry – a strong, controlled poetry that manages the miracle of muscular power and delicate accents of song, much of it inspired by the oral performances of his Ewe homeland in Ghana.[11]

Were one to amend the first and last clauses (Chinua Achebe is better known for his novel-writing . . . much of it inspired by the oral performances of his Igbo homeland in Nigeria), the description of Awoonor's achievements as a poet might well apply to *Beware Soul Brother*.

9

The critic as novelist: *Anthills of the Savannah*

ABOUT ONE-THIRD of the way through *Anthills of the Savannah*, one of the characters writes:

> For weeks and months after I had definitely taken on the challenge of bringing together as many broken pieces of this tragic history as I could lay my hands on, I still could not find a way to begin. Anything I tried to put down sounded wrong – either too abrupt, too indelicate or too obvious – to my middle ear.
>
> (*AS*, p. 82)

This passage suggests several of the distinctive qualities of Achebe's fifth novel – its structural complexity; its self-consciously literary nature; its concern with the problem of finding the right words and the right mode, and the importance of the 'middle ear' in locating that language and style; the role of women not only as subjects, but also as central protagonists and voices – for the quoted passage is written by a woman who acts in some ways as Achebe's surrogate novelist, and who takes over from the men the task of storytelling.

When Achebe wrote his first four novels there was no established tradition of writing in Anglophone African fiction to allude to. His first novel reacts to and departs from the realist, omniscient narrative mode of earlier European fiction, particularly the colonialist fiction epitomized by Joyce Cary's African novels, and turns to the model of oral storytelling to suggest alternative epic and episodic modes – a model which encourages its audience to intervene, to judge and to participate, and which also departs from Cary's unitary narrative voice to suggest a multiplicity of voices, both within the story and within the consciousness of the narrator. His second novel, *No Longer At Ease*, con-

150

trasts the literary consciousness of its chief protagonist, Obi Okonkwo, with the consciousness formed by oral tradition (both Igbo and Christian) of his parents and the majority of his society. Obi is unable to bridge the gap between these two kinds of consciousness. These contrasts are further developed in *Arrow of God*, where stories are told and retold in differing modes not only by the Priest Ezeulu and the District Commissioner Winterbottom, but also by other members of each society, so that once again the reader must become involved in the problem of judging the relationships between knowledge, language and self-interest and the responsible exercise of power. *A Man of the People* posed the problem of these relationships in a rather different way by giving the whole story to an unreliable narrator, Odili, and involving the reader in his gradual but incomplete growth towards self-understanding together with a more finely tuned attentiveness towards language – the realization of the need for a 'middle ear.' *Anthills of the Savannah* continues Achebe's exploration of the same problems, but in relation also to the developing *literary* tradition in Africa, and the critical debate surrounding it. Among the sometimes explicit but more often implicit literary models Achebe reacts and responds to here are those created by Christopher Okigbo, Ngugi wa Thiong'o, Wole Soyinka, Nurruddin Farah, Sembene Ousman, Leopold Sedar Senghor, David Diop, and younger writers such as Chinweizu and Festus Iyayi. His own early works and pronouncements also come under scrutiny.

A Man of the People ends with a military coup; *Anthills of the Savannah* begins after a coup has taken place – and ends with another. But the situation and mood is that of Africa – more precisely West Africa – in the 1980s rather than the 1960s, for the easy optimism and the more vulnerably youthful cynicism which characterized those early years of independence have been replaced by awareness of a deeply diseased society and a more profound determination to understand and cure the illnesses. The main protagonists are not those who aspire to power, and possibly a piece of the national cake in the process, but members of the elite, the been-to's who believed themselves to be among the power brokers. And two of them are men who use the written word to manipulate both the powerful and the powerless. The first of these is Christopher Oriko, like the Chris of *No Longer At Ease* a graduate of the London School of Economics and a lover of debate for its own sake, who moves from the editorship of the *National Gazette* to become Commissioner for Information in the cabinet of his old classmate Sam after a military coup makes Sam head of the West African State of Kangan. (Kangan is a very thinly disguised Nigeria, although, as the name suggests, its politics, its problems, and its political/literary debates are applicable also to Ghana, the Cameroon, and a number of other African states.)

Christopher is the first narrator, and the first witness in the novel, although to begin with the reader is not told who is on trial. The second narrator and witness is Christopher's successor as editor, the crusading journalist, Ikem Osodi, who is also Kangan's leading poet. Both witnesses are partially unreliable narrators and witnesses (we soon realize that they too are on trial), and as in *No Longer At Ease* and *A Man of the People*, the reader is encouraged to question their representation of themselves through their responses to women and women's responses to them. Christopher prides himself on his detachment, his cool reasonableness; but those are the very qualities which irritate and distress Beatrice, his fiancée. Ikem sees himself as the passionate defender of the poor and dispossessed, but we first encounter him contending for a place in the traffic queue with a taxi driver and then quarrelling with Elewa, his proletarian mistress with whom he cannot bear to spend the whole night. His claim that it is in Elewa's own interests that she be sent home in the middle of the night in a taxi appears as questionable to the reader as it does to his mistress. Ikem's praise for 'the people' at the same time reveals his lack of identification with them: 'I was really amazed at their perceptiveness', he tells us without any apparent awareness of how patronizing his comment is (*AS*, p. 47). And a few lines later he proclaims proudly, 'I never pass up a chance of just sitting in my car, reading or pretending to read, surrounded by the vitality and thrill of *these* dramatic people' (my italics). Ikem seems unaware of the irony of the image he presents, sealing himself off from the people in the market by the car and the book, symbols of wealth and education unavailable to them. He seems equally unaware of the closeness of the language he uses to describe 'these dramatic people' of that of John Kent, the English doctor known to his friends as 'Mad Medico', who apostrophizes Kangan thus: 'Sunshine! Life! Vitality. It says to you: Come out and play. Make love! Live', and satirizes 'dusky imitators of *petit bourgeois* Europe'.

The reader may be equally dubious about Christopher Oriko's justification for remaining at his post as Commissioner for Information. Speaking of himself and his fellow members of cabinet and their complicity with 'the suspension of the rules', Chris reflects:

And so it begins to seem to me that this thing probably never was a game, that the present was there from the very beginning only I was too blind or too busy to notice. But the real question which I have often asked myself is why then do I go on with it now that I can see. I don't know. Simple inertia, maybe. Or perhaps sheer curiosity: to see where it will all . . . well, end. I am not thinking so much about him as about my colleagues, eleven intelligent, educated men who let this happen to them, who actually went out of their way to invite it, and who even at this hour have seen and learnt nothing, the cream of our society and the hope of the black race. I suppose it is for them that I am still at this silly observation post making farcical entries in the crazy log-book of this our ship of state. Disenchantment with them turned long ago into detached clinical interest.

I find their actions not merely bearable now, but actually interesting, even exciting. Quite amazing! And to think that I personally was responsible for recommending nearly half of them for appointment.

And of course, complete honesty demands that I mention one last factor in my continued stay, a fact of which I am somewhat ashamed, namely that I couldn't be writing this if I did not hang around to observe it all. And no one else would.   (*AS*, p. 2)

Here, Achebe's perennial question of 'where did the rain begin to beat' is raised for the reader, only to be evaded by the speaker. The passage reveals honest as well as a certain amount of slightly dishonest confusion about motives;

motives which are almost inextricable from questions of responsibility, audience and the role of the writer. For it is Chris who has been partly responsible for elevating his eleven co-disciples clustered about the man who is described satirically as a kind of sun-god, and by his obsequious Attorney General compared to the Messiah, thus bringing to consciousness the buried ironic comparisons with the Last Supper the opening scene might suggest. (Such comparisons are also faintly stirred by the name Chris who additionally, in his relation with Ikem Osodi, recalls the poet Christopher Okigbo.) The theme of betrayal is common to the gospel story and this novel, although the question of loyalty is a far more difficult one here, and it is the would-be messiah who betrays himself. (The president's name, Samson, recalls another biblical strong man, who also brings down destruction upon himself, but here in his attempt to save himself rather than his nation.) Christopher Oriko's decision (if decision is the right word) to write about and for his colleagues, despite his sense of the futility of doing so, is perhaps a continuation of his elevation of them. Chris is at this point unable to see clearly the possibility of other sources of power and change, and so can change neither himself nor his colleagues. Nor is he able to spot the contradiction between his declared 'clinical interest' and his 'interest' and 'excitement', an excitement which scarcely befits one who 'was responsible for recommending nearly half of them for appointment'. It will be only when he has no choice that Chris will begin to understand alternative motives, alternative subjects and audiences, and alternative reasons for involvement. Once he has been declared an enemy of the leader, Chris will begin to listen to his fiancée Beatrice, to Braimoh and his fellow taxi drivers, to the student leader, none of whom have ever been in a position to believe themselves even a part of the game, let alone makers of the rules.

If the opening three chapters focus mainly on the issue of state power – the relations between the governed and those who govern them – relations which often appear as natural, as arbitrary and as awesome as the relation

between sun and rain (or storm as in the case of the distant
rumble of the Abazonians who have come to petition His
Excellency), the three chapters which introduce Ikem also
raise the question of sexual politics and the power relationships between men and women. Chris is subdued by the
authoritative command of His Excellency as his first
chapter opens; Elewa is subdued by Ikem not only as male
owner of the house from which he ejects her, but also as
privileged speaker, talking 'totally and deliberately over
her head.' (*AS*, p. 36). Chris's horrified fascination with
the exercise of power and the complicity of his fellows with
it is matched by Ikem's confessed fascination with his
neighbour's wife-beating ('There is an extraordinary sur-
realistic quality about the whole thing that is almost satisfy-
ingly cathartic') and her behaviour the next morning (. . .
'They were so outrageously friendly and relaxed! She
especially. I was dumbfounded', *AS*, pp. 34–5). As
Beatrice, the third narrator, will argue, Ikem's radicalism,
his concern with altering the politics of the state, is badly
flawed by his failure to envision a role for women in that
changed state.

Nevertheless, Ikem's passion and crusading zeal serve to
counterbalance Chris's 'clinical detachment'. Chris's task
as recorder and observer, as collector and disseminator of
information, is in the right circumstances and put to the right
uses an important and necessary one, as is shown clearly
when he and Emmanuel, the student leader, ensure that the
true story of Ikem's arrest and murder is got out to the media
and 'the Voice of Rumour'. But against mere reliance upon
facts, Ikem argues for passionate commitment:

Those who mismanage our affairs would silence our criticism by
pretending they have facts not available to the rest of us. And I
know it is fatal to engage them on their own ground. Our best
weapon against them is not to marshal facts, of which they are
truly managers, but passion. Passion is our hope and strength,
a very present help in trouble   (*AS*, pp. 38–9)

Ikem then goes on to weigh his own account against 'all
accounts' in his vivid and effective description of a public
execution, and claims the credit for changing popular opi-

nion as well as the law putting an end to such executions. Chris's argument that the law would have been changed anyway may or may not have some substance to it – the reader cannot know, but neither is one encouraged to doubt Ikem's rightness in opposing the executions.

Ikem's poetic passion, his appeal to anecdote and personal insight and intuition rather than statistics as the basis for knowledge and action, is given further weight in the novel, not only by the ways in which its placing allows it to subvert and expose Chris's defensively rationalizing posture, but also by the fact that the title of the novel is drawn from Ikem's poetic prose poem, 'Hymn to the Sun':

The trees had become hydra-headed bronze statues so ancient that only blunt residual features remained on their faces, like anthills surviving to tell the new grass of the savannah about last year's brush fires. (*AS*, p. 31)

The simile here is a complex and oblique one. The anthills are not living trees, but reminders of barely living ones, which warn the 'new grass' of the danger of fire and scorching sun. In the second major myth of the book, the myth of Idemili, here told by the omniscient narrator rather than one of the characters and hence given particular status, the importance of 'invoking the mystery of metaphor' is made more explicit:

Man's best artifice to snare and hold the grandeur of divinity always crumbles in his hands, and the more ardently he strives the more paltry and incongruous the result. So it were better he did not try at all: far better to ritualize that incongruity and by invoking the mystery of metaphor to hint at the most unattainable glory by its very opposite, the most mundane starkness – a mere stream, a tree, a stone, a mound of earth, a little clay bowl containing fingers of chalk.

Thus it came about that the indescribable Pillar of Water fusing earth to heaven at the navel of the black lake became in numberless shrine-houses across the country, a dry stick rising erect from the bare, earth floor. (*AS*, p. 103)

Ikem's male myth of the sun, his prose poem titled 'The Pillar of Fire: a Hymn to the Sun', discovered on the floor of his room by Chris and then passed on to Emmanuel, is a myth of the arrogance and cruelty of naked power, a warning of its consequences, including self-destruction, and a delineation of its 'one-eyed', 'one-wall-neighbour to-Blindness' quality bringing death, sterility and bloodshed to the land. Against it is set the female myth of Idemili, 'The Pillar of Water', bringer of hope to drought-stricken lands, reminder of 'the moral nature of authority', 'wrapping around Power's rude waist a loincloth of peace and modesty' (AS, p. 102). This Igbo myth also contrasts with the Judaic and Christian ones used to deny female power and rejected by Ikem in his letter to Beatrice. Yet, however much power and importance may be ascribed to Idemili on the mythical level, the feminine is given short shrift in the day-to-day life of society, as Beatrice's other given name Nwanyibuife ('A female is also something') reminds her. Examples of male chauvinism are brought into focus throughout the novel. There is the wife-beating which fascinates and revolts Ikem, Beatrice's more compassionate and painful memories of her mother's tears and probable beatings behind closed doors, her father's anger when she behaves as a 'soldier girl', the smug celebration of 'African polygamy' by His Excellency, the invasion of the Women's Hostel by soldiers quelling a student protest, and the attempted rape of the girl on the bus with Chris and Emmanuel. Similarly, the possibility of hope which may come through acknowledgement of Idemili's reminder of 'the moral nature of authority' and life-giving compassion in time of drought is presented not merely on the mythical level, but also on the level of intellectual analysis and plot. Ikem acknowledges in his 'Love Poem' the importance of the insight Beatrice has given him as a means of understanding that the movement towards change must not be simple-minded, answering in kind the 'one-eyed' power of the sun, but multi-faceted, acknowledging the many kinds and many faces of oppression, without blurring the distinctions between them. Chris's final act is significant because he intervenes and acts rather than remaining detached, and also because his intervention is an outraged reaction to the most blatant abuse of male power against a woman.

While the novel is chiefly concerned with the abuse of power, and particularly male power, it also suggests the need for women to acknowledge and take upon themselves aspects of maleness. Beatrice protests far too much against the charge that she is ambitious. We accept that her motive for writing and defending Chris and Ikem is not merely egoistic, but nevertheless detect an all too 'feminine' fear of appearing to be 'aggressive' or to want to hold power. She too has changed by the novel's end, so that she has become the focus of a new nucleus of hope, providing a place and an intellectual testing ground for the discussions of Emmanuel, Captain Abdul, Braimoh, Elewa, and even Agatha – a group significantly more varied in class and ethnic origin than the gatherings to which she, Chris and Ikem had formerly been accustomed. In a metaphor carefully chosen to subvert its usual connotations of gender role, Beatrice is described as 'a captain whose leadership was sharpened more and more by sensitivity to the peculiar needs of her company'. (*AS*, p. 229) The final chapter of the novel emphasizes the changes which women may bring about, thus also answering Beatrice's own despairing thought that Chris and Ikem, and by implication all of them, may have been 'trailed travellers whose journeys from start to finish had been carefully programmed in advance by an alienated history'. For the name she gives Elewa's child, Ameisechina (May the path never close), is not only a prayer responsive to that fear, but also a boy's name for a girl child, promising that a girl may now follow the path Ikem had begun to clear. Beatrice herself takes on the role of the patriarch in naming the child, a right ackowledged by Elewa's uncle, and the women announce that from now on all of them are her father and mother. Again, it is the women who lead the union of different groups and cultures in their ecumenical dance of Igbo, Muslim and Christian.

The role of the writer

Diverse modes of discourse have always been a feature

of Achebe's fiction and poetry, not merely as a means of distinguishing differing speakers and differing cultures, but also as a subject – for celebration, for satire, and above all, for interrogation. The proverbs and anecdotes of *Things Fall Apart* construct and validate the culture of the Igbo, but they also solidify it, creating a series of formulas which can prevent change or fresh perception, just as surely as the District Commissioner's language blinds him. Obi in *No Longer At Ease* is unable to bridge the gap between his English literary world, which brings with it the weary and disillusioned language of T. S. Eliot and Housman, and the traditional Igbo and Christian worlds from which his parents derive their deeply felt beliefs. In *Arrow of God* readers and characters alike are faced with a series of alternate versions of the past, and like Ezeulu must wrestle with the questions relating to language, knowledge and power – questions raised at the very beginning of the novel when Ezeulu ponders his role and responsibilities as priest and herald of the new moon. *A Man of the People* ends with a disquisition on and illustration of the four kinds of language which struggle to be heard in the new Nigerian nation. Achebe's critical essays and lectures reiterate the responsibility of the writer to his community and the danger of his being controlled by communities of interests which are not his own.

Anthills of the Savannah carries on this concern voiced particularly in the essays, for unlike the earlier novels, Achebe is here more centrally concerned with the role of the writer than with the role of the speaker. As the passages I quoted near the beginning of this chapter indicate, there is a recurring meditation on the writer's aims, conscious and semiconscious, on the interrelation of self-discovery and revelation for others, on audience and effectiveness.[1] Whereas the earlier novels exposed or explored the dichotomy between African oral and European literary cultures, *Anthills of the Savannah* is far more concerned with the African literary culture that has grown up since Achebe's first novel was published in 1958. Chris, Ikem and Beatrice, the three chief protagonists and narrators, are all writers. Both Chris as Minister for Information, and Ikem as editor of the

National Gazette have power over the production of the literary word, though both will discover the limits of their power in the course of the novel. It is Ikem who most explicitly addresses himself to contemporary African letters, and even if they do not include Ngugi himself, the unnamed literary antagonists in this novel are the critics and young writers who ally themselves with him. Ikem repeatedly confronts and resists the demand that as a writer he should provide a clear commitment, a simple political solution, preferably a Marxist one, to the troubles of his country.[2]

There is not the space in this chapter to analyse in detail all the many instances or aspects of storytelling which are either used or brought to our attention in *Anthills*. I shall concentrate on a few examples in order to explore the following issues raised within the novel: *Whose* story is of significance? *How* should the story be told – in what language, in what form, and for what audience? For *what purpose* are stories to be told?

Towards the end of chapter 5, which is also the final chapter in which the male point of view is dominant, Chris says of himself, Ikem and Sam: 'We are all connected. You cannot tell the story of any of us without implicating the others.' To which Beatrice replies: 'You fellows, all three of you, are incredibly conceited. The story of this country, as far as you are concerned, is the story of the three of you' (*AS*, p. 66). In the following chapters, the novel will become increasingly inclusive of other stories – Beatrice's especially, but also Elewa's, Agatha's, Braimoh's and Emmanuel's. This inclusion of other stories is closely related to the movement, structure and imagery of the novel as a whole. In the first chapter, the writer, Chris, is claustrophobically shut off in the hermetically sealed world of the cabinet meeting room. The only voice that matters is the President's, and the voices of the people, the delegation from Abazon, are totally excluded, emerging as a distantly threatening murmur only when the President leaves the room. For the President himself, the only voices that matter, other than those of his cabinet who merely echo, or attempt to echo his own thoughts, are those of the western media – he fears above all being portrayed satirically in *Time Magazine*, and it is Louise, the American journalist, who has his ear at the Presidential Palace, thus provoking Beatrice's outburst. Similarly, Ikem has first been introduced to us sealed off in his car, from where other drivers appear merely as rivals and not as fellow human beings caught in the same predicament. In the early chapters the main characters are all isolated from contact with the majority of Kangan's populace either through the deliberate seclusion of their homes or of their work. Telephones become a means of cutting off or excluding communication rather than enabling it; cars delay arrivals and meetings rather than facilitate them; homes are locked and barred. Even within the home, religion becomes a source of antagonism rather than community, as with Beatrice and Agatha. Gradually, however, the novel moves from the cabinet room, the traffic jam, the well-to-do suburbs of the nation's capital, Bassa, to the poorer sections, the Harmony Hotel where Ikem meets the Abazon delegation and begins to hear its story, the university campus, the tiny, crowded one-room home of Braimoh, and finally to the busload of people and the road to the north, before returning to Beatrice's apartment, now far more open and inclusive of far more people than before. Beatrice no longer treasures her isolation, although she still retains some privacy.

The inclusion of other people and other areas also involves the inclusion of other voices. Both Ikem and Chris listen less and less to 'their master's voice' and more and more to the voices of those who have been excluded from power. The turning point for Ikem comes with his meeting with the elders of Abazon, where in one of the major set pieces in the novel, he (and the reader) listen to the long disquisition from the leader of the Abazon delegation on the importance of storytelling. Ikem is overwhelmed by the power and wisdom of the elder's oral art, and by the effectiveness of his tale of the leopard and the tortoise. In a second major set piece, Ikem retells the traditional story, but this time in the context of a written lecture with the paraphernalia, however deficient, of modern technology

161

and in the non-traditional setting of the university lecture hall. The story itself is significant, but so also is Ikem's ability to adapt it to contemporary times, and his insistence on dialogue rather than continued monologue. That message has been brought home to Ikem not only by the delegation from Abazon, but also by the two taxi drivers who come to visit him, and congratulate him on his refusal 'to stay for him house, chop him oyibo chop, drink him cold beer, put him air conditioner and forget we'. Determined to speak their piece, the taxi drivers have inserted their voices and their often inconsistent and uneasily accommodated views into Ikem's private world. Their words and attitudes set off a whole series of reflections in which he expresses his disillusion with 'public affairs' in 'nothing but the closed transactions of soldiers-turned-politicians, with their cohorts in business and the bureaucracy', and finds himself one of those who have been guilty of 'invoking the people's name . . . while making sure of [their] absence', (*AS*, p. 141). The language of the taxi drivers, the voices of the people from the market (including Elewa) become more and more prominent as the novel proceeds, and pidgin takes on a new status as a language not merely to be used for political capital by the Nangas of *A Man of the People*, but expressive of the 'integrity, a stubborn sense of community . . . a teasing affectionateness', a cheerful and ironic humour which allows the poor and dispossessed to survive the corruption and abuse of power which typifies their rulers. It is significant that the very last words in the novel are given to Elewa and that they are in pidgin: 'BB, weting be dis now? . . . Even *my*self I no de cry like dat! What kind trouble you wan begin cause now? I beg-o. Hmm!'

In the early sections of the novel, effective writing and speech are thought to be the kinds which are directed to those in power, as are Ikem's newspaper editorials, or the kinds which seek to manipulate the governed, as are Chris's directives and statements and Professor Okong's political columns. The poetry of Ikem is not published to produce change, but appears as a private paper, a private meditation upon power – though nevertheless more effective, one would guess, than the pieces published in the Soho magazine, *Reject*, for a self-indulgent, self-delighting audience. Chris's journal is also kept as a private record, which allows it to be relatively honest and clear in its reporting of the government's behaviour; but it only becomes useful when incorporated into Beatrice's account of events. It is the Elder from Abazon who gives storytelling 'the eagle feather' and insists on its importance, for 'it is the story . . . that saves our progeny from blundering like blind beggars into the spikes of the cactus fence . . . It is the thing that makes us different from cattle.' (*AS*, p. 124)[3] For the old man, stories are important as reminders of the past, reminders from which future generations can learn. It is significant in terms of the role given Beatrice and the importance of female myth in the novel that he notes the name sometimes given by Abazonians to their daughters – Nkolika: 'Recalling is greatest'. (*AS*, p. 124) Ikem asserts in his lecture that the writer's role is not to give answers, but to ask questions and to 'excite general enlightenment by forcing all the people to examine the condition of their lives because, as the saying goes, the unexamined life is not worth living . . . As a writer I aspire only to widen the scope of that self-examination.' (*AS*, p. 158) Achebe has tended in his earlier fiction to divide the functions of the storyteller: in one novel recalling the past, in the next encouraging self-examination in the present. Here there is some recollection of the more immediate past, but the emphasis is on self-examination, in this case not just on the part of the readers, but also on the part of writers, including Achebe himself. For Achebe, the relationship between author, characters and readers should be analogous to the relationship between politicians and electorate in the ideal state, the leaders in each case accepting the necessity for genuine dialogue with and tolerance of those for whom they are responsible. In short the author must never become a dictator, but like Whitman should be willing to confront and express the contradictions within him- or herself, viewing those selves with self-irony and humour as an antidote to the one-eyed monomania of tyrants.[4] This is the lesson Beatrice recognizes in Chris's enigmatic, rueful, and self-deprecatory reference to the 'last grin', wryly seeing himself as 'the last green bottle' of the old nursery rhyme in his dying moment.

Conclusion

ACHEBE'S FICTION, poetry and essays respond to a series of critical periods in Nigerian history since 1890 – the introduction and imposition of European culture and law in Eastern Nigeria; the unforeseen consequences of the attempt by Igbos to adapt that culture and its technology to their own needs and to keep 'the best of both worlds'; the period just preceding Independence; the end of the First Republic; the civil war; the series of military coups and the struggle to understand and resist dictatorship. Throughout all his works, his continuing concern has been 'the trouble with Nigeria'. His point of departure as a writer was the fiction of Joyce Cary who also sought to expose 'the trouble with Nigeria'. In confronting Cary and the tradition he belonged to, Achebe was aware that he was confronting a culture, a system of values, a complex of power-relations which produced and was produced by colonialism. Drawing upon the model of his own Igbo political and cultural system and its oral traditions, Achebe reconstructed a picture and narrative of Africa and Africans caught in particular moments of history. He also recreated the form and technique of the novel 'to carry the full weight of [his] African experience' with particular respect to the relation between author, subject and reader.

For Cary, historical change was by definition a consequence of the European encounter with Africa. Achebe disagrees with the definition, but in many of his works he does focus his attention on the interaction between Europeans and Africans and/or their cultures. All of his writing is preoccupied with the relationship between the personal and the political, and the question of personal responsibility in a world where individual power must be limited. His novels focus on the conflict between social responsibility and individual feeling or self-expression, demonstrating the ways in which self-knowledge can be obscured by self-interest. Repeatedly they confront the problem of responsiblity for the consequences of one's actions in face of the limitations of individual power and knowledge.

These are concerns Cary shared, although Achebe's novels explore them in greater depth and complexity than Cary's African novels did. Where the two authors differ strongly is on the weight that should be given to individual fulfilment. Cary's overriding interest is in the individual's need to overcome the barriers to self-fulfilment and self-expression, and here he shares with a majority of contemporary European male novelists a valuation of the individual as against his society and its demands. Hence Cary's novels are most memorable not for the worlds and cultures they portray, but for their central characters, as the titles of the novels imply. And those characters are celebrated not as types of their societies, but as eccentrics: Mister Johnson, Bewsher, Aissa and Elizabeth Aladai all create excitement and wonder because they refuse to recognize the conventions which constrain the behaviour and expression of others in the societies they belong to. In this Cary belongs to the tradition of Defoe (in *Moll Flanders*), Sterne, Dickens, Twain, Thackeray, Joyce and, in poetry, Browning and Yeats, rather than Austen, Hardy or Pope. Their central characters are redeemed by their movements away from the cold dogma of their elders. Cary's admired characters are, as Matthew Arnold said of the Irish, rebels 'against the despotism of facts'.

Within the tradition of colonialist fiction about Africa which Cary exemplifies, it is possible for the European characters to change and learn from experience, to reform themselves and their societies, to 'progress'. They are the actors whose drama is staged against an unchanging backdrop or decor in which natives and scenery are merged. The African characters such as Mister Johnson, Louis Aladai or Elizabeth Aladai embody unchanging archetypal forces: the libido, 'blood' instinct, the will. They belong not to history but to the static world of feudal or pastoral romance, and they must be contained or destroyed by those who belong to history, 'civilization' and social order.

In contrast, Achebe's central characters gain their significance not as eccentrics or outsiders, but as types – they are products of the society which has formed them, and they seek to reform and conserve it. All wish, above all, to be insiders, to become significant and acknowledged members of a viable community. The tragedy of Okonkwo and Ezeulu arises both from their failure to become central and the loss that failure represents for the community. Their failure arises from the very trait which makes Cary's characters admirable – their contempt for the opinions of others.

The emphasis on his characters as members of a specific society, formed both by the values of that society and by their particular family and social circumstances, characters who have in them the potential to change, to become something other, given changing circumstances, is one important way in which Achebe challenges the colonialist depiction of Africans. His characters, particularly Okonkwo and Ezeulu, would be for the Hungarian critic Georg Lukács admirable examples of realism and the creation of types as a means of revealing 'the organic, indissoluble connection between man as a private individual and man as a social being, as a member of a community'.[1] Lukács declares:

Realism is the recognition of the fact that a work of literature can rest neither on a lifeless average, as the naturalists suppose, nor on an individual principle which dissolves its own self into nothingness. The central category and criterion of realist literature is the type, a peculiar synthesis which organically binds together the general and the particular both in characters and situations. What makes a type a type is not its average quality, not its mere individual being, however profoundly conceived: what makes a type is that in it all the humanly and socially essential determinants are present in their highest level of development, in the ultimate unfolding of the possibilities latent in them, in extreme presentation of their extremes, rendering concrete the peaks and limits of men and epochs.[2]

Through Okonkwo and Ezeulu, 'in extreme presentation

of their extremes', Achebe succeeds in 'rendering concrete the peaks and limits of men and epochs', discerning also in the transitional periods of history he writes about, 'a contradictory unity of crisis and renewal, of destruction and rebirth, . . . a new social order and a new type of man coming into birth'.[3] Achebe has made the point in his own way, affirming the importance of understanding 'where the rain began to beat'.

Achebe's creation of such types, his reiterated concern with social commitment and analysis, his depiction of crucial historical periods which are moments of transition in African history, no doubt account for the general assumption that his novels fit readily into the category of realism or 'critical realism'. This categorization is argued by JanMohamed,[4] and simply asserted or assumed by Emmanuel Ngara and a number of other critics.[5] However, this view has in my opinion obscured the ways in which Achebe's novels depart from the classic realist form in order to create a new and more radical 'epic' novel with techniques and effects akin in some ways to Brecht's 'epic' theatre.

In his essay on epic theatre, Walter Benjamin points to the elements which distinguish it from the theatre of illusion and suspense, in which the spectator is involved in a closed fictive world, and is not encouraged to question its social or artistic construction while the play is in progress.[6] Epic theatre is purged of the sensational, concerned not so much with the development of actions and suspense as with 'the representation of conditions'. Benjamin insists that this representation differs from mimetic reproduction.

Rather the truly important thing is to discover the conditions of life. One might say just as well to alienate [*verfremden*] them. This discovery (alienation) takes place through the interruption of happenings.[7]

Interruptions in the action of the play are fundamental to its structure, allowing the spectators to participate as critics, to reflect upon the events. Songs and observations are used

to bring about intervals which, if anything, impair the illusion of the audience and paralyze its readiness for empathy. These intervals are reserved for the spectators' critical reaction – to the actions of the players and to the way in which they are presented.[8]

Achebe's cool, dispassionate style, his avoidance of the sensational, is comparable to the style of the epic theatre. But it is above all his use of a variety of perspectives and his choice of narrative technique and structure which allows him to achieve effects similar to those aimed at by Brecht. Like Brecht, Achebe no doubt learned those techniques and concepts of the relation between author/narrator and audience from a non-literary tradition, although an African rather than a European one. So Achebe uses songs, folktales, proverbs, parables and myths to add an ironic or alternative commentary upon the main action. Questions focus and interrupt the action; alternative versions and reasons are given for particular events. This technique reaches its greatest complexity in *Anthills of the Savannah*. Throughout the work, technique and form are inextricably bound up with the author's vision and with the Igbo proverb, often cited by him, that 'Where something stands, there also something else will stand.'[9] He shares with the Igbo people 'a firm belief in the duality of things', and asserts, 'Nothing is by itself, nothing is absolute. "I am the way, the Truth and the Life" would be meaningless in Igbo theology.'[10] As *Anthills of the Savannah* demonstrates more clearly than any other, that rejection of absolutes applies also to political structures.

This 'firm belief' shared by Achebe that no single man or character can or should assume knowledge and judgement that overrides all other views, that arrogance and pride is the worst of all sins, accounts for the failures of his main characters, is the source of his indictment of the British, and also underlies his choice of narrative technique and structure. Whereas Cary chooses a single objective narrative perspective, a fast-paced and detached description of scenes and incidents which leaves no room for the reader to question the narrator's accuracy or judgement, Achebe's novels are remarkable for their variety of perspective and involvement of the reader in the questions and issues central to each novel. *Things Fall Apart* begins with a kind of 'collective voice' reminiscent of oral storytelling, moves flexibly to suggest the point of view and consciousness of characters such as Okonkwo, Obierika and Nwoye, as voices which blend with that of the main narrative voice but maintain individual characteristics, and ends swiftly with the contrasting point of view of the District Commissioner. As seems appropriate to its more intellectual and introspective protagonist and to a historical period when the British presence was acknowledged as a *fait accompli*, the point of view in *Arrow of God* begins with Ezeulu, moves to acknowledge the differing voices and perspectives within Umuaro, and then explores more fully the contrasting assumptions, cultures, attitudes and voices of the Igbo and British communities. In contrast to the two novels with traditional settings, *No Longer At Ease* and *A Man of the People* are generally tied to the limited point of view of the main protagonist. With *Anthills of the Savannah* Achebe combines the techniques explored in earlier works, juxtaposing a series of unreliable narratives and perspectives, and bringing together both traditional and modern storytelling and forms of communication in myth, poetry, lectures, journalism, diaries and fiction and showing their interaction as well as their difference.

Achebe's first four novels seem to be conceived and written in pairs. *No Longer at Ease* continues the response to *Mister Johnson* and explores the themes of thought and feeling, the male and female motifs begun in *Things Fall Apart*; *A Man of the People*, like *Arrow of God*, focuses more closely on the question of responsible leadership, and on the difficulty of disentangling personal and political motives. *Anthills of the Savannah* can be seen as both a summation of the themes and techniques explored in the previous novels, and a new departure. Each of the novels with contemporary settings takes on fuller meaning when read in conjunction with the traditional novel that precedes it in point of composition, and we should set in contrast not only the societies depicted in each novel, but also the *form* of each novel. *Things Fall Apart* is suggestive of traditional epic, speaking for and to a community with shared assumptions, values, traditions, history and legends. The fictive reader is incorporated into that community. As epic, it is primarily

between past and present remained unbridged, perhaps unbridgeable.[12] The contemporary and traditional novels stand as contrasting shores, rather than as points in a river of time into which varying tributaries flow and mingle and continue. Abiole Irele has analysed the tension in *Things Fall Apart* between Achebe's apprehension of and nostalgia for the traditional world and his perception of the forward movement of history, showing how such a tension underlies the structure of the novel as well as its characterization and imagery.[13] Not only *Things Fall Apart*, but the whole *oeuvre* up until 1965 suggests that tension, although in varying degrees. With *A Man of the People* both beneficial and inappropriate continuities with the past are explored. However, it is not until *Anthills of the Savannah* that the tension is fully confronted and explored, so that the traditional is seen to be living and continued in new and viable forms in the present. In this novel too, the 'lost generation' is given some attention, as Beatrice dwells upon memories of her mother and father and her childhood and seeks some reconciliation with them in her consciousness. And here Achebe combines more fully than before romance and community. By placing Beatrice in the foreground, rather than simply making her the object of desire, he is able to suggest a balance between aspiration to individual fulfilment and aspiration to be part of a whole and wholesome community, while also exploring the barriers, political and psychological, to that integration.

In all his fiction and poetry, Achebe calls upon the reader's continuous participation and judgement. It is here, in his refusal to allow readers to suspend judgement and disbelief, that Achebe rejects most firmly Cary's concept of the relationship between reader and writer. The variety of points of view and language, the frequent dislocation of the story line or, in the poetry, the syntax and rhythm, the movement from past to present and present to past, the questions or deliberately unsatisfying answers which end significant episodes, all call upon readers to involve themselves not merely in understanding and sympathizing with the characters concerned, but in thoughtful awareness of the complex problems they face and evaluation of the responses made to those problems. As Achebe argues in 'Truth In Fiction,' the essential benefit of good storytelling comes from the slight detachment it allows the reader or listener in encountering social and psychological dangers. Fiction must 'insist upon its fictionality', constantly reminding readers that it is a pretence, though a serious one, for only then are they free to entertain a variety of possibilities, learning to tolerate the multifaceted and often contradictory nature of existence, while rejecting the 'one-eyed', literal-minded vision which produces prejudice and injustice.[14]

In particular, Achebe has striven to make the reader conscious of language, speech and written discourse. As was Orwell, he is convinced of the inextricable connection between corruption in language and corruption in politics. In an interview during the 1983 elections in Nigeria, he is quoted as saying, 'Language is crucial to our integrity, but here it has been contaminated. If you want to say something in English, you have to learn it properly.'[15] An earlier speech, 'Language and the Destiny of Man', had elaborated on this message, referring to T. S. Eliot's as well as Orwell's 'concern and solicitude for the integrity of words'.[16] As Achebe said in an interview in 1981:

The language of a man is in fact the best guide you have to his character. If you don't listen carefully enough, then all kinds of charlatans and demagogues will steal the show, which is what is happening not only in Nigeria, but in many other parts of the world.[17]

Notes

Introduction

1 Arthur Ravenscroft, *Chinua Achebe*, Harlow: Longman for the British Council and the National Book League, 1969; rev. ed., 1977; David Caroll, *Chinua Achebe*, New York: Twayne, 1970, rev. ed., London: Macmillan, 1980; G. D. Killam, *The Writings of Chinua Achebe*, London: Heinemann, 1969, rev. ed., 1977.
2 *Achebe's World: The Historical and Cultural Context of the Novels of Chinua Achebe*, Harlow: Longman Studies in African Literature, 1980.
3 'The Role of the Writer in a New Nation', *Nigeria Magazine* 81 (1964), 157.
4 Carroll, *Chinua Achebe*, rev. ed., p. 183.
5 See especially E. Obiechina, *Culture, Tradition and Society in the African Novel*, Cambridge: Cambridge University Press, 1975; Robert Wren, *Achebe's World*; M. Mahood, 'Idols of the Den', *The Colonial Encounter*, London: Rex Collings, 1976, pp. 37–64.
6 'The African Writer and the English Language', *Morning Yet on Creation Day*, London: Heinemann Educational Books, p. 62.
7 See essays by these critics in *Critical Perspectives on Chinua Achebe*, ed. C. L. Innes and B. Lindfors, London: Heinemann, 1979; Washington DC: Three Continents Press, 1978.
8 *African Writers Talking: A Collection of Radio Interviews*, ed. Cosmo Pieterse and Dennis Duerden, London: Heinemann, 1972, p. 4.
9 In a talk at the Africa Centre in London, 15 September 1987.

1   Origins

1 'Named for Victoria, Queen of England', *MYCD*, p. 67.
2 *Ibid.*, p. 68.
3 *Ibid.*, p. 68.
4 *Ibid.*, p. 66.
5 Donatus Nwoga, *The Supreme Deity as a Stranger in Igbo Culture*.
6 '*Chi* in Igbo Cosmology', *MYCD*, p. 98.
7 *Ibid.*, p. 103.

8 Quoted from a note to the author from Achebe.
9 Robert W. Wren gives examples of such pacification and discusses Igbo reactions in his study *Achebe's World: The Historical and Cultural Context of the Novels of Chinua Achebe*, Harlow: Longman, 1981, p. 13.
10 'Named For Victoria, Queen of England', *MYCD*.
11 Michael Crowder, *The Story of Nigeria*, 3rd edition, London: Faber, 1973, p. 272.
12 Bernth Lindfors, *Early Nigerian Literature*, New York: Africana Publishing Company, 1982.
13 *Ibid.*, pp. 91–106, 111–42 (chapters on the undergraduate writings of Chinua Achebe and Wole Soyinka).
14 *Ibid.*, pp. 91–4. The essay is reprinted in its entirety in these pages.
15 'Named for Victoria, Queen of England', *MYCD*, p. 70.
16 'An Image of Africa', published in *The Chancellor's Lecture Series, 1974–75*, Amherst, MA: University of Massachusetts, 1975, pp. 31–43. Reprinted in *Hopes and Impediments*, London: Heinemann, 1988.
17 *African Writers Talking: A Collection of Radio Interviews*, ed. Cosmo Pieterse and Dennis Duerden, London: Heinemann, 1972.
18 Robert Wren does compare *Mister Johnson* and *Arrow of God* with regard to their concepts of history in *Achebe's World*, ch. 5 and also in '*Mister Johnson* and the Complexity of *Arrow of God*', *Critical Perspectives on Chinua Achebe*, ed. C. L. Innes and B. Lindfors, Washington DC: Three Continents Press, 1978, pp. 207–18. A more recent book by A. R. JanMohamed, *Manichean Aesthetics: The Politics of Literature in Colonial Africa*, Amherst MA: University of Massachusetts Press, 1983, includes separate chapters on Joyce Cary and Chinua Achebe, but does not make a detailed comparison of the two authors.
19 Frantz Fanon, *The Wretched of the Earth*, trans. Constance Farrington, London: MacGibbon and Kee, 1965, p. 33.
20 *Ibid.*, p. 33.
21 *Black Skin, White Masks*, trans. C. L. Markmann, London: MacGibbon and Kee, 1968, p. 165.
22 *Frantz Fanon: Colonialism and Alienation*, London: Monthly Review Press, 1974, p. 32.
23 The four novels set in Africa are *Aissa Saved* (1931), *The American Visitor* (1932), *The African Witch* (1936), and *Mister Johnson* (1939). For a detailed discussion see M. M. Mahood, *Joyce Cary's Africa*, London: Methuen, 1964; Michael Echeruo, *Joyce Cary and the Novel of Africa*, London: Longman, 1973 and A. R. JanMohamed, 'Joyce Cary', *Manichean Aesthetics*, pp. 15–48.
24 See JanMohamed, *Manichean Aesthetics*, ch. 2.
25 Quoted by Malcolm Foster, *Joyce Cary: A Biography*, London: Michael Joseph, 1969, p. 449.
26 New York: Twayne, 1970.
27 Cary's view that Africa has been isolated from 'history' or change is not only implicit in his stories but is also made explicit in his descriptions of African societies and towns such as Fada (see this

description quoted in note 2 to ch. 3). In his preface to *The African Witch*, Cary writes of the novel: 'My book was meant to show certain men and their problems in the tragic background of a continent still little advanced from the Stone Age, and therefore exposed, like no other, to the impact of modern turmoil. An overcrowded raft manned by children who had never seen the sun would have a better chance in a typhoon.' London: Michael Joseph, 1952, p. 12.

28 *Ibid.*, p. 7.

29 M. M. Bakhtin, *The Dialogic Imagination*, trans. Michael Holquist, Austin: University of Texas Press, 1986.

30 *The Illusion: An Essay on Politics, Theatre and the Novel*, New York: Harper & Row, 1971, pp. 225–6.

31 Cited in the Introduction, *Critical Perspectives on Chinua Achebe*, ed. C. L. Innes and B. Lindfors, p. 6.

2 *Things Fall Apart*

1 'Chinua Achebe', *African Writers Talking*, p. 4.

2 *Things Fall Apart*, p. 51. Subsequent page references to this novel will be introduced in the text.

3 Conversation with Chinua Achebe and students included at the University of Massachusetts, Amherst, 1974.

4 'Chinua Achebe: The Generation of Realism', *Manichean Aesthetics*, pp. 151–84.

5 *Mister Johnson* (Harmondsworth: Penguin, 1965), pp. 248–9.

6 The name Nwoye takes when baptised, Isaac, suggests a parallel with the Old Testament story of Abraham, whose god commanded the sacrifice of his son and who, like Okonkwo, was willing to execute the lad himself. The parallel is an ironic reminder of and commentary on aspects of Christianity of which the 'callow' Nwoye is unaware, and suggests further comparisons with the Old Testament and Igbo traditions.

7 *Mister Johnson*, pp. 102–3.

8 See, for example, B. Lindfors, 'The Palm-Oil with Which Achebe's Words are Eaten' and Gareth Griffiths, 'Language and Action in the Novels of Chinua Achebe', both reprinted in *Critical Perspectives on Chinua Achebe*. See also the relevant chapters in David Carroll's *Chinua Achebe* and E. Obiechina's *Culture, Tradition and Society in the West African Novel*.

9 For further discussion of language as a theme in *Things Fall Apart* see my article in *Critical Perspectives on Chinua Achebe*, pp. 111–25.

10 My use of the term 'Logos' in this context derives partly from its usage by Derrida, Paul de Man and other deconstructionist critics. Derrida argues that western culture, and uses of language in the west, are grounded on a belief in the primacy of spoken over written language, and in the possibility of grounding logically consistent or rational truth and meaning entirely in the spoken utterances of a

particular linguistic system. Derrida seeks to prove such a belief illusory. Achebe's fiction also questions logocentrism, but from a perspective which the deconstructionists, caught as *they* are within western culture, have not been concerned, since they have not discussed the problem in terms of a culture which is entirely oral.

11 Joyce Cary, *Art and Reality: Ways of the Creative Process*, New York: Harper and Bros., 1958, p. 6.

12 *Ibid.*, pp. 30–1.

3 No Longer At Ease

1 *No Longer at Ease*, p. 2. Subsequent references to page numbers in this novel will be included in the text.

2 In a subsequent lecture, 'Africa and Her Writers', in which he is critical of Armah's depiction of the Ghanaian urban slums, Achebe quotes from Joyce Cary's description of Fada in *Mister Johnson*. Cary's description reads thus:

> Fada is the ordinary native town of the Western Sudan. It has no beauty, convenience or health. It is a dwelling place at one stage from the rabbit warren or the badger burrow; and not so cleanly kept as the latter. It is a pioneer settlement five or six hundred years old, built on its own rubbish heaps, without charm or even antiquity. Its squalor and its stinks are all new. Its oldest compounds, except the Emir's mud box, is [*sic*] not twenty years old . . . Poverty and ignorance, the absolute government of jealous savages, conservative as only the savage can be, have kept it at the first frontier of civilization. Its people would not know the change if time jumped back fifty thousand years. They live like mice or rats in a palace floor; all the magnificence and variety of the arts, of ideas, the learning and the battles of civilization go on over their heads and they do not even imagine them. (p. 110)

As Professor Ben Obumselu points out in an unpublished paper given at a seminar at the University of Malawi and kindly lent to me by Landeg White, 'this is the area where a century before Cary's arrival Uthman dan Fodio had waged the jihad. Three centuries earlier the Mai of Bornu corresponded with his counterpart in Tunis and sent him a present of a gazelle.'

3 The title 'No Longer At Ease' takes on complex reverberations as the novel proceeds. It sets up an ironic comparison between the journey of the Magi and Obi's with their return to 'an alien people clutching their gods', but also contrasts Eliot's faith with Obi's lack of it. The title is a continuing reminder that the author of this novel, like Obi, is influenced by modern European literature yet has discarded his almost forgotten Christian name for his African one (Obi was baptised Michael; Achebe was baptised Albert). And given

the title and content of the novel, Obi's Igbo name is painfully inappropriate: 'His full name was Obiajulu – "the mind at last is at rest".' And then, Obi is a back-to-front Ibo! There are echoes also of Greene's hero, Scobie, who takes a bribe so that he can fulfil his commitment to his wife. The fact that Obi's is the *only* African name in the novel makes it all the more obtrusive and continually reminds us that labels are deceptive.

4 For discussions of concepts of tragedy in this and Achebe's other novels see Abiola Irele, 'The Tragic Conflict in the Novels of Chinua Achebe', *Critical Perspectives on Chinua Achebe*, pp. 10–21, and G. D. Killam, *The Writings of Chinua Achebe*, pp. 55–6. Killam, in particular, identifies Obi's view here with Achebe's, and regrets the authorial intrusion. One should note however what Obi fails to take into account: for Greene's Catholic protagonist, Scobie, suicide is an act which will lead to his eternal damnation; hence his suicide is comparable to Okonkwo's act of abomination. Given his own lack of religious belief, it is significant that Obi cannot see the importance of Scobie's faith.

5 David Caroll, *Chinua Achebe*, p. 71.

6 Published in *Morning Yet on Creation Day*. See also note 2 above.

7 A number of critics have disagreed with Achebe's reading of Armah's *The Beautyful Ones are not yet Born*, and have argued that its hero is also criticized by Armah for his detachment.

4 Arrow of God

1 Simon Nnolim, *The History of Umuchu*, Enugu: Eastern Syndicate Press, 1953. Revised by Charles Nnolim, Enugu: Ochumba Press, 1976. Achebe may have learned some details of the story when he interviewed Simon Nnolim and others in Umuchu while working on a programme for the Nigerian Broadcasting Service in 1957, but he was not aware of the written account.

2 *Achebe's World*, Harlow: Longman, 1980, pp. 76–95. See also Wren's article, '*Mister Johnson* and the Complexity of *Arrow of God*', *Critical Perspectives on Chinua Achebe*, pp. 207–18.

3 Joseph Conrad, *Heart of Darkness*, New York: New American Library, 1950, p. 106. This passage is cited by Achebe in his lecture on Conrad, 'An Image of Africa', *Hopes and Impediments*, pp. 4–5.

4 *Mister Johnson*, p. 177.

5 *Ibid.*, p. 177.

6 *Ibid.*, p. 169.

7 *Ibid.*, p. 180.

8 Joyce Cary, Preface to *Mister Johnson*, p. 7.

9 *Chinua Achebe*, London: Macmillan, 1980, p. 123. For a more recent discussion of this issue, and of the use of myth and language in *Arrow of God*, see Simon Gikandi, *Reading the African Novel*, London: James Currey, 1987, ch. 5.

5   *A Man of the People*

1 *A Man of the People*, p. 1. All subsequent references to this novel will be included in the text.
2 See, for instance, Joseph Okpaku, 'A Novel for the People', *Journal of the New African Literature* 2 (Fall 1966), 76-80.
3 With reference to the author's attitude to Kulmax, Chinua Achebe's comments on Marxism and Negritude are of interest. They are taken from an interview with Ernest and Pat Emenyonu, *Africa Report*, May 1972, p. 23.

> Very often people object to foreign ideologies, not because they are genuinely concerned about local and indigenous ideologies but because they resent any kind of change. If someone comes here and says that Marxism is the only form of economic system that will work here, we ought to look at it and not reject it just because its origin is foreign to us. At the same time, if somebody comes and says that in the past we had an economic system that is likely to work better than Marxism and then shows in concrete terms the way it was, and also how the amenities, the fruits, or the national cake was shared in the past, we should not overlook him.
>
> People who talk about foreign ideologies in an exclusive way are often merely saying 'don't upset the system we have got now,' which is the system of 'grab and keep'. That I will accept. In any society you have to work out a system in which people are treated as fairly as possible. If Marxism is going to provide it, then we ought to try it. If, on the other hand, some other system has been proved to be able to solve the problem, then we should look at that. I am not really a politician and I keep an open mind.
>
> As for Negritude, that has been flogged too much. It was a good war cry once upon a time. It no longer is – and one good pointer to the fact that it no longer is, is Senegal, which to my mind is one of the seats of neocolonialism. If this is a result of Negritude, and one of its archpriests is, in fact, running the affairs of Senegal, then obviously that thing no longer works.

4 *Chinua Achebe*, London: Macmillan, 1981, pp. 124-53. David Carroll's chapter on *A Man of the People* is reprinted in *Critical Perspectives on Chinua Achebe*.
5 In 1964, the year before he completed *A Man of the People*, Chinua Achebe had this to say about materialism in Nigerian society:

> Take another example. Anyone who has given any thought to our society must be concerned by the brazen materialism one sees all around. I have heard people blame it on Europe. That is utter rubbish. In fact the Nigerian society I know best – the Ibo society – has always been materialistic. This may sound strange because Ibo life had at the same time a strong spiritual dimension – controlled by gods, ancestors, personal spirits or *chi*, and magic. The

success of the culture was the balance between the two, the material and the spiritual. But let no one under-rate the material side. A man's position in society was usually determined by his wealth. All the four titles in my village were taken – not given – and each one had its price. But in those days wealth meant the strength of your arm. No one became rich by swindling the community or stealing government money. In fact a man who was guilty of theft immediately lost all his titles. Today we have kept the materialism and thrown away the spirituality which should keep it in check. Some of the chieftaincy titles and doctorate degrees we assume today would greatly shock our ancestors!

('The Role of the Writer in a New Nation', *African Writers On African Writing*, ed. G. D. Killam, London: Heinemann, 1978, p. 11.)

6 My analysis of the final paragraph and of the novel is indebted to a paper given by Mark Kinkead-Weekes on 'African Literature in the Universities', published in *OKIKE* 15 (1979), 18–22.

6 The novelist as critic

1 'Writers' Conference: A Milestone in Africa's progress', *Daily Times* (Lagos), 7 July 1962, p. 7. 'Conference on African Writers', *Radio Times* (Lagos), 15 July 1962, p. 6.

2 'Amos Tutuola', *Radio Times* (Lagos), 23–29 July 1961, p. 15.

3 Review of Christopher Okigbo's *Heavensgate*, *Spear* (Lagos), December 1962, p. 41. Review of Jean-Joseph Rabearivelo's *Twenty-Four Poems*, *Spear* (Lagos), January 1963, p. 41.

4 *Nigeria Magazine* (Lagos) 75, 1962.

5 *Morning Yet On Creation Day* p. 47; Achebe's italics.

6 *Ibid.*, p. 48.

7 Originally given as a talk to the Nigerian Library Association and published in *Nigerian Libraries*, 1, 3 (1964), 113–19; Reprinted in *Nigeria Magazine* 81 (1964), 157–60.

8 Originally given as a talk at the University of Leeds in 1964 and published in the *New Statesman* (London), 29 January 1965.

9 'The Role of the Writer in a New Nation', *Nigeria Magazine* 81 (1964), 157.

10 'The Novelist as Teacher', *Morning Yet On Creation Day*, pp. 44–5.

11 See, for example, Leopold Sedar Senghor, *Liberte I: Negritude et humanisme*, Paris: Editions du Seuil, 1971; Ngugi wa Thiong'o, *Writers in Politics*, London: Heinemann Educational Books, 1981; Chinweizu, Jemie and Madubuike, *Towards the Decolonization of African Literature*, Enugu: Fourth Dimension Press, 1981.

12 *Morning Yet On Creation Day*, p. 62.

13 'The African Writer and the English Language', *Morning Yet on Creation Day*, pp. 55–62. Originally published in *Transition* 4, 18 (1965), 27–30.

14 *Transition* 3, 10 (1964), 12–13.
15 Bernth Lindfors, 'Achebe's African Parable', *Critical Perspectives on Chinua Achebe*, p. 249.
16 Bill Dudley, 'Violence in Nigerian Politics', *Transition* 5, 21 (1965), 22. Cited by Lindfors.
17 See 'In reply to Margery Perham', and 'In Defense of English? An Open Letter to Mr Tai Solarin', *Morning Yet On Creation Day*, pp. 85–9.
18 'The African Writer and the Biafran Cause', *Morning Yet On Creation Day*, pp. 83–4. Achebe cites several examples of official British support for the Nigerian Government.
19 In answer to a question after a talk given at the Africa Centre, London, 15 September 1987, Achebe mentioned that the main characters in *Anthills of the Savannah* had been in his mind for a long time, since before the war, but he had only recently been able to find a story for them.
20 See *Okike* 4 and 5 for Mphahlele's 'From the Black American World' and *Okike* 6, 7, and 8 for 'Towards the Decolonization of African Literature'.
21 The *mbari* ceremony was dedicated to the earth goddess Ala, and is described thus by Achebe:

> Every so many years Ala would instruct the community through her priest to prepare a festival of images in her honour. That night the priest would travel through the town, knocking on many doors to announce to the various households who of their members Ala had chosen for the great work. These chosen men and women then moved into seclusion in a forest-clearing and under the instruction and guidance of master artists and craftsmen began to build a house of images. The work might take a year or even two, but as long as it lasted the workers were deemed to be hallowed and were protected from undue contact from, and distraction by, the larger community. (*MYCD*, p. 21)

22 'Work and Play in Tutuola's *The Palmwine Drinkard*', *Hopes and Impediments*, pp. 68–75. Originally published in *Okike* 14 (1978), 25–33.
23 'An Image of Africa'. Originally delivered and published in *The Chancellor's Lecture Series*. Amherst MA: University of Massachusetts, 1975, pp. 31–43. Reprinted in *Hopes and Impediments*, pp. 1–13.
24 The lecture, at which I was present, aroused much indignation in the audience, and strongly felt defences of Conrad. The oral and written debate which Achebe began has continued with extraordinary longevity, as articles still appear in response to the lecture published over a decade ago.
25 'Impediments to Dialogue Between North and South', *Hopes and Impediments*, pp. 14–19. Originally published in slightly different version in *The Times Literary Supplement*, 1 February 1980.
26 *How the Leopard got His Claws*, Enugu: Nwamife, 1972; New York: The Third Press, 1973.

27 Both published Enugu: Fourth Dimension, 1977.
28 *The Trouble With Nigeria*, Enugu: Fourth Dimension, 1983, p. 60.

7 Girls at War

1 See Anthony Kirk-Greene and Douglas Rimmer, *Nigeria Since 1970*, London: Hodder & Stoughton, 1981, p. 119. The authors also discuss the introduction of universal primary education in 1976, when once again the authorities were to find that enrolments were almost a million more than expected, partly accounted for by large numbers of over-age children.
2 Carroll, *Chinua Achebe*, London: Macmillan, 1980, p. 163.

8 Beware Soul Brother

1 *Beware Soul Brother*, Enugu: Nwankwo Ifejika, 1971.
2 This revised and enlarged edition was published in the United States in 1973 by Doubleday Anchor under the title *Christmas in Biafra and Other Poems*. Presumably, the English title was felt to be inappropriate in the United States at a time when the terms 'soul music' and 'soul brother' popularly carried rather different connotations from those in Achebe's poem.
3 Royal Dutch Shell and British Petroleum had begun oil production in Nigeria in 1957. By 1966, production had reached more than 152 million barrels a year. By this time Gulf (USA) and Elf (a French Government consortium) had also become involved in Nigerian oil exploration and production. See Anthony Kirk-Greene and Douglas Rimmer, *Nigeria Since 1970*, London: Hodder & Stoughton, 1981, pp. 82–93.
4 The story of the widow who gave what little food she had to Elijah and was rewarded with an inexhaustible barrel of meal is told in 1 *Kings* 17. Achebe tells the parallel story of Tortoise's miraculous feast in his note to the poem (*BSB*, p. 63).
5 David Carroll, *Chinua Achebe*, London: Macmillan, 1980, p. 171.
6 Misprinted as 'Commandmant' in both the English and American editions of the poems.
7 Philip Rogers, 'Chinua Achebe's Poems of Regeneration', *Critical Perspectives on Chinua Achebe*, ed. C. L. Innes and B. Lindfors, p. 292.
8 Achebe's note concerning this poem reads: '*abia* drums beaten at the funeral of an Igbo titled man. The dance itself is also called *abia* and is danced by the dead man's peers while he lies in state and finally by two men bearing his coffin before it is taken for burial; so he goes to his ancestors by a final *rite de passage* in solemn paces of dance'.
9 Part of Achebe's note to this poem explains: 'The attitude of Igbo people to their gods is sometimes ambivalent', and goes on to

describe an attitude in which bargaining with the gods is encouraged (*BSB*, p. 66).
10 Carroll, *Chinua Achebe*, p. 175; Rogers, in *Critical Perspectives*, p. 290.
11 Originally published by Doubleday/Anchor, New York, 1972. Reprinted in *Hopes and Impediments*, pp. 82-6.

9 *Anthills of the Savannah*

1 In 1986, the year that he completed writing *Anthills of the Savannah*, Achebe gave a lecture at Sokoto on these same issues. Entitled 'What Has Literature Got to Do With It?' the lecture argues forcefully for the role of creative literature and its variety:

> The great nineteenth century American poet Walt Whitman has left us a magnificent celebration of the many-sided nature of the creative spirit:
>
> > Do I contradict myself?
> > Very well then I contradict myself
> > I am large, I contain multitudes . . .
>
> The universal creative rondo revolves on people and stories. *People create stories create people*; or rather, *stories create people create stories.*
> > Achebe's italics (*HI*, pp. 111-12)

In this same lecture, Achebe goes on to discuss the analogies between psychoanalysis and storytelling, and the role of each in creating a coherent self 'eliciting deep or unconsciously held primary values and then bringing conscious reflection or competing values to bear on them.' (*HI*, p. 116). The lecture concludes with this summarizing statement:

> Literature, whether handed down by word of mouth or in print, gives us a second handle on reality; enabling us to encounter in the safe, manageable dimensions of make-believe the very same threats to integrity that may assail the psyche in real life; and at the same time providing through the self-discovery which it imparts a veritable weapon for coping with these threats whether they are found within our problematic and incoherent selves or in the world around us. What better preparation can a people desire as they begin their journey into the strange, revolutionary world of modernization? (*HI*, p. 117)

2 Ikem's lecture to the university students and his refusal to provide them with ready-made formulas to be parroted in the name of revolution replays a scenario with which Achebe himself has been all too familiar – a scenario yet again replayed at the African Centre on 15 September 1987, when Achebe answered questions about this new novel.
3 Achebe makes the point that man distinguishes himself from other

animals by storytelling in the Convocation lecture he gave at the University of Ife in 1978. The lecture, 'The Truth of Fiction', is reprinted in *Hopes and Impediments*, pp. 95–105.

4 In 'The Truth of Fiction,' Achebe distinguishes between malignant and beneficent fictions. The former 'demand and indeed impose . . . absolute and unconditional obedience', asserting their fictions, such as the superiority of white over black or male over female, 'as a proven fact and way of life'. The latter, the useful fictions, insist on their fictionality, and allow us to encounter and understand the world without fear of personal disaster. Achebe concludes by asserting that 'imaginative literature does not enslave':

> it liberates the mind of man. Its truth is not like the canons of an orthodoxy or the irrationality of prejudice and superstition. It begins as an adventure in self-discovery and ends in wisdom and human conscience. (*HI*, p. 105)

Those final sentences appropriately describe the philosophy and structure of *Anthills of the Savannah*.

Conclusion

1 Preface to *Studies in European Realism*, New York: Grosset and Dunlap, 1964, p. 8.
2 *Ibid.*, p. 8.
3 *Ibid.*, p. 10.
4 *Manichean Aesthetics*, ch. 5.
5 Emmanuel Ngara, *Art and Ideology in the African Novel*, London: Heinemann, 1985, 110–12.
6 'What Is Epic Theatre?' *Illuminations*, trans. Harry Zohn, New York: Schocken Books, 1969, pp. 147–54.
7 *Ibid.*, p. 150.
8 *Ibid.*, p. 153.
9 'Misunderstanding', *Beware Soul Brother*, p. 33. See also the note on p. 65 of *Beware Soul Brother*.
10 *Beware Soul Brother*, p. 65.
11 *No Longer at Ease*, p. 63.
12 Achebe speaks of the planned but unwritten novel in 'Named For Victoria, Queen of England', *Morning Yet on Creation Day*, p. 67. For an interesting discussion of the significance of Achebe's silence about this period see Gareth Griffiths, 'Chinua Achebe: When Did You Last see Your Father?' *WLWE* 27, 1 (1987), 18–27.
13 Abiola Irele, '*Le Monde s'effondre* de Chinua Achebe: Structure et Signification', *Littératures africaines et enseignement*, ed. J. Corzani and A. Ricard, Bordeaux: Presses Universitaires de Bordeaux, 1985, pp. 171–86.
14 See *Hopes and Impediments*, p. 110.
15 *The Guardian* (London and Manchester), 16 August 1983, p. 34.

Achebe is not, of course, demanding the use of standard metropolitan English by Nigerians.

16 *Morning Yet on Creation Day*, p. 34.
17 From an interview I recorded with Achebe for the British Council in June 1981.

Bibliography

Works by Achebe

BOOKS

Things Fall Apart, London: Heinemann, 1958; New York: Astor-Honor, 1959.

No Longer at Ease, London: Heinemann, 1960; New York: Obolensky, 1961.

The Sacrificial Egg and Other Short Stories, Onitsha: Etudo, 1962.

Arrow of God, London: Heinemann, 1964; New York: John Day, 1967; revised edition, London: Heinemann, 1974.

Chike and the River, Cambridge: Cambridge University Press, 1966. (Children's novella)

A Man of the People, London: Heinemann, 1966; New York: John Day, 1966.

Beware Soul Brother and Other Poems, Enugu: Nwankwo-Ifejika, 1971; revised and enlarged ed., London: Heinemann, 1972; Rpt. as *Christmas in Biafra and Other Poems*, Garden City NY: Anchor/Doubleday, 1973.

Girls at War and Other Stories, London: Heinemann, 1972; Garden City NY: Anchor/Doubleday, 1973. (Includes in revised versions the stories in *The Sacrificial Egg and Other Stories*.)

(with John Iroaganachi), *How the Leopard Got His Claws*, Enugu: Nwamife, 1972; New York: The Third Press, 1973. (Children's Book)

Morning Yet On Creation Day: Essays, London: Heinemann, 1975; enlarged and rev. ed. Garden City NY: Anchor/ Doubleday, 1975.

The Drum, Enugu: Fourth Dimension, 1977. (Children's book)

The Flute, Enugu: Fourth Dimension, 1977. (Children's Book)

Ed. (with Dubem Okafor), *Don't Let Him Die: An Anthology of Memorial Poems for Christopher Okigbo*, Enugu: Fourth Dimension, 1978.

Ed. (with Obiora Udechukwu). *Aka Weta: Egwu Aguluagu, Egwu edeluede*, Nsukka: Okike Magazine, 1982.

BIBLIOGRAPHY

The Trouble With Nigeria, Enugu: Fourth Dimension, 1983; London: Heinemann, 1983.
Ed. (with C. L. Innes), *African Short Stories*, London: Heinemann, 1985.
Anthills of the Savannah, London: Heinemann, 1987; New York: Doubleday, 1988.
Hopes and Impediments: Selected Essays, 1965–87, London: Heinemann, 1988.
Nigerian Essays. Ibadan: Heinemann, 1988.
Ed. (with C. L. Innes), *The Heinemann Book of Contemporary African Stories*, Oxford: Heinemann International, 1992.

SHORT STORIES

'The Sacrificial Egg', *Atlantic Monthly*, April 1959.*
'Chike's School Days', *Rotarian* 96, 4 (1960), 19–20.*
'The Madman', *The Insider*, by Achebe, Nwankwo, Ifejika, Nwapa, *et al.* Enugu: Nwankwo-Ifejika, 1971, pp. 1–7.*
'Sugar Baby', *Okike* 3 (1972), 8–16.

POEMS

'There Was A Young Man in Our Hall', *University Herald* (Ibadan) 4, 3 (1951–52), 19.
'Flying', *Okike* 4 (1973), 47–8.
'The Old Man and the Census', *Okike* 6 (1974), 41–2.
'The American Youngster in Rags', *Okike* 12 (1978), 3–4.
'Knowing Robs Us', *Okike* 13 (1979), 1.
'Pine Tree In Spring', *Okike* 13 (1979), 2.
'Agostinho Neto', *Okike* 18 (1981), 7.
All but the first of these have been reprinted in *Rhythms of Creation*, ed. D. I. Nwoga, Enugu: Fourth Dimension, 1982. All other published poems are collected in *Beware Soul Brother* or *Christmas in Biafra*.

ESSAYS, TALKS AND MISCELLANEOUS PIECES

'Philosophy', *The Bug* (Ibadan), 21 February 1951, p. 5.
'An Argument Against the Existence of Faculties', *University Herald* (Ibadan), 4, 1 (1951), 12–13.
Editorial, *University Herald* (Ibadan), 4, 3 (1951–52), 5.
Editorial, *University Herald* (Ibadan), 5, 1 (1952), 5.
'Mr. Okafor Versus Arts Students', *The Bug* (Ibadan), 29 November 1952, p. 3.

* Included in *Girls At War and Other Stories* with substantial revisions. All other published stories have been collected in *Girls At War and Other Stories*.

'Hiawatha', *The Bug* (Ibadan), 29 November 1952, p. 3.

'Eminent Nigerians of the 19th Century', *Radio Times* (Lagos), January 1958, p. 3.

'Listening in the East', *Radio Times* (Lagos), January 1959, p. 17; February 1959, p. 17; March 1959, p. 18; April 1959, p. 18; May 1959, p. 33; June 1959, p. 22. (About Nigerian Broadcasting Corporation programming in Eastern Nigeria.)

'Two West African Library Journals', *The Service*, 6 May 1961, p. 15.

'Amos Tutuola', *Radio Times* (Lagos), 23–29 July 1961, p. 15.

'Writers' Conference: A Milestone in Africa's Progress', *Daily Times* (Lagos), 7 July 1962, p. 7; 'Conference of African Writers', *Radio Times* (Lagos), 15 July 1962, p. 6. (Conference held at Makere University College, Kampala, Uganda.)

Introduction to Delphine King, *Dreams of Twilight: A Book of Poems*, Apapa: Nigerian National Press, n.d. [*c.* 1962], p. 5.

Review of Christopher Okigbo's *Heavensgate*, *Spear* (Lagos), December 1962, p. 41.

Review of Jean-Joseph Rabearivelo's *Twenty-Four Poems*, *Spear* (Lagos), January 1963, p. 41.

'A Look At West African Writing', *Spear* (Lagos), June 1963, p. 26.

'Voice of Nigeria – How It Began', *Voice of Nigeria* 1, 1 (1963), 5–6.

'Are We Men of Two Worlds?' *Spear* (Lagos), December 1963, p. 13.

'On Janheinz Jahn and Ezekiel Mphahlele', *Transition* 8 (1963), 9.

'The Role of the Writer in a New Nation', *Nigerian Libraries* 1, 3 (1964), 113–19; *Nigeria Magazine* 81 (1964), 157–60.

Foreword to *A Selection of African Prose*, vol. 1, ed. W. H. Whiteley Oxford: Clarendon Press, 1964, pp. vii–x.

'The African Writer and the English Language', *Transition*, 4, 18 (1965), 27–30. Rpt. in *Morning Yet on Creation Day*.

'The Black Writer's Burden', *Presence Africaine* 31, 59 (1966), 135–40.

Editorial, *Nsukkascope* (Nsukka) 1 (1971), 1–4.

Editorial, *Nsukkascope* (Nsukka) 2 (1971), 1–5.

Editorial, *Nsukkascope* (Nsukka) 3 (1972), 4–5.

Introduction to Kofi Awoonor, *This Earth, My Brother . . .*, Garden City NY: Anchor/Doubleday, 1972, pp. vii–xii.

Rpt. as a review in *Transition* 41 (1972), 69, and in *Hopes and Impediments*, pp. 82-6.

Introduction to Keorapetse Kgositsile, *Places and Bloodstains* [*Notes for Ipelang*] Oakland Ca.: Achebe publications, 1975, p. 7.

'An Image of Africa', *The Chancellor's Lecture Series, 1974-75*, Amherst MA: University of Massachusetts Press, 1975, pp. 31-43. Rpt. in *Hopes and Impediments*, pp. 1-13. (On Conrad's *Heart of Darkness*).

'Contemporary Literature', in *The Living Culture of Nigeria*, London: Nelson, 1976.

'African Writing and the Problem of Translation', *Translation* 3 (1976), 38-43. (Panel Discussion with Rajat Neogy, Donald Herdeck, Joseph Okpaku and Mazisi Kunene).

'Commitment and the African Writer', in *Readings in African Humanities: African Cultural Development*, ed. Ogbu U. Kalu, Enugu: Fourth Dimension, 1978, pp. 181-7.

'Work and Play in Tutuola's *The Palm-Wine Drinkard*', *Okike* 14 (1978), 25-33. Rpt. in *Hopes and Impediments*, pp. 68-76.

'The Bane of Union: An Appraisal of the Consequences of Union Igbo for Igbo Language and Literature', *ANU Magazine* 1 (1979), 33-41.

'The Uses of African Literature', *Okike* 15, (1979), 8-17.

'Impediments to Dialogue Between North and South', *Okike* 16 (1979), 8-12. Also published in the *Times Literary Supplement* (London) 1 February 1980. Rpt. in *Hopes and Impediments*, pp. 14-19.

'Why An Association? Address to the Convention of Nigerian Authors', *Okike* 20 (1981), 7-10, Rpt in *Association of Nigerian Authors Review* (*ANAR*) 1 (1985), 1-2.

'The *Okike* Story', *Okike* 21 (1982), 1-5.

'The Nature of the Individual and His Fulfilment', *The Colonial and Neo-Colonial Encounter in Commonwealth Literature*, ed. H. H. Gowdah, Mysore: University of Mysore, 1983, pp. 205-15.

'The Purpose of Education', *Guardian* (Lagos), 4 December 1983, p. 8. (Excerpts from a speech given at Federal Government College, Lagos, 26 November 1983.)

'Editorial and Linguistic Problems in *Aka Weta*: A Comment', *Uwa ndi Igbo* 1 (1984), 94-5.

Foreword, *Igbo Arts: Community and Cosmos*, ed. Herbert Cole and Chike Aniakor, Los Angeles: University of California Press, 1984.

'I'm an Original Professor . . . Professing Literature', *Sunday*

Concord (Nigeria), 17 February 1985, p. 2. (Letter to editor in response to criticism by Lagos University Professors.)

'Presidential Address 1983', *ANAR* 1 (1985), 7.

'Presidential Address 1985', *ANAR* 2 (1986), 1–2.

'Achebe's Letter from Canada', *Concord Weekly*, 5 September 1985, pp. 16–17.

'What Has Literature Got to Do With It?' Nigeria National Merit Award Winner's Lecture 1986, n.p. [Lagos]: Federal Republic of Nigeria, n.d. [1986]. Rpt. in *Vanguard*, 4 September 1986, pp. 8–9; *ANAR* 2 (1986), 9, 15; and in *Hopes and Impediments*, pp. 106–17.

'Achebe on Editing', *WLWE* 27, 1 (Spring 1987), 1–5.

'James Baldwin; 1924–1987: A Dedication', (with Esther Terry, Michael Thelwell and John Wideman) *Massachusetts Review* 28, (Winter 1987), 551–60. Rpt. in *Hopes and Impediments*, pp. 118–21.

'Our Mission,' *African Commentary*, 1, 1 (October, 1989), p. 4.

'African Literature as Restoration of Celebration'. South Bank Lecture, January, 1990. Rpt. in *Kunapipi*, 12, 2 (1990), 1–10. Rpt. in *Chinua Achebe: A Celebration*, ed. Kirsten Holst Petersen and Anna Rutherford, Oxford: Heinemann International, 1991.

Other previously unpublished lectures and unrevised essays are collected in *Morning Yet on Creation Day* and *Hopes and Impediments: Selected Essays 1965–87*.

SELECTED INTERVIEWS

Anon, 'Entretien avec Chinua Achebe', *Afrique* 27 (1963), 40–2.

Anon, 'Chinua Achebe on Biafra', *Transition* 36 (1968), 31–7.

Cott, Jonathan, ed., 'Chinua Achebe: At the Crossroads', *Pipers at the Gates of Dawn: The Wisdom of Children's Literature*, New York: McGraw-Hill, 1985, pp. 161–92.

Duerden, Dennis and Cosmo Pieterse, eds., 'Chinua Achebe', *African Writers Talking: A Collection of Radio Interviews*, London: Heinemann; New York: Africana Publishing Corp., 1972, pp. 3–17.

Emenyonu, Ernest and Pat Emenyonu, 'Achebe: Accountable to our Society', *Africa Report* 17, 5 (1972), 21, 23, 25–7.

Hayes, Suzanne, 'An Interview with Chinua Achebe (Adelaide 1980)', *New Literatures in English Review*, 11 (n.d.), 43–52.

Lawson, William, 'Chinua Achebe in New England: An Interview', *Yardbird Reader*, 4 (1975), 99–110.

Lindfors, Bernth, Ian Munro, Richard Priebe and Reinhard Sander, eds., 'Interview with Chinua Achebe', *Palaver: Interviews with Five African Writers in Texas*, Austin: African and Afro-American Research Institute, University of Texas at Austin, 1972, pp. 5–12.

Morell, Karen L., ed., 'Class Discussion', *In Person: Achebe, Awoonor, and Soyinka at the University of Washington*, Seattle: African Studies Program, Institute for Comparative and Foreign Area Studies, University of Washington, 1975, pp. 24–32.

Moyers, Bill, 'Interview with Chinua Achebe', in *A World of Ideas*, ed. Betty Sue Flowers, New York: Doubleday, 1989.

Nwachukwu-Agbada, J. O. J., 'Interview with Chinua Achebe', *Massachusetts Review* 28, 2 (Summer 1987), 273–85.

Ogbaa, K., 'Interview with Chinua Achebe', *Research in African Literatures* 12 (Spring 1981), 1–13.

Rutherford, Anna, 'Interview with Chinua Achebe', *Kunapipi* 9, 2 (1987), 1–7.

Searle, Chris, 'Interview with Chinua Achebe', *Wasafiri*, 14 (1991), 12–16.

Wilmer, Valerie, 'Chinua Achebe and the African Novel', *Flamingo* 4, 11 (1965), 27–9.

Works about Achebe

Abrahams, Cecil A., 'George Lamming and Chinua Achebe: Tradition and the Literary Chroniclers', *Awakened Conscience: Studies in Commonwealth Literature*, ed. C. D. Narasimhaiah, New Delhi: Sterling, 1978, pp. 294–306.

Ascherson, Neil, 'Betrayal: *Anthills of the Savannah*', (review) *New York Review of Books*, 3 March 1988, pp. 3–4.

Ackley, Donald, 'The Male-Female Motif in *Things Fall Apart*', *Studies in Black Literature* 5, 1 (1974), 1–6.

Adebayo, Tunji, 'The Past and the Present in Chinua Achebe's Novels', *Ife African Studies* 1, 1 (1974), 66–84.

Amaizo, Elaine, 'L'écrivain négro-africain et le problème de la langue: L'exemple de Chinua Achebe', *Bulletin de l'Enseignement Supérieur du Bénin* (Lome, Togo), 13 (1970), 41–56.

Babilola, E. A., 'A reconsideration of Achebe's *No Longer at Ease*', *Phylon* 47 (1986), 139–47.

Balaogun, F. Odun, 'Achebe's "The Madman": A Poetic Realization of Irony', *Okike* 23 (1983), 72–9.

Boafo, Y. S. Kantanka, '*Arrow of God*: A case Study of Megalomania', *Asemka*, 1, 2 (1974), 16–24.

Bottcher, Karl H., 'The Narrative Technique in Achebe's Novels', *Journal of the New African Literature and the Arts* 13/14 (1972), 1–12.

Brown, H. R., 'Igbo Words for the non-Igbo: Achebe's Artistry in *Arrow of God*', *Research in African Literatures* 12 (Spring 1981), 69–85.

Brown, Lloyd W., 'Cultural Norms and Modes of Perception in Achebe's Fiction', *Research in African Literatures* 3 (1972), 21–35. Rpt. in *Critical Perspectives on Chinua Achebe*, ed. Innes and Lindfors.

Bruchac, Joseph, 'Achebe as Poet', *New Letters* 40, 1 (1973), 23–31.

Carroll, David, *Chinua Achebe*, rev. ed., New York and London: Macmillan, 1990.

Cook, David, *African Literature: A Critical View*, Harlow: Longman, 1977.

Coussy, Denise, *L'Oeuvre de Chinua Achebe*, Paris: Presence Africaine: 1985.

Echeruo, M. J. C., 'Chinua Achebe', *A Celebration of Black and African Writing* ed. Bruce King and Kolawole Ogungbesan, Zaria and Ibadan: Ahmadu Bello University Press and Oxford University Press, 1975, pp. 150–63.

Egudu, R. N., 'Achebe and the Igbo Narrative Tradition', *Research in African Literatures* 12 (Spring 1981), 43–54.

Eko, Ebele, 'Chinua Achebe and His Critics: Reception of his Novels in English and American Reviews', *Studies in Black Literature* 6, 3 (1975), 14–20.

Emenyonu, Ernest, 'Ezeulu: The Night Mask Caught abroad by Day', *Pan African Journal* 4 (1971), 407–19.

Gachukia, Eddah W., 'Chinua Achebe and Tradition', *Standpoints on African Literature:A Critical Anthology* ed. Chris L. Wanjala, Nairobi, Kampala, Dar es Salaam: East African Literature Bureau, 1973, pp. 172–87.

Gakwandi, Shatto Arthur, *The Novel and Contemporary Experience in Africa*, London: Heinemann, 1977.

Gikandi, Simon, *Reading the African Novel*, London: James Currey, 1987, pp. 149–70.

Reading Chinua Achebe, London: James Currey, 1991.

Glenn, Ian, *Achebe and the Dilemma of the Nigerian Intellectual*, Cape Town: Centre of African Studies, University of Cape Town, 1983.

Gordimer, Nadine, 'A Tyranny of Clowns' (Review of *Anthills of the Savannah*), *New York Times Book Review*, 21 February 1988, pp. 1, 26.

Gowdah, H. H., 'The Novels of Chinua Achebe', *Literary Half-Yearly* 14, 2 (1973), 3–9.

Griffiths, Gareth, 'Language and Action in the Novels of Chinua Achebe', *African Literature Today* 5 (1971), 88–105. Rpt. in *Critical Perspectives on Chinua Achebe*, ed. Innes and Lindfors.

Heywood, Christopher, 'Surface and Symbol in *Things Fall Apart*', *Journal of the Nigerian English Studies Association* 2 (1967), 41–5.

Chinua Achebe's Things Fall Apart: A Critical View, ed. Yolande Cantu, London: Collins in Association with the British Council 1985.

Holst Peterson, Kirsten and Rutherford, A., eds. *Chinua Achebe: A Celebration*, Sydney: Dangaroo Press, 1991.

Ihekweazu, Edith, ed. *Eagle on Iroko: Papers from the International Symposium, 1990*, Ibadan: Heinemann Educational Books Nigeria, 1991.

Innes, C. L. *Chinua Achebe's Arrow of God: A Critical View*, ed. Yolande Cantu, London: Collins in Association with the British Council, 1985.

Innes, C. L. and Lindfors, B. eds., *Critical Perspectives on Chinua Achebe*, Washington DC: Three Continents Press, 1978; London: Heinemann, 1979.

Irele, Abiola, '*Le Monde s'effondre* de Chinua Achebe: Structure et Signification', *Littératures africaines et enseignement*, ed. J. Corzani and A. Ricard. Bordeaux: Presses Universitaires de Bordeaux, 1985, pp. 171–86.

'The Tragic Conflict in Achebe's Novels'. *Black Orpheus* 17 (1965), 24–32. Rpt. in *Critical Perspectives on Chinua Achebe*, ed. Innes and Lindfors.

Iyasere, Solomon, 'Narrative Techniques in *Things Fall Apart*', *New Letters* 40 (1974), 73–93. Rpt. in *Critical Perspectives in Chinua Achebe*, ed. Innes and Lindfors.

JanMohamed, Abdul R., *Manichean Aesthetics: The Politics of Literature in Colonial Africa*. Amherst MA: University of Massachusetts Press, 1983.

'Sophisticated primitivism: the Syncretism of Oral and Literate Modes in Achebe's *Things Fall Apart*', *Ariel* 15, 4 (1984), 19–39.

Jervis, Stephen, 'Tradition and Change in Hardy and Achebe', *Black Orpheus* 2, 5–6 (1971), 31–8.

Killam, G. D., *The Writings of Chinua Achebe*, rev. ed., London: Heinemann, 1977.

'Notions of Religion, Alienation and Archetype in *Arrow of God*', in *Exile and Tradition: Studies in African and Caribbean Literature*, ed. Rowland Smith, New York: Africana Publishing Co. and Dalhousie University Press, 1976, pp. 152–65.

King, B. A., 'The Revised *Arrow of God*', *African Literature Today* 13 (1983), 69–78.

Kronenfeld, J. Z., 'The "Communalistic" African and the "Individualistic" Westerner: Some Comments on Misleading Generalizations in Western Criticism of Soyinka and Achebe', *Research in African Literatures* 6 (1975), 199–225.

Kuesgen, Reinhardt, 'Conrad and Achebe: Aspects of the Novel', *WLWE* 24 (Summer 1984), 27–33.

Leslie, Omolara, 'Chinua Achebe: His Vision and His Craft', *Black Orpheus* 2, 7 (1972), 34–41.

Lewis, Mary Ellen B., 'Beyond Content in the Analysis of Folklore in Literature: Chinua Achebe's *Arrow of God*', *Research in African Literatures* 7 (1976), 44–52.

Lindfors, Bernth, 'Achebe's African Parable', *Presence Africaine* 66 (1968), 130–66. Rpt. in *Critical Perspectives on Chinua Achebe*, ed. Innes and Lindfors.

Early Nigerian Literature, New York: Africana Publishing Co., 1982.

'The Palm Oil with which Achebe's Words are Eaten', *African Literature Today* 1 (1968), 3–18. Rpt. in *Critical Perspectives on Chinua Achebe*, ed. Innes and Lindfors.

Mahood, M. M., 'Idols of the Den', *The Colonial Encounter* London: Rex Collings, 1976. Rpt. in *Critical Perspectives on Chinua Achebe*, ed. Innes and Lindfors.

Melamu, M. J., 'The Quest for Power in Achebe's *Arrow of God*', *English Studies in Africa* 14 (1971), 225–40.

Melone, Thomas, 'Architecture du Monde: Chinua Achebe et W. B. Yeats', *Conch* 2, 1 (1970), 44–52.

Chinua Achebe et la tragédie de l'histoire, Paris: Présence Africaine, 1973.

Moore, Gerald, 'Chinua Achebe: Nostalgia and Realism', *Twelve African Writers*, London: Hutchinson University Press, 1980.

Ngugi wa Thiong'o [James], 'Chinua Achebe: *A Man of the People*', *Homecoming: Essays on Africa and the Caribbean Literature, Culture and Politics*, London: Heinemann, 1972; New York and Westport CT: Lawrence Hill, 1973, pp. 51–4. Rpt. in *Critical Perspectives on Chinua Achebe*, ed. Innes and Lindfors.

Niven, Alastair, 'Another Look at *Arrow of God*', *Literary Half-Yearly* 16, 2 (1975), 53–68.

Njoki, Benedict Chiak, *The Four Novels of Chinua Achebe: A Critical Study*, New York: Lang, 1984.

Nnolim, C. E., 'Form and Function of the Folk Tradition in Achebe's Novels', *Ariel* 14 (1983), 35–47.

Nwoga, D. I., 'The Igbo World of Achebe's *Arrow of God*', *Research in African Literatures* 12 (Spring 1981), 14–42.

Obiechina, Emmanuel, *Culture, Tradition and Society in the West African Novel*, Cambridge: Cambridge University Press, 1975.

Ogu, J. N., 'The Concept of Madness in Chinua Achebe's Writings', *Journal of Commonwealth Literature* 18, 1 (1983), 48–54.

Ogungbesan, Kolawole, 'Politics and the African Writer: The Example of Chinua Achebe', *Work in Progress* (Zaria), 2 (1973), 75–93; *African Studies Review* 17 (1974), 43–54. Rpt. in *Critical Perspectives on Chinua Achebe*, ed. Innes and Lindfors.

Oko, Emilia A., 'The Historical Novel of Africa: A Sociological Approach to Achebe's *Things Fall Apart* and *Arrow of God*', *Conch* 6, 1/2 (1974), 15–46.

Okpaku, Joseph, 'A Novel for the People', *Journal of the New African Literature* 2 (Fall 1966), 76–80.

Olney, James, *Tell Me Africa: An Approach to African Literature*, Princeton: Princeton University Press, 1973.

'The African Novel in Transition: Chinua Achebe', *South Atlantic Quarterly* 70 (1971), 229–316.

Omotoso, Kole, *Achebe or Soyinka: A Reinterpretation and a Study in Contrast*, New Perspectives in Literature Series, 4, Oxford: Hans Zell, 1991.

Peters, Jonathan, *A Dance of Masks: Senghor, Achebe, Soyinka*, Washington DC: Three Continents Press, 1975.

Ravenscroft, Arthur, *Chinua Achebe*, Harlow: Longmans, Green for the British Council and the National Book League, 1969; rev. ed., 1977.

Riddy, Felicity, 'Language As a Theme in *No Longer At Ease*', *Journal of Commonwealth Literature*, 9 (1970), 38–47. Rpt. in *Critical Perspectives on Chinua Achebe*, ed. Innes and Lindfors.

Rogers, Philip, 'Chinua Achebe's Poems of Regeneration', *Journal of Commonwealth Literature*, 10, 3 (1976), 1–9. Rpt. in *Critical Perspectives on Chinua Achebe*, ed. Innes and Lindfors.

'*No Longer at Ease*: Chinua Achebe's Heart of Whiteness', *Research in African Literatures* 14 (Summer, 1983), 165–83.

Scheub, Harold, 'When A Man Fails Alone', *Présence Africaine*, 74 (1970), 61–89.

Serumaga, Robert, 'A Mirror of Integration: Chinua Achebe

113; 'The Writer and His Community', 112
Short Fiction: 'Akueke', 123, 127–8; 'Chike's School Days', 121–3; 'Civil Peace', 126–7, 130; 'Dead Man's Path', 10, 11–12; 'Girls at War', 123, 127, 130–3; *Girls at War and Other Stories*, 3, 9, 10, 121–33, 134, see also individual stories; 'In a Village Church', 10; 'The Madman,' 123; 'Marriage is a Private Affair', 10–11, 121; 'The Sacrificial Egg', 121, 123–4; 'Uncle Ben's Choice', 124–5; 'Vengeful Creditor', 127, 128–30; 'The Voter', 125
Achebe, Christie Chinwe, 102, 115
Achebe, Isaiah Okafor, 4
Achebe, Janet, 4
Achebe, John, 8
African Writers Series, 102
Akintola, Chief, 127
Aka-Weta, 120
Ala, 5, 181 n.21
Aluko, T. M., 19
Amadi, Elechi, 8, 19
Ani, 5, 11, 26
Aniebo, I. N. C., 8
Armah, Ayi Kwei, 63, 112, 178 n.7
Auden, W. H., 49, 50
Awolowo, Chief, 107, 117
Awoonor, Kofi, 148, 149
Azikwe, Nnamdi, 9, 107, 117

Babangeda, Major General, 120
Bakhtin, Mikhail, 18, 176 n.29
Balewa, P. M., 107
Basden, G. T., 4
Biafran War, see Nigerian Civil War
Bible, 35
Black Orpheus, 125
Brecht, Bertoldt, 168–9
British in Nigeria, 6–7, 8, 13, 65
Brutus, Dennis, 110
Buhari, General, 119–20

Carroll, David, 2, 53, 73, 94, 129, 141, 147, 174 n.1, 176 n.8
Cary, Joyce, 2, 8, 12, 13, 14, 16, 17–18, 21–41, 43, 63, 64, 65, 66–70, 80, 150, 165, 166–7, 169, 172, 175 n.27, 177 nn.11, 12

Works: *The African Witch*, 14, 15, 16, 26, 30, 43, 64, 70–1, 80, 83, 84, 166; *Aissa Saved*, 14, 30, 166; *The American Visitor*, 15, 166; *Art and Reality*, 41; *The Horse's Mouth*, 24; *Mister Johnson*, 2, 12, 14, 15, 16, 17, 21–41, 42–3, 46, 58, 64–6, 67–9, 166, 170, 171
Caute, David, 18–19
chi, 6, 37
Chinweizu, 105, 111, 151, 180 n.11
Chukwu, 5
Church Missionary Society (CMS), 4, 7, 124
Clark, J. P., 106
Conrad, Joseph, 8, 12, 16, 43, 50, 114
Crowder, Michael, 175 n.11

de Man, P., 176 n.10
Derrida, J., 176 n.10
Diop, David, 151
Dudley, Bill, 181 n.18

Echeruo, M., 175 n.23
Ekwensi, Cyprian, 109, 110
Eliot, T. S., 47, 50, 173, 177 n.3
Emenyonu, Ernest and Pat, 179 n.3
Enaharo, Chief, 107
Equiano, Oloudah, 106
Ezeagu, 64

Fanon, F., 13, 14, 25, 104
Farah, Nuruddin, 19, 151
Foster, Malcolm, 175 n.25
Frye, Northrop, 14

Ghandi, Mahatma, 118
Gikandi, S., 178 n.9
Gowon, General, 108, 116
Greene, Graham, 8, 43, 49, 50, 178 n.3
Griffiths, G., 2, 176 n.8, 184 n.12

Hammond, Dorothy, 16
Heart of Darkness, 65, 114–15
Hill, Alan, 102
History of Umuchu, The, 64
Housman, A. E., 50, 61

Ibadan, University College, 8, 9
Igbos, 5–7, 108–10, *passim*
Ike, V. C., 19, 109

'Indirect Rule', 7
Irele, Abiola, 172, 178 n.4
Ironsi, General, 108
Iyayi, Festus, 151

Jablow, Alta, 16
Jan Mohamed, A. R., 14, 15, 26, 168, 175 nn.18, 23, 24
Jemie, O., 111
Joyce, James, 116

Kano, Aminu, 118
Killam, G. D., 174 n.1, 178 n.4, 180 n.5
Kinkead-Weekes, M., 180 n.6

Lindfors, B., 2, 19, 175 nn.12, 13, 176 n.8, 181 n.15
Lugard, Lord, 7, 64, 67
Lukács, Georg, 35, 167–8

Madabuike, I., 111
Mahood, M. M., 174 n.5, 175 n.23
Mbari, 11–12, 181 n.21
Milne, Van, 102
Milton, John, 8
Mphahlele, E., 111
Muhammed, Murtala, 116, 118
Munonye, John, 19, 109

Naipaul, V. S., 115
Niger River, 5, 124
Nigeria Magazine, 103
Nigerian Broadcasting Corporation (NBC), 102, 108
Nigerian Civil War, 2, 108–10, 113, 130, 134 ff.
Ngara, E., 168
Ngugi wa Thiong'o, 19, 105–6, 118, 151, 160, 180 n.11
Nnolim, Simon, 64, 178 n.1
Nsukka, University of Nigeria at, 110, 115, 120
Nsukkascope, 110
Nwankwo, Nkem, 19, 109
Nwapa, Flora, 19, 109, 110
Nwoga, Donatus, 111
Nzekwu, Onuora, 19, 109

Obasanjo, 116
Obiechina, E. N., 110, 111, 174 n.5, 176 n.8
Obumselu, Ben, 177 n.2

Ogidi, 4, 5, 7
Ojukwu, Lt. Col., 108
Okara, Gabriel, 8, 109, 110
Okigbo, Christopher, 8, 103, 106, 109, 113, 115, 136, 137, 151
Okike Magazine, 3, 110–11, 115, 120, 126
Okpaku, Joseph, 179 n.2
Onitsha, 5, 124
Orwell, George, 173
Ousman, Sembene, 118, 151
Owerri, 7

Parrinder, J., 7
Perham, Margery, 109
Pilgrim's Progress, 7

Rabearivelo, J., 103
Radio Times (Lagos), 103
Ravenscroft, A., 174 n.1
Rich, Adrienne, 42
Riddy, F., 2
Rogers, Philip, 144, 147
Sartre, Jean-Paul, 63, 105
Senghor, Leopold Sedar, 93, 105, 106, 113, 151, 179 n.3, 180 n.11
Shagari, Shehu, 117, 119
Shakespeare, W., 7, 8, 19
Shelley, P. B., 46, 144
Solarin, Tai, 109
Soyinka, Wole, 9, 109, 110, 151

Tennyson, Alfred, 35, 46
Tutuola, Amos, 103, 106, 114

University Herald (Ibadan), 9, 10
University of Biafra, see Nsukka, University of Nigeria at
University of Connecticut, Storrs, 111
University of Massachusetts, Amherst, 111
Uwa ndi Igbo, 120

Wali, Obi, 106
Waugh, Eveleyn, 49, 50
West African Pilot, The, 9
White, Landeg, 177 n.2
Whitman, Walt, 112, 163, 183 n.1
Wordsworth, William, 8, 10, 41
Wren, Robert, 1, 64, 174 nn.1, 2, 5, 175 nn.9, 18, 178 n.2

Yeats, W. B., 13, 35, 143, 144

Zahar, Renate, 14, 25

Lightning Source UK Ltd.
Milton Keynes UK

178616UK00001B/29/A